To Ada —

Best personal regou

Ben Bell

Amazing Secrets

of

Psychic Healing

Amazing Secrets
of
Psychic Healing

Benjamin O. Bibb, D.D.

and

Joseph J. Weed

Parker Publishing Company, Inc.

West Nyack, N.Y.

©1976, by

PARKER PUBLISHING COMPANY, INC.
West Nyack, New York

Library of Congress Cataloging in Publication Data

Bibb, Benjamin O
   Amazing secrets of psychic healing.

   1. Mental healing.   I.   Weed, Joseph J., joint
author.   II.   Title.
RZ400.B5   615'.851   76-16041
ISBN 0-13-023846-5

Printed in the United States of America

To my wife,
Margaret,
whose loyalty and unselfish efforts
have been a major help to me
throughout my work.

Benjamin O. Bibb, D.D.

We acknowledge with thanks
the generous contribution of artist
ROY W. HILL
who supplied the drawings for
the MEDIPIC series.

Ben O. Bibb, D.D. and Joseph J. Weed

THE SONG OF THE HEALER

The sons of men are one and I am one with them.

I seek to love, not hate;

I seek to serve, not exact due service;

I seek to heal, not hurt.

How this book will help you to radiant health

Are you completely healthy? Always? If not, you should be. Are any of your family, friends or acquaintances suffering from poor health, injuries or even long standing afflictions? They need not, if you decide you want to help them—for help them you can, and yourself as well.

How? you ask. This book will tell you how—for you do have the ability to heal. Right now you may not be aware that you have it, but you do. This gift of God is part of the birthright of every man and woman; it lies dormant in you waiting to be awakened. Only a small effort on your part is required to stimulate it to powerful and effective action, so just read on and discover for yourself

THE AMAZING SECRET WAYS TO

- —Relieve pain in a matter of minutes (see Chapter 2)

- —Heal wounds, cuts and abrasions the day they are suffered (see Chapter 2)

- —Repair bone fractures quickly (see Chapter 2)

- —End the pain of arthritis by eliminating its cause (Chapter 3)

- —Dramatically change and improve the appearance of blemish-ridden skin (Chapter 5)

- —Correct ailments of the ears, nose and throat (Chapter 6)

- —Treat failing eyes and bring them back to normal sight (Chapter 7)

- —Strengthen the heart and repair any malfunctions that may hamper its action (Chapter 10)

- —Wash out infections from the intestines and bowels and re-establish their normal functioning (Chapter 13)

—Search out and correct liver and gall bladder problems (Chapter 11)

—Relieve prostate pain and restore normal action (Chapter 12)

—Clear impurities from the blood, a very important treatment which everyone can employ with profit (Chapter 15)

—Balance glandular functions and thus heal diabetes (Chapter 16)

—Relieve toothache and clear out tooth infection (Chapter 14)

—Instruct your inner mind to automatically correct any malfunction that may develop (Chapter 18)

—Effect many other surprising and marvelous healings (Chapter 17)

Right here in print for the first time you will find the step-by-step procedures whereby hundreds of people with no previous medical knowledge of any kind have been taught to become successful healers. These are men and women from all walks of life, most of them no different from you. Some are secretaries, salespeople, bookkeepers, mechanics, teachers and students, and some are professional people such as lawyers, ministers and doctors—yes, doctors. Read on and let them tell you in their own words what they have learned and how this knowledge has served them, enabling them to accomplish seeming miracles of healing. Along with their reports are explained the exact techniques taught them in the classes of one of the world's greatest healers, Benjamin O. Bibb, D.D. This man is outstanding not only for the great number of remarkable cures he has effected, but chiefly because he is able to describe in detail just what he does and to teach others how to do it. This book is based upon his class teachings and supported by the case histories of a vast number of confirmed healings. By following the instructions given herein, you too can become a successful healer.

THE TEACHING OF BEN BIBB

Ben Bibb's methods are simple and easy to understand. Most of his pupils learn them in two to three weeks and some even more quickly. Once a student has the amazing secret technique explained and understands it, the development of skill is then only a question of practice. If you would know what this secret is, just read on. You will find in the chapters to follow not only a complete description of the method employed so successfully by Benjamin O. Bibb, D.D. but also his personal instructions in how to use it to heal psychically or mentally—for this book describes the complete course taught by Ben Bibb in his classes. The step-by-step instructions make it seem easy, as you will soon discover. First, however, you should know and appreciate to some extent the scope of this ability of yours once it is unfolded. For this reason there is explained herein what can be done, what is possible for you to do and what has been done by the graduates of Ben Bibb's classes. These students are no more gifted than you are; anything they can do, you also can do.

INSTANTANEOUS SELF-HEALING

For example, here is a case of instantaneous self-healing. One student of Bibb's was attempting to repair a stall shower that didn't work. Endeavoring to get at the valves, he discovered that someone had cemented them over. Annoyed at the stupidity of this, he started to chip away at the cement with a hammer and cold chisel. Due partly to the cramped quarters in the small shower stall and partly to his irritation, the hammer slipped on the head of the chisel and struck him on the wrist. Ignoring the pain, he continued, but he struck his wrist again, and then again. The fourth blow was so severe he thought he might have damaged the bone. Coming out of the shower stall into the light he saw a purple welt about four inches long swelling up along his left wrist and forearm. The pain was intense, so he ceased work and started a healing treatment as instructed in the Ben Bibb class. Almost immediately the pain began to subside. In a few moments the throbbing ceased, the swelling diminished and the discoloration started to fade. Within ten minutes all pain was gone, the welt had disappeared and there was no indication his wrist had been so severely damaged a few moments before.

A miracle, you say? No, just an example of what the mind can do when properly directed. This man is no different from you and his abilities are no greater than those you possess. He just knows the Secret. His name is Glenn Whitten and he lives in Statesville, North Carolina. He has given permission for this report to be published and will confirm it if requested.

YOUR MIND CAN HEAL

In the foregoing example the mind is mentioned as the healing agent. Powerful healing ability resides in that little understood and often underrated faculty of yours called the mind—not the brain, the mind. There is a vast difference. The mind uses the brain like a tool, but is limited all too often by the brain's erroneous convictions as to what can be done and what cannot. The human mind is capable of doing many surprising things, as science is just beginning to discover, and the ability to heal without medicine or surgery is one of them. We are blessed today with many men and women who are able to heal and help others. Some are called psychic healers; others, who operate in a religious atmosphere, are called faith healers. Recently it has become clear that all use their minds to heal even though most of them act instinctively and do not fully understand the process involved. They thus have great difficulty in transmitting to others a comprehension of what they do. Few attempt it and those who do have but little success. Yet Ben Bibb knows quite clearly what he does and how he does it and can transmit this amazing secret to others. In this book he will disclose it to you.

There are on file literally hundreds of reports of healings by the pupils of Ben Bibb and confirming acknowledgments from the people who have been helped. These pupils are men and women like yourself with little or no medical knowledge or training. This is emphasized because it is normal for you to question your own ability to heal. The knowledge that so many people, literally hundreds, have already learned to heal themselves and others should encourage you to try it yourself—so read on.

A SINUS HEALING

Let us look at the case of May McLoughlin. She had been troubled for years by chronic sinus attacks. At times her head would ache so badly behind the nose and eyes that she would be unable to see. These attacks would also weaken her legs so she could hardly stand. This debilitated condition would usually prevail for about twenty-four hours after the actual pain in the head had subsided. Edith Jacques, who had been trained by Ben Bibb, gave her a treatment and within one hour the pain was gone. Three hours later she was walking without difficulty and hungry for her dinner. Since then, four months prior to this writing, the sinus attacks have not returned.

RELIEF FROM PAIN

Everyone who has given this system a fair trial is willing to endorse it. They all say "It works!" A letter from Vera Gatto of Paterson, New Jersey to Ben Bibb is an example—

I was in constant pain in my lower back due to many extreme bouts with surgery. My physicians all told me I would have to live with it because they could no longer give me anything but temporary relief from my constant agony of pain. But now, since my treatment by you six months ago, I have been without pain. What a miraculous healing!

Blessing you always,

Vera Gatto

Thus writes a grateful woman.

In the pages that follow are detailed instructions together with practical examples to support every phase of this Medipic technique, as the students refer to it. The phrase Medipic is used because pictures are sent mentally from the healer to the sufferer in a manner which will be explained to you as you read along.

THIS IS A SCIENTIFIC METHOD

Bear in mind that this healing method is not to be classified as inspirational, religious or spiritual. It is scientific, and in all probability will be incorporated into standard medical practice within the next few years. Most doctors already agree that the patient is largely responsible for healing himself and that their efforts are bent toward removing the blocks to that self-healing. The Medipic technique is but an extension of this idea and consists in part of an intelligent, well-directed stimulation of the inner mind toward that end. This is not meant to imply there is no place for Divine Power in this healing method. On the contrary, no work of man, great or small, can be accomplished without Divine Assistance—but some human effort is required. If one desired to build a bridge, how foolish he would seem if he requested Divine Assistance and then sat back doing nothing as he waited for the bridge to appear. What person planning a dinner would just ask for Divine Assistance and then relax in an easy chair while waiting for the table to set itself and the dinner to manifest. Buildings and bridges and yes, even cathedrals and cakes are created by human hands, human minds and human effort. Divine Assistance, yes—but not without human planning and work. So it is also with healing. Such is the Medipic Technique.

In the chapters that follow this technique is explained in complete detail and the Amazing Secrets of Psychic Healing are revealed.

You have only to put the miracles of psychic healing into practice to realize restored health and peace of mind for yourself and those you love.

Ben O. Bibb, D.D.
Joseph J. Weed

Contents

How This Book Will Help You to Radiant
Health 6

Chapter 1. Discover the Amazing Secrets of Psychic
Healing Now 17

Chapter 2. Dramatic and Rapid Psychic Repair for
Accidental Injuries. Learn how to repair
damaged bones and injured tissue with
surprising speed by employing the secret
Medi-Pic treatment. Examples of success-
ful healings by students like yourself. 38

Chapter 3. The Miraculous Psychic Healing Treatment for Relief and Frequent Care of
Arthritis, Rheumatism and Similar Problems. Case histories given that you can
follow and duplicate. 52

Chapter 4. Remarkable Psychic Healing Cures for
Asthma and Other Respiratory Ailments
Including Emphysema, Pneumonia and
Tuberculosis. Supporting case histories. 63

Chapter 5. Psychic Healing Harmonies for Correcting
Skin Ailments Including Shingles, Boils,
Warts and Similar Skin Infections. Specialized treatments with case history
examples of successful cures are included. . . . 76

Chapter 6.   The Secret Psychic Technique for Diagno-
sing Ear, Nose and Throat Problems. Ailments affecting these areas are described
and successful psychic treatments given in
detail, with supporting examples and case
histories.   85

Chapter 7.   Seventh Sense Psychic Healing Methods
for Eye Troubles. This is a most important chapter. Here we consider the various
eye afflictions such as cataract, glaucoma,
etc. and give detailed instructions in the
remarkable psychic healing treatments for
their relief and cure. Supporting case histories are inclued.   95

Chapter 8.   Instant Relief From Headaches: How
Televisual Healing Can Cure Their Causes.
Various reasons for headaches are examined in detail and psychic healing techniques given with explanatory actual case
histories.   104

Chapter 9.   Secret Medi-Pic Methods for Handling
Tumors and Parasitic Internal Growths,
Leading to Their Elimination. Case histo-
ries   113

Chapter 10.   Medi-Pic Methods for Strengthening and
Healing the Heart. How you can repair
heart damage and related problems by
mental instruction given to the inner
mind   122

Chapter 11.   Secret Psychic Healing Treatments for
Banishing Gall Bladder and Liver Ailments. These problems are sometimes
related and frequently stem from the
same general causes. Here you are given
effective methods to successfully cure
these problems with supporting case histories   130

Chapter 12. Amazingly Successful Psychic Healing
             Treatments for Kidney, Bladder and Pros-
             tate Malfunctions. Learn how to psychic-
             ally flush out the kidneys, repair bladder
             ailments and reduce prostate pain and
             difficulty. 142

Chapter 13. Psychic Healing Remedies for Stomach
             and Bowel Disorders. How the causes are
             sought, corrected and healing effected by
             Medi-Pic. 158

Chapter 14. Psychic Healing Treatments for the Relief
             of Toothache, Tooth Infection and Spinal
             Afflictions. The ache and pain can usually
             be relieved in a matter of minutes by
             proper psychic treatment. Repair and
             complete correction may take longer. 167

Chapter 15. How To Psychically Analyze and Correct
             Vein, Artery and Blood Problems. Correc-
             ting techniques are described and sup-
             ported by actual case history examples of
             successful treatments 180

Chapter 16. New Seventh Sense Glandular System Bal-
             ancing Secrets for Correcting Diabetes
             and Serious Ailments of the Thyroid and
             Pancreas. 190

Chapter 17. Healing Colors and Their Various Medi-
             Pic Applications for Miraculous Healing
             of People and Animals 203

Chapter 18. Amazingly Simple Self-Healing of Self-
             Assisted Psychic Healing Methods and
             Secrets, Including the Medi-Automatic
             Twenty-Four Hour Program. 212

1. Discover the amazing secrets of psychic healing now

Right here, in the very first chapter of this book, you will be given the secret of psychic healing. You will discover what you must know, and how to apply that knowledge. In the chapters that follow specialized treatments for various ailments will be described, but in this first chapter is the basic technique of Televisual Healing, as it has been called. Here in simple language is what you must do and how to do it.

The *first secret* is to learn how to contact the inner or subconscious mind of the person to be healed. When you learn this you will be able to "see" the subject mentally and to identify the illness, injury or other distress, including the parts of the body affected. This "in-picture" visualization can be triggered by expanding your imagination from an ordinary daydream condition. There are several ways in which this can be done. Some of the easiest and simplest will be described here. Please do not concern yourself now with *why* these methods work. This will be explained later. Learn *how to* first. This is important. For a learning psychic, theories can be very confusing and preoccupation with them may block success. Right now *methods* are all important—so follow the instructions given and successful results will be yours.

It is not difficult to learn to contact and instruct the inner or subconcious mind of the person you wish to heal. Actually it is far simpler than it may seem at first. Most learn it in a very short time—two or three weeks at the most—providing a sincere effort is made. We have on record the case of a man who after only one day's instruction went home and performed a successful bursitis healing that very night. His name is Fred Miller and he lives in Plainfield, Connecticut. He will verify this.

In the foregoing paragraph it is indicated that a "sincere effort" on your part is required. Everyone with common sense realizes that you don't get something for nothing. Life is like this. Sincere effort is required to heal successfully just as it is needed to achieve any other worthwhile objective in life.

HOW TO REACH THE SUBCONSCIOUS MIND

First in your training is to learn how to dissociate your attention from your conscious mind, your normal thinking apparatus, which registers the smells, sights and sounds that impinge upon your senses. This conscious awareness must be temporarily distracted if you are to reach your own subconscious or inner mind and through it communicate with the inner mind of the person you wish to heal. Today many people who have no interest in becoming healers have learned through practice how to quiet the outer or conscious mind and slow it down to a meditative level where the inner mind can be contacted. Meditation is certainly an excellent way to achieve this, but learning to practice it successfully takes time, usually more than students will devote to it. Another quicker method was therefore sought and found. This is to distract the conscious mind by giving it some ordinary everyday task to perform. Here is one device many have found to be effective. There are several others, but it is suggested you try this Mental Telephone as a starter.

The *Mental Telephone* system was conceived and developed by Ben Bibb to help his students reach the inner mind of the person to be healed. It is really quite simple. All it requires is imagination and a little concentration. Some make a successful contact at their first attempt; others take a little longer. Like anything else worth learning it takes some practice, but not a great deal—nothing at all like the practice required in learning to play even the simplest musical instruments. It is more of a trial-and-error method, like learning to ride a bicycle. Once you get the knack you can become skillful in a short time.

Befort attempting a mental telephone contact, or a mental contact by any other method, the following three conditions should be present.

BASIC REQUIREMENTS

1. Really *want* to make a mind-to-mind contact. If you don't want to, don't try. As you can imagine, a negative attitude of mind can lead only to failure.

2. There must be a definite individual that you want to contact. This person need not be an acquaintance or friend; indeed, he or she need not be known to you at all. But you must have the name, age, sex and the address or location of an actual person (not an imaginary one) that you intend to contact.

3. This person must have an ailment or an injury that you wish to heal. Your mental contact must have a purpose, an intention to do good or to help that person. There is no point in attempting a contact just to say hello or to prove it to yourself. Your inner mind will regard such as frivolous and refuse to cooperate.

THE MENTAL TELEPHONE METHOD

Let us now assume you correctly understand the foregoing conditions and are following them. You have a specific person in mind who needs help and you desire to mentally contact him or her in order to give that help. Sit where you will not be disturbed, take three deep breaths and then relax. When you are calm, *mentally* pick up a telephone and dial the number of the person you wish to reach. If you know the actual number, dial it mentally, if not, dial any number with the appropriate number of digits (7 or 8 or 10). If you don't dial, then mentally ask the operator to get you the party you wish to contact. Just give the name and location.

After a ring or two (imagined by you) you should get an answer. The one requiring healing will be on the line. If at first you don't get a recognizable reply, just imagine that your patient has replied, state your name and ask if he or she wishes to be healed. Some students make a good contact after three or four tries; others require a week or more of practice until they get the knack. Remember, in each contact attempt you must have a definite person in mind, one who actually needs help.

When you start this work and are learning to make mental contacts it is helpful to work on a number of different persons, maybe twenty to thirty. Switch from one to another so that you don't attempt to reach any one person more than twice a day. It is suggested that you use the system the Ben Bibb students employ in their classroom work. This is as follows.

HOW TO PRACTICE

Get a package of three-by-five inch cards from a stationery store. Ask your relatives and friends for the names of people who may need help. It matters not whether this be the result of a recent accident or an ailment of long standing. Put each name on a separate card along with the address (or general location) of the sufferer, his or her approximate age and the problem requiring correction. Twenty to twenty-five name cards should be enough. Then work on each of these names in rotation until you begin to get good contacts. You will learn by doing. Within a week or two at the outside, you will begin to realize a response from the inner mind of one of the persons you are trying to contact. Most often it will welcome your help and your suggestions. Some will be apathetic; with these you will have to use your ingenuity to get their interest. Very seldom will you get an outright rejection. In such cases there is almost always an emotional reason involved. If this happens, look for some emotional clue to guide you to a solution. Here is an example.

A RARE PROBLEM

A Mrs. S. has three small daughters. When they were six, four and two, their mother called from Chicago, where they lived, and asked help for the second daughter, Juanita, the four-year-old. About once every two or three days she would go into convulsions. She would cry out, then alternately stiffen and shake uncontrollably. Between these attacks she seemed normal. The pediatrician confirmed this and said he was at a loss how to help her. I took the responsibility of the case and when I contacted little Juanita mentally I was surprised to hear her answer me in an annoyed adult voice saying, "Let me alone. I know what I am doing."

At first I was puzzled, but then I understood. As the middle child, neither the oldest nor the youngest, she felt neglected and was subconsciously employing these tantrums to get attention. I explained to the mother my interpretation of the situation and suggested she give little Juanita special love and fuss over her for a while. Mrs. S. did so. Apparently this was all that was needed, for the paroxysms ended and have not recurred since.

To get back to your name cards: Some of these will be people you know while others will probably be people you never before heard of and know nothing about. There is no need to talk to any of them about what you are doing or trying to do. In most cases it is better that you don't. When you are learning in this way and before you have acquired the confidence that comes from repeated success, an increased self-awareness on the part of the subject, coupled with normal skepticism, will effectively block your efforts to make contact with his or her inner mind.

Go through the cards in rotation and make an attempt to contact four or five of the names at least once a day. Spend about five minutes on each name. Start by imagining you are talking on the telephone to the person you wish to contact. Remember the events you create in your imagination have reality of their own. This is not a three-dimensional reality to be picked up by your five senses. It may therefore be rejected as nonexistent by the conscious mind. Your inner mind, however, sees and accepts your imaginary creation for the type of reality that it is and, what is important here, so will the inner mind of the person you are trying to heal.

FIRST CONTACTS

Having placed your telephone call, imagine that someone answers. When they do, even if you do not understand what is said, state your name, say you are a healer and ask if he or she needs help. Say, "I believe your physical body may be suffering. Would you like me to try to heal it?"

If in your imagination you receive a reply, any reply except an outright "No," then ask, "Will you indicate the part of your physical body that requires attention by placing your hand over it?"

If in your imagination you then see a hand move to a particular spot, you will know you have actually made contact. Don't doubt this but accept it as a fact.

It is important to find out the cause of the trouble. You can determine exactly what is wrong by asking the inner mind of the subject and also by examining the subject's etheric body. Do not depend upon the way the problem has been diagnosed by hospitals and doctors. Most often they are exactly right, but sometimes their judgment is in error. You can get accurate firsthand information just by looking at the afflicted person, as will be explained later. Make sure to examine him or her thoroughly and ask the inner mind to point out to you the area where lies the seat of the problem. When this has been done you will *know* what must be done to effect a healing.

ANOTHER CONTACT TECHNIQUE

The *Mental Telephone* is an excellent device to employ when first learning to make contact with persons requiring healing, but there are other methods which may be more to your liking. Here is one: Sit calmly in an easy chair. Take three or four deep breaths and when you are fully relaxed, allow yourself to drift into a sort of daydream in which you find yourself standing next to the person requiring help. This is purely imaginary, of course, and your conscious mind, regarding it as no more than a daydream, usually will not interfere. Once you have created this imaginary picture of you standing alongside the person to be healed, take time to observe him or her and something of the surroundings. In this subtle way you can transport yourself from the purely imaginary to the real.

FORGET YOURSELF

In both of the foregoing methods and indeed, in all mental contacts, any self-consciousness on your part will break the contact—so forget yourself. Think only of the person you wish to aid and how you may provide the help needed. Any sort of a flashback to check how you are doing or even to rearrange your chair or cross your knees can be fatal to the success of a mental contact. Your purpose is to employ your inner mind to make contact with the inner mind of the subject to be healed and even the slightest deviation from that purpose will tend to break the contact. Good concentration is necessary, therefore. It may be difficult at first to maintain your dreamlike state but after a few successful contacts you will become so engrossed in what you are doing and the reactions you are getting from the person you are helping that you will no longer have to worry about the intrusion of your conscious mind.

HOW YOU MAY CREATE THOUGHT FORMS

At this early stage in their training some students have said, "As far as I'm concerned, this is purely imaginary. I don't see how it can do any good." Not so. There is no such state as "purely" imaginary in the sense that it exists only in the imagination of the thinker and nowhere else. The human mind is automatically creative, which means that every thought and every imagining held in the mind has a factual existence. The solidity of that factual (or material) existence depends upon the power of the creative thought and the force of the emotion behind it; thus the greater your desire to make a successful inner mind contact, the more forceful will your imagining be. But don't get tense or uptight, for this will defeat your purpose. Stay in the calm relaxed dream state, but see your imaginary pictures more clearly and sustain them longer in your inner mind. The longer a clear thought is held, the more it "solidifies" and the nearer it comes to materialization. When the same thought is repeated clearly at intervals an enhanced and strengthened effect is produced.

Keep a file of three-by-five cards on which you have listed the name, sex, age and location of the various people who need help. As you learn of others make cards for them as well and set all these people up for healing treatments when you start this next phase of training. Before going on to the instructions for healing, you may find helpful some reports of actual experiences in making mind-to-mind contacts. Here is one from a graduate, Julia Whitten, who lives in Statesville, North Carolina.

THE AMAZING EXPERIENCE OF MRS. WHITTEN

The first time I concentrated deeply enough to make mind-to-mind contact in order to "see" what the trouble was with the subject, I felt as if I were reaching out, somewhat like groping outward with hands and arms in a dark room—only I wasn't groping with my hands but with my mind. As my objective neared I began to feel quiet and then a feeling of awe came over me as my mind reached that of the subject. How did I know I had reached that point? This is most difficult to describe: I experienced a feeling of warm, glowing energy, complete peace, and above all, a feeling of oneness with all things at that moment. As our individual inner minds met for a common goal, I could see what appeared to be tiny fine copper wires connecting us as I was permitted to join with this other mind. Once I had made the connection, the physical body of the subject seemed to become as a shadow, secondary to the problem at hand—but the minds were real.

Mrs. Whitten's colorful description of her first mind-to-mind contact should help you understand some of your own experiences.

Here is another report, this one by a successful graduate healer, Mrs. Joyce Dix of West Palm Beach, Florida.

First I look at the person's aura. This gives me a standard against which to weigh all subsequent observations. Next I try to get the "feel" of the person's frame of mind—does he or she want to be healed? Is he or she "enjoying" poor health? Will he or she be cooperative? All this comes before asking any questions. Based then on the impressions thus obtained, I proceed to seek out the ailment and how it may be corrected.

Mrs. Dix here mentions the aura of the subject. Auras will be explained and a method for interpreting the information they convey will be described in a later chapter. Before going now to healing instruction, you should know something about the human mind, or minds. You can become a perfectly competent healer without this specific information, so you may skip this part if you wish and go right on to the heading "How to Heal" on page 26. If you would understand how the mind works, however, read this section before going any further.

HOW THE HUMAN MIND WORKS

Every human being is comprised of three thinking entities. Most psychiatrists agree to this. All three are "you," but each of these entities is distinct from the others and appears to function apart from the other two. These three thinking entities are:

1. The conscious mind.

2. The inner or subjective mind.

3. The higher mind, sometimes referred to as the soul.

Since it is important for you to understand how each functions, they are here described as follows.

The *conscious mind* is the only one of which most people are ever aware. It is wholly dependent upon the brain, which is our contact with the physical world through the senses of sight, hearing, touch, taste and smell. These senses record the impressions they receive from outside physical stimuli and then send them on to the brain which records them and then translates them in turn to the conscious mind. These impressions are also permanently impressed upon the inner mind without the concious mind being aware of it.

We are all inclined to the perfectly natural mistake of assuming that the conscious mind is the only mind, and therefore the entire "self." *It is not.* There is no question but that it is in control of you, your life and most of your voluntary actions. Because the impacts on our five outer senses are so powerful and often so dramatic, we have a tendency to ignore our other senses, our other sources of information. One leading psychiatrist, Dr. Lindsay Jacob, says we have at least thirty senses and cites as examples, a sense of balance, a sense of both physical and emotional exhaustion, a sense of muscular fatigue and so on. All of these senses send their information to the subconscious mind as well as to its conscious counterpart, but all too often the conscious mind ignores it. Another frailty of the conscious mind is that it works entirely through the brain, and if this organ is damaged or inhibited in any way, the functioning of the conscious mind is likewise impaired.

These limitations of the conscious mind are emphasized in order that you may better realize the important part in human life that is played by the subconscious or inner mind. The inner mind has equal importance with the conscious mind and in many ways it is more powerful, so it is necessary for you to know about it and understand some of its functions.

The *inner mind* can do amazing things, many of them impossible from the viewpoint of the conscious mind. It constructed the human body, your body, from a single cell. Compared to this, healing a wound or correcting a bodily malfunction is a relatively insignificant task. Can you imagine your conscious mind, your present sense of awareness, achieving such a miracle? The inner mind not only made your body but keeps it functioning twenty-four hours a day. Have you any idea what a masterful job this is? Can you imagine just trying to keep your heart beating via impulses from your conscious mind? You wouldn't live more than five minutes. Don't make the mistake of regarding your heart beat as "automatic." It only appears that way to your conscious mind. All of your bodily functions, including breathing, digestion, elimination, etc., are intelligently and continuously directed, but since this activity is below the awareness level of the conscious mind, it dismisses the entire wonderful performance as "automatic," with little more than passing curiosity.

There is nothing wrong with this arrangement. In fact, this is the way it should be in order to give the conscious mind and its tool, the brain, a chance to develop. This developing process has still a long way to go, as is indicated by the fact that we use, on the average, less than ten percent of our brain's capacity. When we ignore the inner mind, we neglect a most powerful instrument which is there for us to use, if we but try. For one thing, we can use it to heal ourselves and to heal others. The whole purpose of this course of instruction is to teach you how to do this.

When you came into being, your inner mind was programmed to create a certain type of body and to keep it functioning smoothly, or as smoothly as your conscious mind and your emotions would permit. The inner mind does not reason nor form judgments and make decisions, but usually accepts without question the attitudes adopted by your conscious nature. It can be reached, however, and will usually follow constructive suggestions. It is this willingness to accept instruction that we employ in our healing work.

The *higher mind or soul* is where the "I," the real self, usually resides. This part of you is most powerful and, when called into action, can wield physical matter and events as easily as your hands can shape wet clay. In the present stage of the average human's development—and this applies to most of us—it stands aloof so that the conscious mind, through trial and oft-repeated mistakes, may learn the true nature of energy and how to put it to the best use. Only rarely do we approach the soul in our healing work. You will learn as we proceed when and how to do this.

HOW TO HEAL

It is necessary to realize that you yourself, and everyone else, has these three mental entities functioning within. As we have said, few people are aware of anything but what their conscious minds hold before them. To work with our healing methods you must learn to distinguish the inner mind from the conscious mind and be able to contact it. For it is the inner mind of the subject that in most cases does the healing. It will also communicate to you, the healer, the exact nature and location of the injury or malfunction so that an accurate appraisal may be made. The methods to make this contact and obtain the necessary information have been described earlier in this chapter. Now we will study the various healing techniques which may be employed in Televisual Healing.

Here is a brief outline of the method most frequently used.

1. Contact the inner mind of the subject and observe the true nature of the injury or malfunction.

2. Use mental pictures to show the subject's inner mind how to correct this.

3. Supply healing energy and instruct the subject's inner mind how to obtain the energy necessary for it to perform and sustain the healing.

4. See the subject perfectly healed, then break contact gently and give it no further thought *at that time,* although the treatment may be repeated later.

We have seen how to contact the subject's mind and learn from it the true nature of the ailment and its cause. Now, armed with this information proceed to step 2, the actual Televisual healing technique. As you will come to realize, the name Televisual is most fitting, as is also the descriptive name, Telepic.

Mind-to-mind contact is the oldest form of communication between humans. It existed long before speech was developed and is actually the transfer of impressions from one mind to another. Initially these were only feelings but in our present sophisticated day, pictures convey the impressions far more clearly than feelings, or even words. Words are particularly unreliable because they, too, are symbols and often mean different things to different people. A picture clearly shown is unmistakable, however. The technique of sending a picture from one mind to another is called the Televisual method or Telepic.

HOW YOU CAN EMPLOY
TELEVISUAL HEALING

This is not difficult. You first create a picture in your mind, not a still one, but a moving, living picture of the procedure you wish the inner mind of the subject to follow in order to heal the physical ailment. Here again, as in the first steps at making contact with the inner mind, the imagination is brought into play. The human imagination is more powerful and has far greater capabilities than we, as a race, have ever conceived of, much less recognized. I'm not talking about fantasy, which is but a loosely knit by-product of the imagination, but of the hard core creative imaginative process. You must certainly know that every great invention, every discovery of science, every great creation of man, first existed in someone's imagination as an idea. Every forward step of the human race started in the imagination of one or more persons. These facts alone should give you some concept of the power of the imagination. What is suggested here is that you give your imagination the respect due it and then learn to employ it usefully, instead of carelessly as most people do. If you start by imagining that you are making a contact with the patient, you will, if you persevere, actually make that contact. If during that contact you give certain suggestions to the patient's inner mind, it will comprehend them and usually act them out as you gave them. Remember, the conscious mind *always* thinks and communicates in words, but the inner mind uses impressions, usually pictures.

A PRACTICE HEALING SESSION

Let us assume now you have succeeded in making a contact with the inner mind of a person you are trying to help. You have started by visualizing a person of the same sex and approximate age of the subject whose name you have, and now you are noticing some additional characteristics not put there by you in your initial visualization. So you speak, not aloud, but mentally. Meanwhile, let your conscious mind believe you are still daydreaming so that it will temporarily relax its strict censorship of the inner mind; then start an imaginary conversation.

Do not try to figure out *why* this method works. It does—and you can make it work. Too much introspection will lead you back into the realm of the conscious mind which will result in doubt and then failure. Instead of thinking about what you are doing, just *do it.* Always see yourself as busily doing something even if it is only talking to the patient. So don't analyze—*act.*

HOW TO EXAMINE THE SUBJECT

Once you have made a successful contact and are "locked in," so to speak, on the inner mind of the patient, you can begin your examination. See and examine the etheric body of the one desiring your help. It will be perfectly visible to your inner mind and will appear normally as a pale gray-blue figure, corresponding in detail to the patient's physical body, but slightly larger. As you look at it you may observe a dark area, possibly a dark gray or brown or dull red patch in the otherwise shimmering etheric body. If so, you will know that this corresponds to the part of the physical body which needs to be healed. In most cases this indication will corroborate the diagnosis of the attending doctors, or if the person has not been treated by a physician, it will probably indicate the place where he hurts. Should your observation differ from the medical diagnosis, by all means keep your impressions to yourself. You are not ever, under any circumstances, to announce that you have diagnosed a condition to be such-and-such. Your observations are purely mental and are solely for your aid in mental healing. Never set yourself up in opposition to the medical profession even though you may be convinced that you are right and the medical diagnosis incorrect. To state so openly will be sheer vanity on your part. Surely your ego does not need that kind of support. Cure the person if you can and say nothing.

ALWAYS OBEY THE LAW

Most states have very stringent laws designed to protect their citizens from quacks and charlatans. These laws must be respected; in this connection I wish to give you the following advice before proceeding further.

1. It is not necessary to touch a person you have been asked to heal. In our mental work this is not necessary, but where such contact seems advisable, use the finger tips lightly. No massage!

2. Never tell a patient, or anyone else, what you believe to be the cause of the patient's trouble if it should be contrary to the medical diagnosis. Keep your observations entirely to yourself, to be used only as a guide to your own healing efforts.

3. Never prescribe exercises or massages, and never recommend medication of any sort, internal or external. Remember, you are a *mental* healer.

4. If you should believe that a line of physical treatment not recommended by the doctor might speed recovery, have the patient ask the doctor if, in his opinion, it might help—for example, maybe an external massage with warm castor oil as a remedy for arthritic pain. Usually his reply will be, "I don't know, but if you want to try it, go ahead. It can do no harm." He might say,"Under no circumstances," though, and in that case, never mention it again.

Keep the foregoing admonitions in mind at all times. Remember, you are not in competition with the medical profession and any such attempt on your part will come more from a desire to inflate your ego than to help the patient. Cooperate with doctors and support their efforts in every way you can. Their knowledge and experience is far greater than ours. In this country alone they treat and help to cure millions of people a year. You will come to learn that our work is occasionally with people who have not responded to normal medical treatment. Sometimes their afflictions are labeled incurable; sometimes they are described as terminal. It is then our job to visually present to the patient's inner mind a technique of repair which it can employ to free its body from the recalcitrant growth, injury or disease. If you are successful where standard medical procedure apparently failed, be thankful for this privilege. Under no circumstances make comparisons. It won't be too long before the medical profession will include our mental healing methods along with their present chemical and surgical treatments.

Meanwhile, do what you can to help others. You will find, I am sure, that most of your treatments will be for relatively minor ailments—a sore throat, a tennis elbow, a bad tooth and so on. When your friends and relatives learn that you can help them, they will probably seek you out before they consider going to a doctor. This is all right. It is good for you, and if you help them to robust health, it is good for them, too.

HOW TO INTERPRET THE PROBLEM

Now, after this digression, let us go back to the person to be healed. You have established mental contact and are ready to observe the nature of his or her trouble. Don't expect to find a companion all ready for a heart-to-heart talk. You will be lucky if your first few contacts will give you a few fleeting impressions, sometimes *symbolic impressions* which you will have to interpret according to your own background of experience. For example, you may get the impression that the patient is in a wheelchair. Since this might mean heart trouble or arthritis or just a broken leg, you should meditate on this picture and try to learn from your earlier and more impressionable years just what this means to you. Oh, yes, you say, it must be arthritis. From my earliest childhood I remember my granduncle was always in a wheelchair because he had arthritis.

You might visualize a pipe with a thick brown, syrupy material flowing through it. For many this would signal diabetes, yet another person might for the same ailment see white specks in red blood symbolizing sugar crystals. Of course, as you proceed to handle twenty or thirty cases you will be able to get a picture of the patient and then his or her actions will convey more clearly what the problem is. Most healers get symbolic impressions before they achieve good mental vision, however. This is the fault of their own conscious mind, which is inclined to fight what it regards as an intrusion of the inner mind into its own domain. In a way, it is necessary for the inner mind to use subtlety in presenting information gleaned in a mental contact. If the conscious mind regards these impressions just as daydreams, it will let them pass into your awareness. Later on, when you gain more confidence and greater control these subtleties will no longer be necessary.

WRITE DOWN ALL
YOUR IMPRESSIONS

Whatever your early impressions may be, record them or write them down on the card, no matter how trivial or irrelevant they may seem. They may later be verified as quite accurate. Some healers register their first impressions on themselves. One of the students working on a woman patient she did not know and had never seen suddenly felt a pain in the left side of her neck. After a little thought she came to the conclusion the patient had a "wry neck." This proved to be exactly true. The patient's head was fixed in a twisted position down over her left shoulder and she could not move it without suffering pain.

Since each of you is an individual, different from everyone else, you must expect that most of the symbolic impressions you receive will be definitely your own. Don't throw out any impressions. Try to understand what your inner mind is attempting to convey to the conscious mind. In this work you must learn to trust your imagination. Sometimes you will get a mental picture of the patient as he or she appears physically. More often, though, your impression will be of the inner physical and etheric workings of the patient's organism. We must work with what we get. This is not fantasy, as two or three successful healings will soon prove. Just withhold judgment of your impression. Give it a fair chance and you will be surprised at how soon you will get tangible results.

When you get a mental picture of the physical appearance of the patient, it is usually best to start a mental conversation. You might give your name, say you want to help and politely ask if the patient would like your assistance. If the answer is affirmative, then say, "Where is your distress? Show me by pointing to its location." The resulting indication, if it agrees with the report the doctors have made, should guide you from that point onward. Often, though, you will get only an impression of the etheric or energy body of the patient. In a healthy normal person, this energy body is bright and scintillating, so if you observe a dark or turgid area you will know that this is where the problem lies. Sometimes the etheric body will appear to have one or more holes in it. These usually indicate that a malignancy exists in those spots.

In order that you may have a general idea of the name and location of the various organs in the human body, I am including here some charts which show the bone structure and the major organs. You should study these until you are familiar with their names and functions.

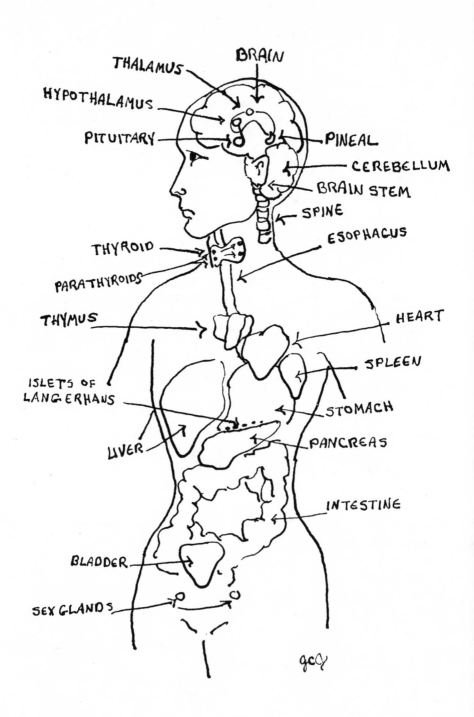

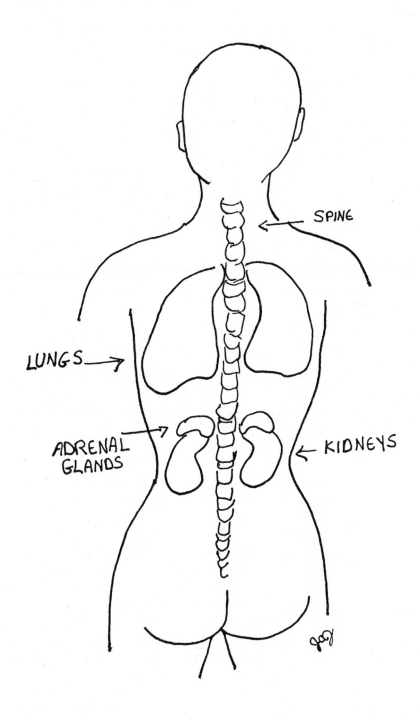

MEDIPIC: YOU TEACH THE SUFFERERS
TO HEAL THEMSELVES

Most of the healing we accomplish is performed by the patient, by his or her inner mind. I hear the question, "If this is so, why doesn't it heal without us and do that long before we are notified that a healing is required?" The answer is that the inner mind is programmed to guide all normal bodily functions, to rush blood to a wound, to increase the supply of white corpuscles to fight an infection, to grow a broken bone together and so on—but there are certain conditions which it accepts as normal and does not act upon. It does not fight against a malignant cancer, for example, because these cancer cells are native to the body and, even though violently destructive, are regarded by the inner mind as "belonging." In the case of a broken bone the healing process will automatically go to work, but unless the break is properly aligned, the healing may result in a malformation. Also, in arthritic conditions where the cause is emotional distress, the inner healing process is helpless as long as the emotions continue their harassment of the physical.

. . . AND TO PROTECT THEMSELVES

Recently one student came to me for help. For a reason that will soon be obvious she refused the use of her name, so we will call her Mrs. A.M.T. She said she had a severe headache and asked if I could relieve her of the pain. Knowing her ability as a healer, I asked her why she didn't heal herself. She replied that she could ease the pain but it would come back in a couple of hours. When I remarked that obviously the cause of the headache was still present and asked her why she hadn't eliminated it, she said she couldn't. It then became clear to me that her headaches were the result of emotional distress caused by the violent and unreasonable temper tantrums of her husband. Calming her would give only temporary relief and her headache would be back again the very next time her husband "blew his stack." After a puzzled moment a solution occurred to me: to insulate her against undesirable emotional impacts. I taught her to strengthen her aura by increasing its psychic energy reserve and thus building up a wall of resistance. The method was to see herself surrounded by a pink cloud, the outer perimeter of which would be solid enough to prevent the intrusion of unwanted emotional violence—like being inside of a large pink egg. She was instructed to create this herself and to renew it once a day. When I asked her how she felt some weeks later she said, "Oh, fine thanks. No more headaches, and when the old man explodes I just relax and let it run off me like water off a duck's back."

REACH THE SUBJECT'S INNER MIND WITH MEDIPIC SYMBOLS

It is well to remember that when you contact the inner mind of a person in distress, you communicate in symbols, and the simpler they are, the better. There are no words required in mind-to-mind contact; if you should use words they would be solely for your own benefit as a device to keep you concentrating on the idea you wish to convey. You will recall that mind-to-mind communication is via impressions. The nearest our concrete mind can get to this is pictures, so most of your instruction to the inner mind of a patient will be by means of pictures—motion pictures.

The pictures or scenarios you send are not offered in the expectation they will be slavishly followed. The inner mind of the subject has its own methods for handling the situation once it gets a general idea of what must be done to effect a cure. The simplest pictures are best. If a muscle is torn, tie it together. If a subject's lungs are filled with mucus, use a vacuum cleaner. If there is a growth to be removed, pluck it out with your fingers. Never, never visualize the use of a knife: there should be no cutting. You are to heal tissues, not destroy them. If a tooth is loose, take it out with your fingers mentally, clean it thoroughly and return it after first packing the cavity with glue (mental, of course).

LEARN THROUGH PRACTICE

Our experience with various groups of students indicates the need to remind them occasionally how important it is for them to get to the meditative or detached level of thought before attempting contact. Once you learn this it is quite simple, but the conscious mind will always offer resistance. Practice is required. It is suggested, therefore, that in addition to the telephone technique you also repeat the exercise for reaching the meditation level. For practice you might get twenty or thirty names of people you do not know who need help and try to contact them. You should not be told their difficulty. This you are to find out by contacting them mentally. Put what you learn on a card with his or her name and then try later to find out the accuracy of your appraisal.

We are aware that some students find it difficult to get their active consciousness down to the meditation level, the so-called alpha level. As you know, there are several different methods; what one person will find easy will not work well for another. Before going any further with actual healing instruction, I will describe some other meditation techniques which have been found to be effective. If what you have been doing for a week or two has not brought satisfaction, then try one of these methods. Give it a chance; it is not easy to still the conscious mind. Practice is required, and some must work at it longer than others before success comes.

OTHER PROVEN MEDITATION METHODS

One very wonderful healer says that she employs the "shutting out the world" method recommended by Hindu teachers. She sits quietly with back erect and eyes closed and then performs the classic ballet gesture of sweeping first the right arm and then the left arm out across her body. This is a symbolic gesture designed to indicate a pushing away of all worldly things. Then she listens, not to the physical sounds, but to the thoughts that run through her head. Gradually their mad rush slows down and eventually the conscious mind becomes still. At this point start your contact with the person you desire to heal. She says it will help greatly if you feel an affinity for all life, all living things. This realization will make it easier for you to contact the patient, to flow to him or her in a stream of living energy.

Another successful healer suggests that in the beginning the student set aside at least fifteen minutes each day to develop a contact with the inner mind. He says it is best to sit upright in a chair where you will not be disturbed and with eyes closed proceed to relax completely. In addition to consciously relaxing your muscles, one at a time if necessary, you should take several deep breaths, exhaling each very slowly. Then, when relaxed, offer a petition to God, or the Cosmic, for aid in reaching the person to be healed. He goes on, "This attunement is a subtle thing, not easily described in words. It is like being semiconscious, halfway between waking and dreaming."

Another healer advises the student to sit poised and balanced avoiding both rigidity and sloppy posture. Every muscle should be consciously relaxed including particularly the muscles of the neck, jaws and even eyebrows. "When the body is relaxed," he says, "then turn to the mind. Gently move the center of your attention from the outer to the innermost part of your head. If your thoughts stray, as they are likely to do, bring them back carefully and gently, not abruptly. Sometimes it helps to focus on some high abstraction like wisdom, beauty, goodness, or gratitude for some extraordinary help you have received. Thus you lift your conciousness from the everyday things about you to the blue heavens above."

You will notice that the methods recommended to their pupils by these three different and very successful healers are all quite similar. They are all pathways to the same beautiful garden, the garden of attunement with the inner self. Try them all and select one of them or any other method, and practice it daily until you succeed. This should not take too long. Some achieve good attunement in a week; others in two or three weeks depending on how hard they work at it. There is nothing taught by Ben Bibb that you yourself cannot achieve if you only try. Hundreds have—why should you be different?

In the chapters that follow, various difficulties, ailments and other human problems will be analyzed and their treatments described, each separately. Basic to all success with this method, however, is the ability to get your own inner mind to contact the inner mind of the one seeking help, and then show it in mental pictures what needs to be done. This is the secret.

May success crown your efforts!

2. Dramatic and rapid psychic repair for accidental injuries

You now know the secret technique, the basic healing principle employed so successfully by Ben Bibb and his graduate students. As you practice this and find that it really works, you will gain in self-confidence, your technical skill will improve and you will obtain quicker and more impressive results for the people who ask your help. You will be amazed at how quickly the knowledge of your ability will spread. Friends and relatives will ask you for aid and you will even receive requests from people you have never met. Helping others is a great work; be thankful to the Lord that this privilege has been granted you.

THE INITIAL STEPS IN HEALING
ACCIDENTAL INJURIES

As you proceed with your healing work, you will find that on the average, the largest number of people who request your help will be the victims of accidents. The busiest place in any general hospital is always the accident ward. Apparently a great many people are not properly equipped to cope with the multitude of various mechanical devices on the market today and are often careless in handling them. Witness the number of auto accidents over any weekend. It is for this reason that a whole chapter is devoted to accidents and special instructions given on the best methods of healing the injuries that may have resulted from them.

Cuts or tears in the skin, both surface and internal bruises, and bone fractures are the commonest injuries in accidents. Regardless of what damage may have occurred, there is almost always pain, so in discussing the best ways to heal these accident injuries, we will first of all consider pain and how to alleviate it.

Pain. It is obvious that the best way to get rid of pain is to find and eliminate its cause. Often you can do this fairly quickly, as in the case of flesh wounds. Some injuries, like bone fractures, take longer, though—sometimes two to four days depending upon the complexity of the fracture and the amount of life energy the inner mind of the victim is able to apply to the problem. In these cases, pain continues unless you take action to reduce it or stop it entirely.

In general, the best procedure after making contact with the inner mind of the victim is to instruct it to become calm and to soothe the agitated nerves. As you now know, this is done by visualization. There are many ways in which this may be done. As you proceed with this work and gain experience you will develop for yourself the technique which suits you best. Here, for example, are some of the methods used successfully by students like yourself. If any one of them suits your own thinking, use it.

A PSYCHIC HEALING CASE STUDY

This report is from Joyce Dix of West Palm Beach, Florida. She is married, has two grown children and currently teaches school. She has had great success in relieving headache pain. When asked about her method, she responded as follows:

> Usually my treatment for a headache is first to make contact with the subconscious mind of the sufferer and talk gently to it. When I get its attention, I give it instructions to shrink the blood vessels in the head until the blood supply returns to normal. This almost always reduces or entirely eliminates the ache within a few minutes. In addition, if I am with the person, I place my hands on his or her head as my own inner mind instructs me and then pour white healing energy into the area indicated. I don't hear the instructions but "sense" the position.

THE MIRACULOUS CURE OF PAIN

Frans M. Eyberse of Lisbon, Ct. when asked about simple pain said,

> I have several times stopped the pain of headaches, earaches and colds, by pouring white healing energy into the area affected. On two occasions I stopped earaches in my son by merely placing my hands over the boy's ears and pouring white energy down through my arms

and into his ears. I have successfully taken away the pain of headache in several different people in the same manner.

In a slightly different situation I found I was able to relieve the distress of a severe hacking cough. One evening as I was about to leave the house, my ten-year-old daughter complained of a cough. I gave her a cough drop and put her to bed before I left at 7:30 p.m. When I returned at midnight I found that she had been unable to sleep. Her cough had become progressively worse and twice was so violent she became nauseated and threw up. I turned her onto her stomach in her bed and placed my right hand on the back of her neck with my fingers touching the skull area; then I poured powerful blue-white energy down my arms and into the area covered by my hand. After I started this she coughed only once more and in five minutes was sound asleep. She slept throughout the rest of the night and awoke feeling bright, fresh and very much relieved.

From the examples given, you can see that these two healers employ white healing energy to reduce pain. When the injured person is present, this energy can be transmitted to the affected area through the hands of the healer. Here's what you do. Take a deep breath, hold it for a moment and then release it slowly. Repeat this three or four times and as you do so, mentally visualize psychic energy accumulating around your head and shoulders in the form of a brilliant white cloud. You will begin to feel a tingling sensation. When you notice this, send the energy out by visualizing it flowing from the white cloud across your shoulders, down your arms and out your hands in a shining white stream right onto and into the place where the pain is located.

The foregoing cases all involved physical contact or close physical approach. Some people feel more confident of success when they are able to see and touch the one in pain. However, most healers work equally effectively at a distance, sometimes helping a person they have never seen—and may never see in the flesh.

CURING PAIN OVER GREAT DISTANCES

Mrs. Jacqueline Gonnella, who lives in Ringwood, N.J. gives the following report of the method she used to reduce and ultimately eliminate pain from a person who was more than fifty miles distant. Since there is also a subsequent very interesting healing involved in this case, the entire report is included. Jackie Gonnella writes:

My sister Joyce Bogdan is 29 years old and lives in Fairless Hills, Pa. For some years she has had what she calls a Joe Namath knee. It occasionally slips out of joint, always unexpectedly and frequently at the most awkward times and places. The resulting pain and distress usually last about six weeks. She wears a knee support but since she is a beautician and has to spend much of the day on her feet, she has found this small insurance.

After I had learned the Ben Bibb healing secrets and had achieved some successful cures, she called me one day in distress and asked my help. She had thrown out her knee that day and was in so much pain she could not stand, much less do any work, so I went to work on her immediately. First, I put mental ice-packs on her knee to ease the pain and reduce the swelling. Then I treated her etheric body by flooding all of the dark red (painful) areas with white healing energy. Then I proceeded to oil all of the bones in her knee using olive oil and honey. Moving then to the ligaments, cartilages and muscles, I reinforced all of them, using narrow strips of rubber which I tied in place. Finally I wrapped the knee (still mentally) with porous tape to give it support until her inner mind completed the repair work.

She told me later that the pain left her about an hour after she talked to me on the telephone and two days afterward she was able to go back to work.

PAINT A HEALING PICTURE
IN YOUR MIND

It is important that you pick up and adopt the positive ideas you find in the many healing reports in this book. These techniques fully exemplify that "what you see is what you get." In less simple language, this means that whatever you clearly visualize for the person asking help, that is the direction and form the help will take. So if your visualization is half-hearted or less than complete, the results will be proportionally diminished. Think positively; always be confident in the success of your efforts and they will be richly rewarded.

The following case is simple, but because of its simplicity it will help you to understand how really easy the Ben Bibb healing method is to employ. It concerns a woman, a housewife and mother who heals her small son and does not regard it as unusual in any way. She is Mrs. Frances Miller of Plainfield, Connecticut. Here is her report:

One morning I tapped my six-year-old son Timothy on the shoulder to awaken him and told him it was time to get up. He sat up and swung his feet over the side of the bed but when he stood up and put his weight on his feet, he let out a scream of pain and fell back on the bed. I examined his feet and his right ankle looked like someone had put a golf ball under the skin. I carried him to the living room and set him on the couch where he sipped orange juice while I prepared breakfast.

About a half hour went by before I checked his foot, but there was no change. If anything the swelling was larger and darker. So I went to my room and shut out all other thoughts while I mentally examined his foot and lower right leg. There were black lines running down the leg and into the ankle while the ankle area itself seemed to be filled with fluid. I proceeded to expel the fluid with my mental hands and then scraped all the black lines clean. Following this, I suffused the whole area first with pain-killing energy and then with healing energy.

The entire operation took less than five minutes. I rose and went to the kitchen to take the coffee off. I then checked Tim's foot and found the ankle had been reduced in size to about one half what it had been. Five minutes later it was back to normal. I asked Tim to stand up but he was still fearful of the pain he had experienced earlier. However, after a little urging he rose and put his weight on it. What a surprise! No pain! The pure joy on his face as he strutted about the room was a sight to behold.

PINPOINT THE CAUSE OF
THE PAIN

In the healing work you will do, you will find that pain always has a cause. You will be shirking your responsibility if you do not seek out that cause and do your best to correct it. In each of the foregoing reports on pain, a cause is indicated or its presence inferred. To relieve the pain of a headache is a fine goal which frequently can be effected in two or three minutes, but the headaches always have a cause which should be sought out and corrected.

ELIMINATION OF 25-YEAR-OLD PAIN

This case is reported by Yolande (Mrs. Ted) Scott of Lake Worth, Florida.

My teacher and counselor, Dr. Ben Bibb, had remarked that generally the most difficult cases are those concerning persons with whom you are emotionally involved, such as a husband, wife, child or parent. I had achieved several good healings, so in spite of this less than encouraging statement, I decided to try and help my husband, who for twenty-five years had suffered from very severe headaches. These headaches were neither occasional nor mild. While the attacks came in an erratic pattern, they were frequent: sometimes every day, sometimes every other day, rarely less than twice a week. The doctor had given him a prescription sedative so that when they were very bad he could get some measure of comfort.

The headaches had started twenty-five years ago when he was in the military service. He was stricken then by what was diagnosed as a hepatitis virus and confined to the base hospital for three weeks. His headaches continued afterward and after many tests, the doctors told him that over a period of time the frequency and severity of the headaches would gradually subside—but they did not.

During the ensuing years many physical examinations were made and tests given—x-rays from head to toe to assure the nonexistence of tumors, chiropractic treatments, etc.—until finally he was sent to a prominent neurosurgeon. This required further tests and x-rays. When the results had been studied by the neurosurgeon, he told Ted that in the neck portion of his spinal column there was an accumulation of calcium which had hardened between nine of the vertebrae. This was pinching the nerves and causing the headaches.

Two courses were offered. One was surgery to remove the calcium; the second was traction. The traction treatment consists of putting the head in a harness which, by means of pulleys and a ten-pound weight, tends to draw the head away from the body and thus relieve the pressure on the spine and the nerves entering the base of the skull. This traction treatment was selected as the lesser of two evils since surgery could always be performed as a last resort.

For one full year Ted was in traction for two hours every day. He had no pain or headaches and felt he was cured. He started to skip the treatment for a day, then two, with no ill effects, but when he daringly skipped two weeks the headaches came back with a crash. It seemed then that surgery was necessary, but because of the obvious risk involved, we kept putting it off.

It was about this time that I heard of Ben Bibb and went to him for instruction. I attended the lectures and participated in numerous discussions. Eventually I was successful in effecting several cures and it was then I decided to try to cure my husband.

I gave him four treatments at two-day intervals. In each I followed the same procedure. I first surrounded him with a blue aura to soothe his nerves and ease the pain; then I mentally performed an operation to remove the calcium by delicately filing away the calcium deposits with an abrasive paper similar to a manicurist's emery board. Following this I applied lubricating oil between the surfaces of the vertebrae to facilitate a smooth easy flowing motion. After each operation, I engulfed the entire spinal column in an aura of white energy followed by a flow of golden healing energy. To assure a carry-over of the energizing effect, I ordered Ted's subconscious mind to periodically reapply these energies until the next operation. After the fourth mental operation, Ted said he felt fine, so I stopped the treatment. Now over two years have elapsed with no recurrence of the headaches. Apparently he is cured. I am happy to have been instrumental in helping my husband, but I take no credit. This is God's work; I am only a channel through which He has performed a miracle. You too can do the same. Study, confidence and persistence are the keynotes.

HOW PSYCHIC HEALING
POWER EXPANDS

Mrs. Scott has worked hard and has developed into an excellent healer but as you are probably beginning to realize, you will at first have better success with people you have never seen than with those close to you. Gradually, as you become more experienced, this will change, and you will be able to heal anyone who comes to you for help. It is usually wiser to start with less difficult problems, however, until such time when your confidence in your own ability is solidly established, because assurance and confidence play as large a part in success in healing as they do in achieving success in any other endeavor. Can you imagine a champion tennis player worrying about his service, or a top flight golfer worrying about his drives? They both *know* they are going to work. So must you. If you follow the methods described in the preceding chapter you will shortly be successfully healing three or four people a day. This is the foundation of confidence. Don't worry; it will become easy.

CUTS AND ABRASIONS

The commonest injuries incurred in accidents are cuts and abrasions. These are healed in different ways, depending upon the nature of the wound and also on your own background of knowledge and experience. It might be well at this point to go back to Chapter 1 and read again Ben Bibb's instructions on the methods to be employed in making contact with the inner or subconscious mind of the injured person. Once this contact has been established, you should then employ the Televisual technique and send to that person's inner mind by mental visualization a short scenario describing the best method of healing as you understand it. Use the simplest of pictures to convey the idea. If bleeding is excessive, stuff the wound with cotton to restrain the flow of blood while you proceed to seal off the injured arteries and other blood vessels. If there are pieces of glass or metal fragments in the wound, pick them out with your fingers—all of them—and put them in a small sack which you will later destroy. All these actions take place only in your own mind, but the inner mind of the injured person accepts them as suggestions and then carries out the pictorization in its own way and by its own methods.

A STOMACH INFECTION
QUICKLY BANISHED

Here is a case history which may make this clearer. June Amlin of Boynton Beach, Florida had been troubled with a stomach infection accompanied by diarrhea for five days when at 2 a.m. she fainted in the bathroom. In her fall she sustained a concussion and a badly damaged face. She was taken to Bethesda Memorial Hospital in Boynton Beach, Florida, where it was ascertained that the bridge of her nose was fractured and that a portion of the nasal bone had broken off and was touching the brain. She was bleeding profusely from both nose and mouth and could breathe only with difficulty through her mouth. When her brother was informed of her condition, he telephoned Margaret Bibb, wife of Ben Bibb, and asked for help. Margaret agreed to help. Shortly after his call, the bleeding stopped suddenly, but June's breathing was still difficult. However, the pain eased gradually and shortly thereafter June fell asleep. She awoke at midnight with a clear head and no pain, and was able to breathe freely through both nose and mouth. Furthermore, her stomach no longer bothered her and the diarrhea had ended.

Here now is Margaret Bibb's report of the part she played in this healing.

> On the morning of April 3, I received a telephone call from a young man who said that his sister, June Amlin, had had a serious fall and was then in the Bethesda Memorial Hospital in Boynton Beach. I said I would try to help her. When I made mental contact I saw she was bleeding quite a lot through both nose and mouth. On looking further I saw that the bridge of her nose and another nasal bone were broken and a portion of bone had entered her brain. Three blood vessels in the nose and two in the throat had been severed; this caused the bleeding. After resetting the bones I sealed up the nasal blood vessels with cotton strips. The throat bleeding was so bad I used sanitary napkins to shut it off. Before I broke contact I saw that she had an intestinal infection which I cleared out by combing the area with psychic energy.

Later Mrs. Amlin called to thank Mrs. Bibb for her wonderful help. She said her face now shows no evidence that her nose was broken and that she has not suffered from stomach trouble for four months. She said she can breathe well and there has been no recurrence of bleeding. She concluded by saying her name could be used and that she will gladly confirm the foregoing should anyone inquire.

All of the real-life people cited in this book have given permission for their names and experiences to be documented. In the few cases herein where this permission was not given, an X or some other letter of the alphabet has been substituted. In other words, no fictitious names like Mary Smith or Tom Malloy are employed.

TELEVISUAL COMMUNICATION

Remember that when you contact the inner mind of a person, you communicate in symbols. There are no words required in mind-to-mind contact; if you choose to use words they are solely for your own benefit as a device to keep you focused on the idea you wish to convey. Mind-to-mind communication is via impressions. The closest our concrete mind can get to this is pictures. So your instructions to the inner mind of the person seeking help is by means of pictures— motion pictures, if you will.

These pictures, the scenarios you send, are not offered in the expectation they will be slavishly followed. The inner mind has its own methods. What you as a healer must do is convey a general idea of what must be done to effect a cure. In the foregoing example, Margaret Bibb's approach to stopping a gush of blood from June Amlin's throat was certainly unorthodox. It was what one woman might think of to convey to another woman's mind the pressing need to suppress a rapid flow of blood—a sanitary napkin. The important point was to get across to June Amlin's inner mind that the bleeding must be stopped quickly—and it was, but in a manner known only to her inner mind and certainly far different from the method the picture suggested.

In accidents, and indeed in all healing, the simplest picture is the best. If a muscle is torn, tie it together. If a cut has widened to an open wound, press the edges together and seal them that way with imaginary tape.

Here is an account of the healing of an accident injury by a woman who uses a slightly different technique. She is Nell Crossan of West Palm Beach, Florida. This is her report.

AN AMAZING CASE OF AN
INJURED HAND HEALING

On Sunday night, Peter S. Hoobyar, my daughter's husband, who works for Disney on Parade, had a tent pole snap and go through his left palm just below and between the knuckles of his middle and ring fingers. The pain was excruciating. He was rushed to the hospital, where the wound was sterilized and bandaged. The doctor there told him not to use the hand for three weeks and to check back with them in four days, but the show was moving to another city and he went with it.

Gail, my daughter, called me Monday and asked if I could help. I said I would try and went to work. First I calmed the nerves throughout Pete's entire body starting from the head and working down to the feet. I psychically placed my hands on his body and told the nerves to calm down. After completing this soothing procedure, I told his pituitary gland to keep them calm. My belief is that a calm body responds better to treatment than one which is tense and in pain. Also, a clean body is important, so I did a body washout with washout lights and energies. Next I elevated Pete's left hand to drain the blood from it while I massaged it gently. I then cleaned out the wound with peroxide and poured in healing oil and honey, after which I packed it with green aura paste and sealed it closed with human tape. Next I poured in white-gold healing light to meet and combine the honey, oil and paste and begin the healing, and then I inserted an anaesthetic around the hand to stop the pain.

I gave him a similar treatment twice a day for the next four days, but it turned out it wasn't needed because he was back at work on Wednesday. On Friday he and Gail came to visit us here in Florida. When I looked at his hand it was entirely healed. Only a small pink scar remained.

YOU CONTROL THE VARIATION IN
TELEVISUAL METHOD

Here now is an example of still a different method, evidence that each person is an individual who will employ the Televisual technique in the manner which seems easiest and most effective. Find out which of these many healing methods works best for you and use it, or design your own imaginative approaches to healing as many students do.

This case is reported by Annie Gvengilas of Plainfield, Connecticut. She writes

It always amazes me when I do something like this. We were at a Labor Day picnic when a bottle exploded in my brother's hand. He is Edward

Colbridge Jr. of Plainfield, Connecticut. One of his fingers was cut very badly and the blood flowed profusely from the open wound. Before I gave it any more thought I was leading my brother into the house. He kept asking, "What are you going to do?"

I sat him down on a kitchen chair and started working on him. I must admit I had a few nervous minutes because his daughter-in-law stood there watching with a skeptical look on her face. I went into the case like this: I asked the Universal Mind to fill me with healing energy and then to transmit the energy into the cut finger while commanding the blood to get thicker. I kept my eyes closed so that I could concentrate better. While I was doing this I saw in my mind's eye red and white swirls. Slowly the red ones disappeared; when they were all white, I opened my eyes and saw that the finger was completely healed. Only a white line remained on the finger. I must confess I got a lot of pleasure from this not only because of the healing but also because my brother and others kept asking all day, "How did you do that?"

HEALING BONE FRACTURES

Accidents frequently result in bone fractures, so now we will consider different ways to tackle this problem. Remember that the victim really heals himself in most cases; your part in the healing is to show his or her inner or subconscious mind what it is required to do. When a bone is broken, the normal tendency of the human system is to heal the fracture. This may take three weeks to three months depending upon the size of the fracture and the recuperative powers of the victim. Even then, unless treated surgically, the end result may be a badly aligned bone and a crippled leg or arm. It is important, therefore, that you work on the victim as soon after the accident as you can.

As soon as your attunement is established, examine the fracture with your mental eye. See just how the bone is broken and if any muscles or ligaments are involved. Proceed then to properly align the broken edges and splinters and fasten them securely with mental body tape. When the bone is wrapped in place, tie up the torn ligaments and muscles, reinforcing them with elastic tape. With everything back in its proper place send green nourishing energy into the area to lubricate and heal the bone, muscles and surrounding tissue. Finish off by flooding the entire area with white healing energy. Tell the subconscious mind to repeat this treatment every six hours until you check on it again the following day; then dismiss the entire matter from your mind.

The foregoing is a standard pattern, but as has been indicated, students soon find they get good results with their own type of treatment, sometimes following this pattern in part and sometimes abandoning it entirely to employ a method all their own. Whatever works for you is best for you to use.

John Schilter of Kinnelon, New Jersey healed a leg fracture this way:

> Isabel Gatto had a fall and injured her leg. She found she could stand on it, so she never considered the possibility of a fracture and did not seek medical assistance. After two days, the pain was so severe that she could no longer put her weight on it and asked for my assistance. When I first made mental contact and saw the leg, it looked to me almost like a mechanism with a lot of twisted wires. Gradually it became clearer and the wires became ligaments tangled together. One by one I untangled them with my fingers and straightened them out. Then I found I had to realign the nerves and blood vessels before I could get to the fractured bone. Fortunately, the bone break was not extensive, so I patched it with bone cement and used my "auric flashlight" to dry this quickly in place. It was when I started working on getting the blood to circulate at an even rate and was checking out the nerves to make sure the impulses were timed properly that I had the experience of perceiving the complete functioning of the leg at this higher level of consciousness. I knew then that she was healed, so I swept the entire leg with psychic energy and withdrew. Isabel Gatto's leg gave her no more trouble and she was able to walk immediately without pain or any other difficulty.

John Schilter apparently follows the standard pattern fairly closely. However, he introduces to us his "auric flashlight" which he uses as a device to concentrate etheric energy on a particular spot. This has no value in itself but serves as a most effective tool in John's hands, enabling him to focus additional energy where it is needed. It is an aid to his own concentration.

THE POWER OF HEALING MEDITATION

The man in the following case report takes an entirely different approach to healing a bone fracture. He is Glenn F. Whitten of Statesville, North Carolina. Here is his report:

> During a meeting of graduates from Ben Bibb's class, a girl with a walking cane limped into the room. She said her name was Alice and wondered if someone could help her. Her trouble had been diagnosed at the hospital as a feathered fracture of a bone in the arch of her foot which

she was told would in time heal itself. It was too painful to stand upon, however, and since she was a salesgirl in a store, she hoped that someone at the meeting might relieve the pain or cure the fracture. I said I would try.

I had a relaxed feeling as I went into meditation and this encouraged me to ask the One Great Universal Power for energy to heal this girl's foot. At the same time I thanked the Power for giving me the required energy to pass along. All at once I became aware of another me. This other self moved away from my body and became huge as it rose up into space. It (I) caught a huge ball of golden-white pulsating energy in the left hand. I then saw very clearly this other me standing very close to the girl. While holding the ball of energy in the left hand, I passed the energy to the right hand and moved it back and forth above her foot. At the same time I told the One to fix and normalize the foot because It knew far better than I just what needed to be done. In a few moments the girl said in an amazed tone, "The pain is gone!" She left the meeting not limping and in no pain. About a week later she reported to the chairman of the meeting that the pain had not recurred and she had been able to resume her work in the store without any trouble.

In this case Glenn Whitten employs the direct transfer of healing energy as described in Chapter 1. In most cases, however, it is more effective to send picturized suggestions on the healing process to the inner mind of the injured party. Sometimes all the injured person requires to speed up healing is additional energy, as in this case, but far more often the inner mind has to be directed to the best and most rapid healing procedure before it will stir itself.

MEDIPIC FOR HEALING ACCIDENT INJURIES

It is recommended that in accident cases you follow the standard healing procedure. This may be described as follows:

1. Make contact with the inner mind of the injured person as described in Chapter 1.

2. Examine the physical and etheric bodies of the injured in order to be absolutely sure of the nature and extent of the injuries sustained.

3. Clean out open wounds, then seal them up with body tape. If an area should be scraped raw, cover it with new skin torn from a roll, like plastic wrap. Make sure first that the exposed area is completely cleansed and all foreign matter removed; then apply the new skin, making sure it lies smooth and fits properly.

4. Replace all bruised and discolored areas with new flesh and muscles. Make sure the muscles are elastic. If you deem it necessary, reinforce them mentally with rubber bands.

5. Be most careful with broken bones. Make sure you do not overlook any splinters; then carefully fit the pieces together properly. Some healers mentally glue the pieces together; others wrap them in tape before surrounding them with green rebuilding auric energy and white healing energy.

6. Always finish your work on an injured person by flooding the damaged area with blue calming and pain-killing energy. Usually it is advisable to instruct the inner mind of the subject to repeat the healing process at definite intervals (three to six hours) until your next treatment.

7. Always check back in a day or two in order to make sure that a proper healing has taken place. This will enable you to tie up any loose ends that may exist and finish your work in a proper and efficient manner.

If you will read this chapter again, I think you will realize that the healings described were performed by people no different from yourself. Indeed, they are the kind of people you might meet in a supermarket or a movie theatre. This in itself should give you confidence and help convince you that you can also heal as they do.

3. Miraculous psychic healing treatment for relief and frequent care of arthritis, rheumatism and similar problems

Here is the marvelously effective psychic treatment for the relief and frequent cure of arthritis, rheumatism and similar problems as employed by individual students. Also included are case histories that you can follow and duplicate.

A stiffness and swelling in the joints resulting in restricted movement and often accompanied by pain is a fairly common ailment in people over fifty years of age. Usually this is called arthritis but it is sometimes referred to as rheumatoid arthritis. Your task as a healer is to discover just what is causing this stiffness, swelling and pain, and to eliminate it. Begin by making contact with the inner mind of the sufferer in order to observe the painful area directly.

HOW TO RELIEVE ARTHRITIC PAIN

Let us assume that in this case a woman about sixty has come to you complaining about pain and swelling in the joints of her fingers. You put her in a comfortable chair and tell her to relax and be quiet for a moment or two while you "study her case." Then you seat yourself, take three deep breaths and reach out mentally to contact her inner mind. Focusing your attention on her hands, you observe that minute calcium crystals, like tiny grains of sand, have attached themselves to the bones in and around the first and second joints of each finger. This has restricted motion in the joints, resulting in pain and inflammation of the surrounding tissues. Your task is now clear. To remove the pain you must first remove the calcium deposits and restore the fingers to normal mobility. Proceed as follows:

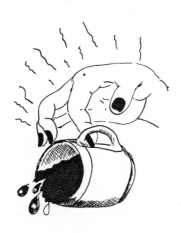

1. Observe and identify all of the crystalline deposits on the bones of both hands.

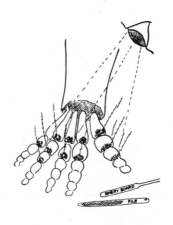

2. Mentally separate each joint and, with a nail file or emery board, clean the bones of all crystal deposits.

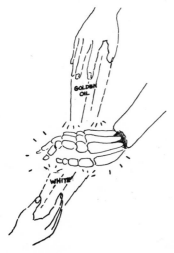

3. Before reassembling the joints, lubricate them well with golden oil; then saturate them with white healing energy as you fit them back in place.

4. See all fingers completely healed, all strong and supple once again, then slowly withdraw your mind.

This is the standard pattern for correcting painful and restrictive arthritic conditions. Of course, the foregoing is just an imaginary case designed to guide you, but here is an actual report from a student healer which, you will notice, is quite similar. The healer is Mrs. Yolande Scott of Lake Worth, Florida. Here is her report.

A MIRACULOUS ARTHRITIS HEALING

When I went to France last year, my friend, Helene Dupont, met me at the airport to take me to her home. On the way I noticed that she seemed to be favoring her right arm and when I asked her about it, she said, "It hurts so much I can hardly move it. The doctor said it is probably arthritis in my shoulder, but if it goes on I won't be able to drive any more. Right now it is very hard for me to drive. I don't know what I am going to do."

Then I told her about my work doing healing and she asked me to try to help her. I started that evening and continued the next day. After three treatments she was cured. She raised her arm up and down and sideways. "This is fantastic," she said.

Here's what I did: I cleaned the bones in the shoulder with sandpaper to take off the calcium. Then I put warm oil in between the joints and sent white energy into the shoulder and upper arm to make sure all parts were properly healed. Finally I put her on automatic, which means I told her inner mind to send energy to this area each day for the next seven days. I was in touch with Helene recently and she tells me the pain never came back since I treated her in Paris nearly two years ago.

In this report Mrs. Scott followed the practice of showing the inner mind of the subject just what needed to be done and how to do it with mental pictures. Usually this technique gets the best and quickest results. However, some healers, once they have pinpointed the cause of the trouble, will dissolve it with a powerful ray of healing energy. Not every healer has this much psychic energy at his or her command, but you may be one of these fortunate ones. Here is a report from a young woman who has this gift. She is Patricia Gleason of Plainfield, Connecticut.

ANOTHER ARTHRITIS HEALING

This case concerns my neighbor, Pauline Dugas. She has had a very painful knee for several years. When I learned to heal in the Ben Bibb class, I asked if I could help her and she said, "Yes, please." I went mentally into her knee, checking out all the bones and muscles. My inner mind directed me to go to a certain bone in the knee which appeared red to my inner eye. I started pouring pure white energy into this painful area, using the sun's rays and then painting it blue to soothe it. When I finished, Pauline said the pain had gone. That was three months ago and she has had no pain since.

You too may have this gift of extra energy which will enable you to effect rapid and permanent healings. Experiment with it; try it out. About one out of every three graduates of the Seventh Sense school has it. But do not be disappointed if you do not—you will still be a very successful healer, only it will require that you give more thorough application to the problem by giving visual suggestions to the subject's inner mind. Also, it may sometimes take a little longer.

There are many forms of arthritis stemming from a great many different causes. The commonest cause of all is the subject's harboring over a period of time one or more of the lower destructive emotions like fear, anxiety, resentment, jealousy, anger or frustration. These all create poisonous particles in the blood which cluster about and deposit tiny crystals in any area that has been damaged or possibly overworked. A fall in which a knee, arm, shoulder or hip is hurt could result at a later date in arthritis at that point. Likewise certain strained or overworked areas present convenient drop-off points for these crystals. Sometimes arthritis may develop following a disease or an ailment like scarlet fever, typhoid or blood poisoning. Our job is to relieve the pain as surely and as quickly as possible, so that is what we concentrate upon. Correct what is wrong even though it may appear different from what you expected to find. Here is a case in point:

A GROUP HEALING

One spring evening, a group of Seventh Sense graduates, all healers trained by Ben Bibb, had gathered in West Palm Beach to treat as a group several people who had asked their help. While they were there, the telephone rang and a young woman, Mrs. Margaret Keel of Lake Park, said she had a very painful leg and thigh and asked if they would help her. The group agreed to help her and was successful. Here first is Mrs. Keel's report as she gave it to me recently. Following her report will be the report of the group on what its members found and how they corrected it. Here is Mrs. Keel's letter describing her experience.

I had been having a great deal of pain in my right leg from my heel to my buttocks for many months. I was unable to sleep on my right side. The pain was not always present but a weakness in the leg seemed to be growing each day. There were times I could hardly climb the stairs to our apartment. The doctor could not find a reason for the pain but suspected arthritis, and said if it didn't improve that he would do a bone scraping.

A few days after my session with the doctor, I read about Ben Bibb, the healer, in a local paper. On that day the pain was intense, so I called him and asked for help. He told me about a meeting of some graduates from his Seventh Sense classes and said they would be glad to help.

I fixed my family's dinner and sat down with my husband to read. Suddenly, at about 8:35 p.m., I felt a peculiar feeling in my leg as if fingers were rubbing the long bone. Then a sensation of movement began. It started on the right side of my buttocks and travelled down the leg to my heel. I began feeling warm spots, first just above the outside of the ankle and then in the hip. I told my husband what was happening and he asked about the pain. At that moment I had several feelings like mild electric shocks down my side. I couldn't believe what I was experiencing.

The next morning I awoke refreshed and free from pain. In fact, I found I had been sleeping on my right side! I was afraid to stand then for fear the pain would return—but it didn't and it hasn't, and it is now two years since that group treatment.

As can be expected, a group of competent healers can exert more energy than one alone, which accounts for the unusual experience of Mrs. Keel and the rapid healing of her painful condition. Here now is the report of the healing taken from the records of the Seventh Sense group.

There were fifteen present and Bill (last name withheld by request) was designated to lead, speaking aloud. Under Bill's pacing, we found the painful nerve, symbolically red and hot, running along the right leg from low in the calf upward, and traced it curving partially around the right side of the thigh, then more inward in the buttock area, and then swerving to enter the sacrum at the end of the spine. Following Bill's timing, we each found the point of pressure and irritation where the pain nerve left the sacrum and we each corrected this by our own means (putting sponge rubber pads in mentally, or covering the irritated area with "human tape," etc.) To "cool down" the painful nerve running down the leg, we variously used iced cloths, blue energy or "blue paint" to bring it to normal temperature, each healer doing what seemed best to him. We then completed the treatment by raising the vibration rate of the energy body in order to speed up the healing.

You will notice in this report that certain energy colors are mentioned. These will be described in detail in Chapter 16 where instructions on when and how to employ them are given. In this report mention is also made of "raising the vibratory rate of the energy body" in order to speed up the healing. After the inner mind of the subject has been instructed by pictures on the healing method that it is to employ, it may occasionally appear to you to be low in energy. In these situations you can help it by raising the vibratory rate of the energy body. You are given detailed instructions in this technique in Chapter 10.

Aside from its interest as a group healing effort, this case history is included because what appeared at first to be arthritis, and was apparently so regarded by Mrs. Keel's doctor, actually turned out to be inflammation of the sciatic nerve caused by friction in the sacral area. You can see from this example how important it is to view the injured or affected area through the medium of the patient's inner mind. This is the surest and best way to appraise the location and extent of the trouble, so be sure to look in each case.

WHY YOU SHOULD ALWAYS MAKE
A CAREFUL EXAMINATION

Here is a remarkable healing by Harold Ames of Canterbury, Connecticut, which proves how important it is to examine the subject carefully. The subject is H.R. (name withheld by request). Here is Mr. Ames' report.

> It seems to me that some people find it very hard to accept the fact that they have been cured psychically. Apparently it is not easy to accept something one doesn't understand. Such is the case of H.R.
>
> About eleven one night the phone rang. It was my daughter. She told me she was visiting a friend whose husband was in pain and she asked if I would try to help. I agreed; then she explained that this man had severe pain in his right shoulder and had great difficulty in moving his right arm. This condition had existed for over three weeks. The doctor said it was probably a pulled muscle and had prescribed pain pills which gave H.R. little relief.
>
> I went into my conscious working state and put H.R. on my mental screen. My purpose was to send him soothing energy to relieve his pain, but as I proceeded, my vision of the subject was impaired by what seemed to be a pane of glass which began to crack into many little web-like cracks.

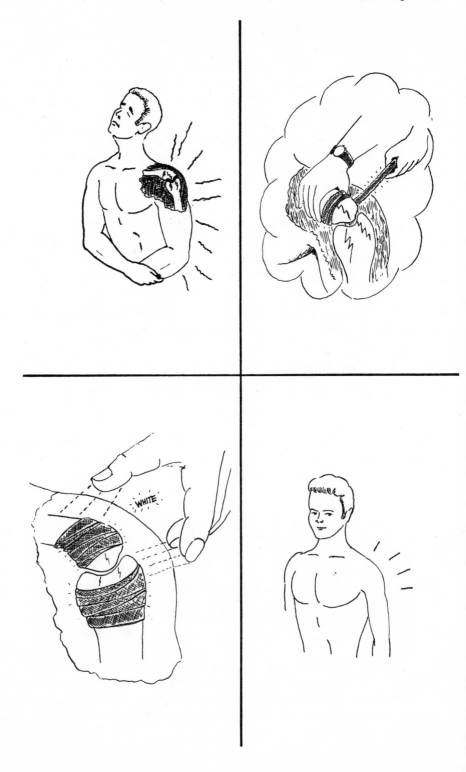

This was immediately followed by a picture of an arm with red waves running up and down from the elbow to shoulder.

Since it was late and I was tired, I ignored this clue and just sent calming soothing energy to H.R. But on waking the next morning, I realized that what I had seen the night before were symbols. The pane of cracked glass was telling me that there was a fracture in the shoulder which was causing the inflammation and pain symbolized by the red waves running up and down the arm.

I went back to my mental screen and when I succeeded in getting H.R. into focus, I found there were tiny hairline cracks all around the shoulder socket. This lead me to the assumption that he had been in an accident of some sort. I proceeded to heal the cracks, sealing them with imaginary tape and concluding by sending him healing energy and white energy to relieve the pain.

I later asked my daughter if H.R. had been in some sort of an accident recently. She replied that he had been playing baseball about a month earlier and suffered a fall after colliding with another player. Apparently he had hit the ground on his right shoulder and, while it had hurt at the time, he put it aside and did not connect it with the more serious pain that started a couple of days later.

About a week later when I met H.R., he told me the pain had eased after the night my daughter had telephoned me. He stopped taking the pain pills then and had no more trouble since. "Apparently it was only a pulled muscle," he said.

It is clear that H.R. will not agree that he received psychic help, but Harold Ames' daughter, Mrs. Angela M. Bourque, is aware of what took place and confirms it. You will find this will occur more often than not. Good health is a normal human condition. Every healthy person takes his condition for granted and is inclined to feel abused when even the slightest ailment strikes him. Likewise, when he feels well again, he assumes this to be normal and soon forgets his previous trouble along with any assistance he may have received to overcome it. There are, however, some people who have suffered over a longer period of time, or have been told they could not be cured. As a rule, these people are grateful for your help and will tell you so. Here is one such case.

A GRATEFUL PATIENT

Judy Jones of West Palm Beach, Florida is an excellent healer. Among her many successes she numbers her own father, who had suffered for some time from a crippling case of arthritis in his knees. Here is Mrs. Jones' report.

My father is 55 years old and has had arthritis in his knees for several years. At times it was so painful he could not get out of bed, and he always had trouble walking. When I learned to heal and had some confidence in my ability, I went to work to try to help him. I polished his knee joints and removed all crusty material. As I fitted them together once again, I flooded each joint with healing oil and then covered it with white pain-killing energy. I did this once each day for a week; then I got word from Nashville, Tennessee, where he lives, that he was walking. In checking I found he was no longer taking any medication and all the pain and stiffness was gone. He no longer needs the special shoes he used to wear and is now able to work in his garden once again. My mother says he is able to dance the way he used to years ago. I worked on him over a year ago and he has been all right ever since.

Here is a letter he sent confirming this remarkable cure:

This letter is a statement concerning a condition I have had for several years. I have had bad rheumatoid arthritis in both knees, so bad at times that it was an effort to walk, or when I sat down I could hardly get up. Our daughter, Judy Jones, has helped me so very much that I have had no pain in six month. This I can hardly believe and I am so very thankful. Sincerely, William Copeland, Jr., Nashville, Tennessee.

Sometimes you can give remarkable relief to an older person suffering greatly from arthritis and similar bone and muscle afflictions. Such is the case in which Emil Girard of Baltic, Connecticut was able to help a 67-year-old woman named Charlotte Baltram of Woodstock, Connecticut. When Emil Girard, a Seventh Sense graduate, encountered her, she had spent most of July, August and September in bed. She had arthritis in her back and could only sit in a chair for ten minutes at a time three or four times a day. When he saw her she was sitting so bent over that he had to sit on the floor in order to see her face. She had seen an orthopedic doctor at Day Kimball Hospital in Putnam, Connecticut who said nothing could be done since her spinal discs were soft and disintegrating. She then went to the Lahey Clinic in Boston and, after a week there, was told the same thing—that she would have to be a bed case for five or six years with no guarantee that she would get better. Emil Girard felt sorry for her and visited her weekly. He mentally sent blue energy into her spine when in her presence, without touching her. Between visits he gave her similar treatments at least once a day.

At the end of October he had to discontinue the visits and was not able to get to Woodstock to see her until Thanksgiving. He was amazed at the change. She was up, walking around and helping her husband in the kitchen. At Christmas time, when he next saw her, she was doing the cooking and some of the lighter housework. By summer she was doing canning. Her head was up in a normal position and her back was straight. Emil is delighted with the success of his effort and says he will continue to work on her at least once a week. He says:

> I learned to do this healing through the classes with the Seventh Sense group, and I believe that if we use this ability to do good, God will help us in many ways that we never expect. We ask God for energy to heal and He sends us more than we need, so there is always some left over for us. God is good!

As you can judge from Emil's words, there is a great deal of personal satisfaction to be gained by healing others. Every successful healing—and this should be most of those that you attempt—will give you a sense of achievement, the feeling of a difficult task well done. Believe me, this is very rewarding.

HOW TO RELIEVE BURSITIS

As you know, bursitis symptoms are similar to those of arthritis and are sometimes mistaken for them. Actually, arthritis pains are caused by crystalline deposits on bones, usually at the joints, which limit their mobility and result in pain. Bursitis results in most cases from injury or a prolonged strain on certain bones and muscles. It consists of inflammation of the bursa, a sacklike cell near or connected with a joint which contains synovial fluid, the liquid which normally provides the lubrication required at each bone connection such as a knee, shoulder, elbow, etc.

Rapid relief can be afforded a bursitis sufferer by mentally emptying the offending bursa and refilling it with fresh lubricant. You can visualize this lubricant as warm olive oil. The inflammation is then corrected by visualizing a blue healing energy replacing the red in the painful area and finally, by sending a white energy charge to speed the healing. As a rule, the sufferer will be free of pain within an hour or two after this treatment, but sometimes there is immediate relief.

HOW THE MIND CAN CURE
TENDINITIS

Tendinitis is inflammation of a tendon or tendons and is usually accompanied by muscle pain. It may be caused by a blow or may be the result of strain or physical abuse. Like bursitis, it can be cleared up quickly, usually within an hour or so, by Medipic methods. One student healer said that after he made mental contact with the sufferer, he saw a number of tiny red threads or strings all tangled up with the tendons and muscles in the victim's shoulder. He removed these red threads pulling them out with his fingers until he could find no more. He put these into an imaginary plastic bag he found handy and later destroyed. Continuing his mental contact, he wiped the tendons clean and then rubbed healing oil into them and into the surrounding muscles. After checking once again to make sure all tendons and muscles were properly aligned and in place, he flooded the area with golden sun energy and withdrew. At the time of this treatment, the healer was in Connecticut and the patient in New Jersey, one hundred miles away. About an hour later, they made contact by telephone and the subject reported, "No pain at all. I can move my arm and shoulder freely without any difficulty."

The causes of these muscle, tendon and joint ailments are many and varied, far too numerous to attempt to analyze here. They range from the aftermath of disease, poor blood and emotional strain, to blows, muscle strain and similar injuries. Fortunately, a study of causes is not your problem. You are a healer; your responsibility is to relieve pain and discomfort and to prevent their recurrence. It is important, therefore, that you examine carefully with your inner mind every one you are asked to help. In this way you will be able to ascertain with surety just what is causing the pain or discomfort and proceed from there to suggest with Medipic the best method to correct it.

4. Remarkable psychic healing cures for asthma and other respiratory ailments- including emphysema, pneumonia and the common cold

Frequently you may hear that this or that ailment cannot be cured but must "run its course." This kind of judgment is due to the incompleteness of our present medical knowledge. Actually, every human malfunction can be corrected, sometimes very quickly, if you as a healer can gain the cooperation of the subject's inner mind. With children and young people this is usually quite easy, but sometimes in older people the conscious mind will offer resistance. It is therefore better to treat people over fifty without their conscious knowledge whenever possible.

How often have you heard, "There is no cure for the common cold?" But there is—the subject's inner mind can cure it, often within minutes. Here is a case history of just such a healing performed by the Rev. Martin L. Grissom, Vicar of St. Paul's Episcopal Church in Plainfield, Connecticut.

CURING THE COMMON COLD

This is the Rev. Grissom's report in his own words:

I present this case as one which is quite simple, and with which almost any mother can identify. I believe many mothers heal their children of childhood aches and pains, for what mother has not had the experience of

63

"kissing it all better"? I present this case, also, as a possible help for mothers who at times become frantic when their child has a "common cold."

One evening, Brenda, my daughter's little girl, aged two, was left in my care. She was suffering from a bad cold, had a tight chest and was breathing with difficulty. I took her in my arms, laid her head on my shoulder and placed my right hand on her back. Mentally, I took a small golden sponge and gently brushed down the lung, throat and nasal passages. Next I used a mental fluid to coat the brushed areas, to keep them from becoming sticky and dry. I used white gold energy for healing and soft pink energy for peace and calm. Almost immediately little Brenda's breathing became easier, but I had more to do, for then I remembered that the mucus in the lungs had to be eliminated. The only way that I could see to discharge it was to induce her to vomit. I had just concluded this thought pattern when my daughter returned. I gave Brenda to her arms and immediately she threw up the mucus all over her mother—but her cold was gone.

This healing was not a fortuitous circumstance. It is but one of hundreds of similar cold cures performed by the graduates of Ben Bibb's classes. You, too, can cure colds merely by giving the proper instructions to the inner or subconscious mind of the sufferer. The instruction can take whatever form your own imagination may suggest, just as long as you get across the basic idea.

To make this clearer, a far different method to reach the same end is described. The healer is Vi Holtberg, a healthy mature woman who is in the real estate business in Boynton Beach, Florida. She sits on a committee with other realtors that meets every two weeks. One of these, a man she identifies only as Dick, seemed to have a perpetual cold in the head. After she had observed his distress and runny nose for several months, she asked him about it and he told her he had been to several doctors and two specialists but none was able to help him. Feeling sorry for him she decided she would try to help him, so that night and for several nights thereafter, she made contact with his inner mind and sent it the following mental suggestion. She visualized an assembly line of tiny absorbent sponges running through his nose and nasal passages. She had it picking up dry sponges as it entered one nostril and dropping off wet sponges as it came out the other. Along with this picture she sent white healing energy.

At the very next meeting, Dick's sniffles seemed to be gone, and when she questioned him he said, "I don't know what happened, but it dried up a few nights back and I've been okay ever since."

It seems in most cases that the inner mind of the patient needs only a small suggestion, a tiny shove, to get it started in healing the ailment. We have on record many histories that bear this out. Frequently, as in the case of the common cold, medicines have been tried without success. Here is a report on the successful treatment of infected tonsils and adenoids by Diane White of Chattanooga, Tennessee.

CURING AN ADENOID INFECTION

My little girl is two and one-half years old, writes Mrs. White. About six months ago her tonsils and adenoids started to bother her and as time went on, the infection got steadily worse. We tried three kinds of medicine prescribed by her doctor but none helped. Finally about a month ago, her adenoids started draining so badly that she couldn't lie down without choking. I had to get up several times every night to sit her up so she could get her throat cleared out.

She needed sleep so badly that although I don't consider myself a healer, I thought I would try to help her psychically. When she lay down for her afternoon nap I started putting white healing energy into her head and throat. In about five minutes she sat up and started spitting out yellow mucus by the mouthful. About half a cup came up and then she lay back and fell asleep. It was the first time in over a month that she slept for more than an hour without waking up in a coughing fit.

That was a month ago and she hasn't coughed since. She looks better now than she has in several months. I realize this is only a small thing, but it is something I know I did.

I cite these reports because I want you to realize that these people—Diane White, Vi Holtberg and the others quoted—are no more gifted than you. What they can do, you can also do. All that is required is an understanding of the secret of how to make contact with the inner mind of another, plus a little practice in sending mental pictures via the Medipic method. If you apply yourself you can become a competent healer in a few days—two weeks at the most. Get to work!

HOW TO CURE OTHER
RESPIRATORY AILMENTS

In curing colds, pneumonia, asthma and similar respiratory ailments there are two problems to be solved. The first is to remove the congestion; the second is to reduce and eventually eliminate the inflammation, soreness and irritation. You turn these two tasks over to the inner mind of the afflicted one, accompanied by a visual suggestion as to how each may be accomplished. As you now know, it is up to your imagination to supply the details. For example, you might see the fluid in the lungs of a pneumonia patient being pumped out, or running through faucets, or being siphoned off, just so long as you convey to the patient's inner mind that the fluid has to be removed. Obviously the inner mind cannot and will not use any of these methods, but will employ its own technique to empty the lungs once it understands what must be done.

Once this is under way, turn your attention next to the infection, soreness or irritation that caused the fluid congestion. Your attunement with the subject's inner mind will enable you to detect this cause. As soon as it is ascertained you can then put in motion suggestions for its correction and cure. This technique will be conveyed vividly to you in the report of a self-cure of pneumonia made by Seventh Sense graduate Frances Miller of Plainfield, Connecticut.

Here is her report.

RELIEVING AND CURING
PNEUMONIA

Early in Thanksgiving week I caught a bad cold. At first it seemed to be only an ordinary inconvenience and being busy, I paid little attention to it. But on Thanksgiving Eve while I was attempting to complete my pie-making, I began to feel terribly ill. My chest felt on fire, my throat was raw and I had a constant very bad cough which tore through my chest like a poorly honed blade. Even shallow breathing was difficult. There were many other uncomfortable symptoms, but it was the 104-degree temperature and the severe chest pain that posed the real threat—pneumonia.

I certainly needed help—but what to do? A group of twelve, family and friends, was due for noonday Thanksgiving dinner the next day, so I just couldn't be sick! I could go to a doctor on Friday if necessary, but for tomorrow I would have to heal myself.

As I sat with closed eyes, slumped in a parlor chair, I made contact with my inner mind and "saw" my lungs half filled with fluid and flames fiendishly dancing atop the fluid. I drained the lungs with faucets making sure all the mucus-like fluid had run out before I proceeded to put out the internal blaze with an improvised fire extinguisher. Then I soothed my raw throat and bronchial tubes with healing oil and projected pain-killing and

MEDIPIC FOR TREATMENT
OF PNEUMONIA

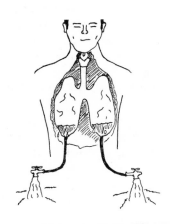

1. This is the way a pneumonia sufferer's lungs will usually appear to the
   inner mind of the healer—heavy
   with fluid and aching.

2. Start the draining suggestion. Here
   we show the fluid running out
   through faucets, one for each lung.

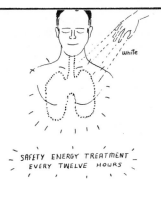

3. Now the lungs are empty of fluid
   and you can start the healing process by visualizing healing body tape
   covering sore areas and soothing,
   pain-removing oil being passed
   through and around all the tubes, as
   well as over the inner lining of the
   lungs themselves.

4. This shows throat, bronchial tubes
   and lungs all healed and functioning
   normally as you, the healer, give
   them a final shot of white energy
   and instruct the inner mind to
   repeat the procedure at twelve-hour
   intervals until a relapse is no longer
   likely.

soothing energies to the afflicted area. Finally I gave my entire body a
stimulating energy charge and told it to be ready for tomorrow.

Suddenly I realized I had been sitting there about ten minutes without
moving and I had not coughed once the entire time. I was beginning to
breathe more easily even then and felt a great deal better when I rose the
next morning. I prepared a complete holiday meal and partook at the table
along with everyone else. To me the most remarkable part was that I never
coughed once the entire day. Friday I did, about a dozen times, and each
time coughed up mucus, but with no pain. It seemed as if my inner mind
kept me from coughing until my respiratory system had healed to the
point where it could stand the type of cough necessary to rid the lungs of
the fluid. It struck me then that while it was necessary to clear my lungs, it
was a distinct advantage to do this when the body was better able to stand
the stress of coughing. Besides, I had been able to prepare and enjoy a
great holiday dinner!

Whether you are healing yourself or another of pneumonia, the
foregoing is a good example of the best method to employ.

All respiratory afflictions are related. The causes may differ from
pneumonia in a child on to emphysema in an octogenarian, but
shortness of breath and obstructions in the bronchial passages leading
to rasping and wheezing are the common distress symptoms. It is
your responsibility as a healer to first relieve the distress of the
afflicted person and then clear up the malfunction. Regardless how
complex the ailment may appear under medical diagnosis, your task
is relatively simple. You can see and thus go directly to the heart of
the problem. Two of the afflictions generally considered to be most
difficult to correct medically are asthma and emphysema—yet you
can relieve sufferers from both of these problems and frequently
effect a permanent cure by employing the Seventh Sense Medipic
methods. Here's how this may be done:

HOW TO TREAT AND CURE
ASTHMA

In about one half of all asthma sufferers the cause is an allergy or
allergies, usually inherited. It is well for you to first determine if this
is the case with the person who comes to you for help for, while you
can give him or her relief, this will be only temporary unless you can
"balance out" the system's objections to the pollens, molds, animal
hair, lint, insecticides or whatever it may be that excites the
membranes. The balance of the asthma sufferers—the other one

half—are the victims of internal infections. With these, the irritated areas may be in the nose and sinuses, or they may be in the lower respiratory tract or bronchial tubes. We thus have two general types of asthma which must be treated differently: they are the external or allergic asthma and intrinsic or infective asthma. Both are examined in the following pages and Medipic methods for correcting both types are given.

THE MEDIPIC METHOD TO TREAT
AND CURE ALLERGIC ASTHMA

The immediate causes of discomfort, wheezing and shortness of breath characteristic of all types of asthma are the heavy mucus deposits in the nose, sinuses, throat and bronchial tubes. The first need in all cases, therefore, is to clear out these passages so the sufferer can breathe properly. You must make contact with the inner mind of the patient and observe just where the clogging exists; then you should remove the mucus from those areas by the method that seems best to you at the time. This may be by blowing them clear, by siphoning off the mucus, by washing it out, or by whatever method your imagination suggests. Trust your intuition in these matters—it will frequently amaze you.

When you have satisfied yourself that all of the passages are clear, then continue with your treatment, this time to remove the cause of the mucus congestion—the allergy to certain foreign matter such as lint, mold, animal hair or even certain household cleansers or insecticides. These allergies are actually fears implanted in the subconscious at birth, usually as an inheritance from some ancestor. By this is meant that the inner mind, because of this early programming, regards the allergy-producing ingredient as dangerous and tries to prevent its entrance into the human system. It floods the whole area with mucus which is designed to surround, absorb and carry off the offending particles. Actually these particles of hair, lint, grass or the odors of disinfectants are no more dangerous to the patient than they are to anyone else. In order to effect a true healing this idea must be conveyed to the subject's inner mind.

The best method is to first ascertain the substance or substances to which the subject is allergic. Once these are identified you must explain in mental words to the inner mind of the patient that they are actually not harmful but merely unpleasant. Tell it that in the future it must regard them as relatively harmless and cease its strenuous efforts to reject them. This can also be accompanied by an endocrine gland balancing as described in Chapter 16. Since you are working to dislodge a prejudice of long standing, and nothing more than this, you may find it necessary to repeat this treatment two or three times before the subject's inner mind finally accepts it. In the many cases of allergic asthma treated by Ben Bibb and the Seventh Sense graduates, all have eventually responded to this treatment.

HOW TO TREAT AND CURE
INFECTIVE ASTHMA

There is another type of asthma which is not due to allergies. This is called intrinsic or infective asthma and is caused by a virus or some other infectious element settling in either the upper respiratory area (nose or sinuses) or the lower (bronchi, lungs, etc.). The frequency and severity of these asthma attacks may be greatly influenced by rapid temperature changes, fatigue, endocrine changes or emotional stress, but these provocations need not be considered by you, the healer, since once you have relieved the distress and eliminated the cause, they will have no further influence on the patient.

As in cases of allergic asthma, your first task is to drain off the mucus and relieve the congestion. Once you have made contact with the subject's inner mind, send it an appropriate Medipic scenario showing it how the drainage should be performed. It can be visualized as being drained off, pumped out or siphoned out, whatever way seems best to you at the time. When you can see that all the respiratory passages are clear, you should then proceed to eliminate the infection. Usually this is best done by mentally suggesting a complete washing out and disinfecting of the entire respiratory area, followed by a generous bath of healing oil and concluded with a powerful stimulation of white healing energy. It is best then to put the patient on repeat, which means you should instruct his or her inner mind to repeat this disinfecting and healing process at twelve-hour intervals until a complete cure has been effected.

Another pulmonary affliction usually found in older people is emphysema. Its symptoms, coughing, wheezing and shortness of breath, are similar to those of infectious asthma. It may even develop from chronic bronchitis, as asthma often does, but as an ailment it is vastly different and requires different treatment. Here is a description of the very successful Seventh Sense Medipic method of coping with emphysema.

THE MEDIPIC TECHNIQUE FOR
CURING EMPHYSEMA

As soon as you make contact with the inner mind of the emphysema patient, instruct it via Telepic to expel the accumulated mucus, softening it to a loose liquid form and then removing it by draining it off. Use whatever visualization occurs to you in order to convey this instruction; then bathe all of the pulmonary passages with a soothing, healing warm oil. When you are satisfied that the subject can breathe without difficulty and can really take deep breaths if desired, then proceed to the next step.

As you now look mentally into the bronchial passages and the lungs of the patient, you will observe that the lung area seems distended, stiff and larger than normal, while the internal walls appear dry and covered in spots with what seem to be blisters, little bubble-like extrusions. Tiny distended air sacs may also be visible in one or both lungs. These plus the blisters inhibit proper lung action and create a demand for an oversupply of mucus. They must be removed and the pulmonary walls restored to their original elasticity. Using your imagination, this can be suggested in any number of ways. You might mentally pluck out all the bullae (little bubbles) and all the air sacs with your fingers and then rub a softening healing oil into the walls of the lungs in order to restore their proper elasticity. Finally, send white healing energy to saturate the entire afflicted area, put it on repeat at twelve-hour intervals, and then withdraw. Check it again forty-eight hours later and repeat the same procedure, if necessary. This should do it.

In a person over seventy, or possibly in his sixties but prematurely aged, you will occasionally find a condition called senile emphysema. The treatment in these cases is almost the same as that already described. In order to illustrate the visualizations you may create to help emphysema sufferers a series of pictures that might be employed is provided.

Note that once you make contact with the inner mind of the sufferer and it has indicated a willingness to help or cooperate, all healings are equally attainable. It is no more difficult to cure an ailment currently regarded as medically incurable than it is to heal a burned finger or a sore knee. The inner mind can correct *any* malfunction of the body it inhabits, provided it receives the proper incentive or guidance. Always remember this, and don't look upon emphysema, or other serious ailments often regarded as terminal, as

AN EMPHYSEMA TREATMENT

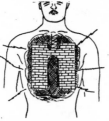

1. This is the way the subject's lungs may appear to your inner eye when you first make contact. It is an exterior view of the lungs themselves, showing their lack of elasticity.

2. Here is a visualization to suggest the need to clear the lungs of all foreign matter, sacs, bullae, etc.

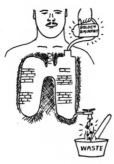

3. This picture shows the disinfecting and cleansing of the interior of the lungs.

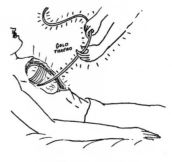

4. Here begins the repair work. The stiff walls of the lungs have to be made elastic once again. In this case you suggest that they be wrapped in elastic gold thread.

5. White healing paint is now applied to the entire area—both the inside and the outside of the lungs.

6. Now you see the lungs completely healed and in perfect working order before you withdraw your attention from the patient.

insurmountable obstacles. If you give the inner mind proper suggestions and the subject's soul has not already made a decision to depart the body (a rare circumstance), your healing effort will be successful. Always keep in mind that for you, no healing is impossible.

A healer with this right attitude is Edith Jacques of Juno, Florida. Here is her firsthand account of how she gave quick and lasting relief to an emphysema sufferer:

> Last summer I visited a friend in Massachusetts who lives with her mother. In spite of her age, 84, L.T.'s mother is completely active, but suffers from emphysema. She explained that at times this created quite a problem, but at other times there was but little discomfort. She was particularly sick when I was there and had been going to the hospital twice a day to get relief.
>
> The morning after I arrived, L.T. and I planned to go out into the nearby fields to pick blueberries, but before we left the house she reminded her mother to call the hospital to find out what time she should go there. It was then that I decided to see if I could help. I asked her if she would like me to try and she said she would try anything in the hope of getting relief. Before we went out I put my hands over her throat and chest and flooded them with white healing energy. I could see the clogged mucus and mentally siphoned it off. I then mentally massaged her lungs to make them more flexible.
>
> After we returned, L.T. asked her mother if she had called the doctor. She said, "No. After you left I went to the bathroom and coughed up a lot of phlegm. I didn't cough any more after that and I was breathing so easily I didn't call the hospital." From that time until I left, she only coughed twice a day and was breathing just fine.

There was never any doubt in Edith Jacques' mind that she could help this emphysema sufferer. Because of the woman's age, she did not hope for a cure, but only relief. Apparently her efforts were more successful than she believed possible. From this it is obvious that it is always best to look for and expect the maximum results.

HOW TO PINPOINT AND CORRECT
AN ALLERGY

As a fitting conclusion to this chapter, an allergy correction performed by Ben Bibb himself is described. The subject was Patricia M. Bates of West Palm Beach, Florida. As she explains in her letter, she had been suffering for about two months with severe respiratory allergies when, about a week before Christmas, she decided to ask Ben Bibb for help. She had taken prescriptions for her stuffy head and her itchy, sneezing, drippy nose, but over the two-month period, nothing gave her any relief. Some days she says she could not raise her voice above a whisper, which was quite a handicap since she is a science teacher in the local middle school.

When early in Christmas week a woman friend gave her Ben Bibb's telephone number, she decided to call him and ask for help. She says he gave her a quick appraisal of her condition which made sense to her, then suggested she lie down and relax and call back in four or five days. She says she lay flat on her back as instructed, but suddenly became aware of strange sensations in her arms and legs, almost as if she could feel the blood pumping through them. After a moment or two she fell into a light sleep. Forty-five minutes later she was suddenly awakened by what sounded like someone snapping fingers in her left ear.

She says she followed her daily routine for the next few days, feeling somewhat better, but still bothered by the troublesome allergy. She then called Ben Bibb and reported as he had requested. He gave her another treatment and suggested she call back in another five days, which she did. It was now after Christmas and she had been improving slightly day by day. On the twelfth day after the original treatment, all traces of the allergy were suddenly gone and she felt fine. She says there has been no recurrence of the trouble up to the time she wrote the letter, which was over a year later.

You will be interested, I know, to read Ben Bibb's report on this case, so here it is:

> When Pat Bates called I was able to tell her that her respiratory allergies were the result of a false response by her autoimmunity system. (In contrast to this, some allergies are from a perfectly proper response, but the antibody with which the response is made has been wrongly constructed and is therefore ineffective.)
>
> With her cooperation, I contacted her inner mind. Mentally I placed the fingertips of my left hand on her pituitary and hypothalamus glands, in the center of the head underneath the brain, while I put my right mental fingertips on her thymus gland on the forewall of her chest just below the collarbone juncture. (The thymus is the governor of the autoimmunity system working through the lymph glands and spleen.) I began a rhythmic pulsation of energy to harmonize the action. With my left hand as originally placed, I would then go mentally with my right hand into the lungs as well as the windpipe and nasal passages, mopping out the mucus

emission from the tissues and using a blotter to soak up the natural histamine in the tissues which was reacting and creating the mucus. The right hand would then go back mentally to the thymus gland, energizing it, and then go into the neck and chest to jolt the lymph glands with energy.

To round out, I mentally projected a sun-colored aura around her and sent this sun-gold energy into her nasal passages, windpipe, bronchial tubes and lungs, causing them to "dry out" to the proper moistness.

I then gave her inner mind a strong automatic reminder that the entire process would be repeated daily until she reported. When she reported the first time by telephone, I revised the routine again, giving her an automatic reminder that the routine was to be repeated each day until she was completely cured. This apparently resulted in a healing about twelve days after the original contact.

You can see from the foregoing treatment that an allergy is usually a pretty deep-seated conviction that the inner mind does not surrender very readily. It is thus frequently necessary in these cures to repeat the treatment several times until the inner mind finally accepts the suggestion offered. Also, remember that in older people, there is a greater resistance to change, a fact which must be considered when treating them.

5. Psychic healing harmonics for correcting skin ailments including shingles, boils, warts and similar skin infections

This chapter offers Medipic solutions for banishing skin ailments of all kinds. There are some thirty-one basic classifications of skin problems, most with many subdivisions. For example, there are at least ten types of superficial fungus infections alone. You can see, therefore, that to deal with these as a dermatologist would—by trying to find out by observation and tests just what type of affliction might be causing the difficulty and then correcting it—would require a couple of books this size. Because of your unique opportunity for direct observation, however, your concern with skin ailments can be narrowed down to two types: those caused externally and those resulting from internal causes. This, in turn, means that for you there are but two general approaches to be adopted in healing them.

First let us look at the externally caused skin problems. As you suspect, there are many types, but with our Televisual method all can be handled by basic Medipic treatments.

MEDIPIC HEALING FOR EXTERNALLY CAUSED SKIN PROBLEMS

Most superficial skin infections are caused by contact with germs, staphylococcus and streptococcus being the most common. The infection resulting from such contact is usually impetigo, but it may take the form of ecthyma, erisipelas, carbuncles or some similar skin eruption. Here is the best way to correct these or any other germ-induced skin affliction:

76

1. Make contact with the mind of the sufferer and ascertain the *exact* cause of the skin ailment.

2. If, as suspected, it is germ induced, proceed at once to a thorough mental washing of all the affected parts with a powerful germicide. Do not be afraid of damaging the tissue. Remember that you are sending a mental suggestion and you want the inner mind of the subject to realize that it must take vigorous action to counteract and clean out the offending germs. Once it gets the idea, it will use its own method of getting rid of the germs.

3. Once you are sure the subject is free of all external irritation, you should then proceed with the healing. Here you can use your own imaginative technique, but most healers have found it best to mentally remove all the old damaged skin and replace it with perfect new skin, binding it all in place with what is called "people tape," a mental form of flexible tissue.

4. Finally, flood the entire affected area with white healing energy, green energy to speed the growth of the new skin, and light blue energy to soothe and remove all pain. Before leaving, instruct the subject's inner mind to repeat the entire process every six hours until the external physical condition is back to normal.

Sometimes, when the subject has carbuncles or cysts as a result of infection, it may be advisable to mentally lift out these growths with your fingers before moving to stage 3 in the foregoing healing procedure. You will find this will present no difficulty.

There is a different type of superficial skin infection which is caused by fungi and not germs. This, as in the case of germ infection, may take many different forms. The commonest are know as ringworm and athlete's foot. Also fairly common is a rash commonly called "the itch," which results from a parasitic skin growth. All of these superficial (surface) skin disturbances may be treated and healed by the same Medipic technique described in the foregoing as the proper method to correct skin infections from germs.

More than one half of all external skin afflictions are classed as dermatitis, and in the case of chronic dermatitis they are described as eczema. The best method of relieving and, in most cases, curing any form of exteriorly induced dermatitis is to follow the Medipic outline given earlier in this chapter. This covers all the necessary steps, the removal of the cause, the replacement of the affected and injured skin areas and the final healing stimulation. It must be noted, though, that a high percentage of eczema cases are the result of allergies. Unless the tendency to react to the allergy stimulants is sought out and eliminated, the dermatitis will in time return. The methods for combating allergies are described in Chapter 4.

Here is a case history of a self healing by Mrs. Donnabel Carter of Glastonbury, Connecticut. As you read her account you will realize that Mrs. Carter underestimated the true character of her skin ailment and failed at first to correct it, but once she discovered her error, she gave herself a thorough treatment which resulted in a complete cure. Here is her testimony:

> I recently developed an itching rash on my hips and in the pelvic area. It was very uncomfortable! I took antihistamines and applied different ointments, but these gave only temporary relief from the itching and no improvement in the large swollen red blotches. I bathed off the ointment and quit taking the pills, deciding to see if I could correct it via Medipic.
>
> First I used theraesthia locally (the laying on of energy through the hands) sending healing energy into the affected area. I watched as in treatment after treatment the red blotches paled and the itching subsided. But then I noticed that other blotches were appearing, and I realized that a healing was required in the entire blood stream and not just in the areas that appeared to be affected. So I changed the treatment.
>
> I imagined a great white light coming into me from above my head and filling my body with its healing energy. As I sent this energy to the affected parts I visualized it changing into blue to soothe the itching and into green to purify the blood and cleanse the irritants from it. Finally I combined the green and white for a most dramatic instantaneous healing of the entire condition.

In her letter Mrs. Carter comments that this treatment was so successful that when she caught athlete's foot at a local swimming pool a couple of weeks later, she used it again with the same dramatic success.

In her report Mrs. Carter refers to different colors of energy. These are symbolic of different vibratory levels. As you know, all energy is in vibratory form and the human energy associated with the head center, the pineal gland, etc., is regarded as having the highest vibratory rate. It is therefore described as "blue" energy because in the solar spectrum the blue rays vibrate the most rapidly. Next on the human vibratory scale is green energy, while red energy vibrates at the lowest or slowest rate. These and all human energies will be discussed in detail in Chapter 16.

Because burns occur very frequently when doing household chores, a method of dealing with them has great interest for many people. For this reason Dr. Bibb includes from his files an account by Joyce Dix of West Palm Beach of how she healed a burn on her hand. Here is her report:

> While working in the kitchen preparing dinner I had just finished frying potatoes and had put the large iron skillet to one side of the stove when, in order to get additional working space, I decided to put it in the sink. With my mind on the next step of the meal, I reached to pick it up with my bare hand. It wasn't until I had it half-way to the sink that I realized how very hot it was and that I was indeed "frying." The fingers of my right hand felt cold at first and then almost immediately so hot that I almost screamed. I dropped the skillet into the sink and went to work immediately to heal the burn on my fingers.
>
> I sat down and stilled my mind. Then I put the thumb and first two fingers of my left hand against the burned fingers and visualized white light surging into my forehead, down my left arm and out my left hand into the burned fingers. At the same time I said over and over to myself, "Normalize, normalize." I continued this for three or four minutes and when the pain stopped, I went on preparing the meal. Since there was no pain and I was busy, I gave it no thought until the dinner was over. Suddenly I recalled what had happened. I looked at the fingers and saw that there was still a trace of redness in them, but felt no pain. The next morning even the redness was gone and my fingers were completely normal.

In this report Mrs. Dix relates how she used white healing energy to rapidly ease the pain of a severe burn and to subsequently repair the tissue within a matter of a few hours. This is a healing that you, too, can perform almost immediately. Try it.

At the beginning of this chapter you were cautioned not to jump to conclusions as to the cause of a skin affliction but to mentally examine the subject before starting the treatment. The importance of this is well illustrated in the case of little Jason Russell, age four. Here is what happened.

On Sunday while Jason and his mother were in church, his father saturated the back garden with weed killer. After lunch little Jason went out to play and wandered into the area in which the poison had been spread. Some time in the afternoon he scratched his face. It is not known whether the poison entered his bloodstream through the scratch or by inhalation—but poisoned he was. On Monday huge blisters appeared all over his body and he was rushed to the hospital. He got steadily worse. It appeared that the several doctors attending him could do nothing to help, for on Friday morning they announced that he could not survive another night. The entire epidermis had blistered and peeled off his body and the dermis had started blistering. It was not until then that his mother sought the help of her friend, Julia Whitten, a graduate Seventh Sense healer. Calling from California where Jason and his family live, Mrs. Russell finally reached Mrs. Whitten at her home in West Palm Beach, Florida. She explained the condition of the boy and said that doctors had been unable to ascertain the cause of his distress because he had no fever at any time and no signs of a cold or sore throat. Mrs. Whitten wasted no time in getting to work on little Jason, with amazing success. Here is her report:

> I first asked the Divine Mind to grant me the guidance, energy and wisdom so that this little boy could be saved to live a normal life with his parents, grandparents and relatives who so dearly loved him. I then slipped into a deep velvet state of mind where I could see Jason clearly. It was almost as though I was watching a movie—completely apart from what I was doing. I saw the soul of the boy pulling away from the head area. It looked like a large brilliant cone of swirling energy with just the tiny tip in contact with his head. I felt a cool calmness come over me as I spoke to it humbly but with determination to give it valid reasons why it should wish to stay with the physical body of this child. The soul then took on a more dense appearance and changed shape so as to surround the head of Jason.
>
> At this point, and without any conscious effort on my part, I watched the little boy go back in time, through the days he had been in the hospital, then at home, then out in the back yard some time before he became ill. The movie-like regression stopped at this point and I could see a misty vapor coming from the ground around Jason. His pores seemed larger than normal and I could actually smell the vapor. It was an unpleasant odor and seemed acid. At this point I received a message to pack him in baking soda, which I did. It seemed to me that the vapor was either insecticide of some sort or a fertilizer.
>
> This picture then faded and returned to Jason in the hospital. I used more baking soda and sent energy to him. I held the pulsating golden-white energy in live golden hands, provided so generously by the Creator, until I could feel the life force returning to the boy's body.
>
> I gave him another complete treatment again the same day and still another on Saturday. It was then that I saw that Jason's blisters had subsided, and that he was sitting up eating and retaining food. On Sunday I took another look and saw he was nauseated and unable to retain food. I telephoned his mother at once and asked her to have all medication

stopped, which she did. After they stopped giving him antibiotics he
was once more able to eat and retain solid food.

A few days later Jason was released from the hospital totally
healed and without scars, although his entire back and bottom had
been without either layer of skin. Interestingly, the doctors on the
case assumed from the start that Jason had a staph infection
contracted through the scratch on the boy's face. They are convinced
that the antibiotics they administered orally finally effected a cure.
One of the doctors said, "We have only been able to cope with this in
the last five years. He is lucky the antibiotics took hold in time."
True, this might have been the case, but it does not coincide with
what Mrs. Whitten actually *saw* in her contact with the inner mind of
the boy. This points to the importance of "looking." To be a successful healer you must know as much as possible about the cause of the
ailment. This means you should look and see as Mrs. Whitten did.
Once her contact with the boy's inner mind disclosed the fact that
the poisonous vapor rising from the ground had entered his system
through his pores, the next step was to counteract the acid invasion—
which she did by mentally coating his body with baking soda.

HOW TO CLEAR UP INTERNALLY
CAUSED SKIN PROBLEMS

When you mentally examine sufferers from skin ailments you will
find in a great many cases that these disorders are the result of
internal causes. You can always provide fairly quick relief in all such
situations and sometimes, as in the case of warts, moles and
sebaceous cysts, no further treatment is necessary. As you have seen,
one method is to just wash the troubled parts in an antiseptic,
remove the warts, moles or cysts with your fingers and then bathe
the entire area with healing energy.

Another technique, which some students prefer, is illustrated.
It can be successfully employed to clear up moles, warts or any other
blemish not due to a deep-seated blood disorder.

This treatment will correct all but the most stubborn stiuations.
However, if after a reasonable time, not exceeding twenty-four
hours, a complete healing is not evident, go through this Medipic
treatment again and at its termination, instruct the inner mind of the
subject to repeat this healing every twelve hours until it is no longer
necessary. This will be effective.

MEDIPIC METHOD TO
RELIEVE SKIN RASH,
MOLES AND WARTS

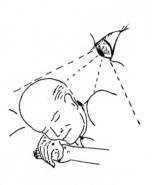

1. After establishing mental contact, make sure that the blemishes to be removed are not the result of a serious internal disorder. If this is not the cause, then proceed thus:

2. Wash the area in disinfectant and then apply violet skin peeler to the entire surface.

3. Using a tweezers or your fingers, carefully peel off all the skin from the affected area.

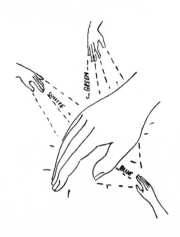

4. Examine the area carefully to make sure all blemishes have been removed; first flood it with white healing energy, to speed the growth of new skin and finally with blue energy to soothe and prevent any painful reaction. Withdraw then and recheck in twelve hours.

Sometimes blisters, rashes and skin eruptions are but the external evidences of more serious internal disturbances, as in the case of surface tumors, psoriasis and shingles. In all such ailments an internal cleansing and balancing process is required in addition to the surface healing if a permanent cure is to be achieved.

In the case of a surface tumor, a female breast tumor let us say, the cause may be a deep-seated malignancy or it may be nothing more than a glandular maladjustment. If the latter, the following case history, described by Seventh Sense graduate Harold Ames of Canterbury, Connecticut, is a good healing procedure to adopt.

HEALING A BREAST TUMOR

Recently my daughter-in-law, Norma Jean Ames, asked me if I could do anything about a breast tumor. I told her I would try. She had a lump in her left breast and since she had a similar tumor in the same breast removed surgically three years previously, she was worried.

That evening I put her on my mental screen and found the tumor. I checked to see if it was malignant and found it was not, since there were no dark or vacant areas in her etheric body. I therefore just proceeded to shrink it mentally until it was completely gone and then bathed the area with healing energy. I also projected different beneficial colors into her aura before finally releasing her from my mental screen.

Two days later she called to tell me the tumor had completely disappeared.

In a letter from Norma Jean Ames, who gives permission to use her name, she says that the healing took place exactly as stated.

In treating people who suffer from psoriasis or shingles, an inner treatment is required in addition to the surface cleanup. In the case of psoriasis this requires the glandular balancing described in Chapter 16. Where shingles is the offender, first clear up the surface blisters and sores and then purify the blood. Shingles is a blood infection, a virus, which must be eliminated by employing the blood cleansing Medipic method described in Chapter 15.

A letter from Mrs. T. Raymond Hagle of Ripley, New York illustrates a case of special interest. Mrs. Hagle had shingles. After determining what her ailment was, she sought the help of a Seventh Sense group in Florida who had previously cleared up a toxic condition in her pregnant daughter. Here is Fran Hagle's letter:

Since you gave me your help, I've had no further problems with my shingles (what a name!). But they were rough when I had them.

As you know, I had been in deep misery around my right ear for several days before I decided to call a doctor to tell me what was the matter and what to do about it. The diagnosis was <u>shingles.</u> He said they would last at least six weeks and predicted the path they would take as they progressed. He said there was no medicine or salve that would do me any good, but he did prescribe some pain pills. Upset that such a ridiculous disease was bothering <u>me</u> I wrote to you.

Four days later I noticed I had no pain whatsoever and that the horrible sores were not spreading as the doctor had said they would. There have been no more sores from that day to now. You Seventh Sense people have certainly a better way to heal. I think it is wonderful! Take care. Love, Fran Hagle

Since about fifteen per cent of all diseases seen by family doctors and internists are skin ailments, this chapter is important to you as a healer. Once you have established satisfactory mind-to-mind contact with the sufferer, you can clear up surface blemishes, rashes or other unsightly skin disturbances very quickly. You will be amazed at the rapidity with which these problems will respond to the Medipic treatments described here. Usually these surface cleanups will be all that is needed, but always give the patient the benefit of a good mental examination. If the cause is internal and serious, you should then proceed to correct it as indicated by one of the methods described in this book.

Always remember to make your picturized instructions to the subject's inner mind as simple as you can. No matter how complicated the medical diagnosis may seem, the correction or cure is easy for the subjective mind once it understands what must be done. If you find a torn muscle, therefore, tie it together. The patient's inner mind will understand and make the repair in its own way. Likewise, if an artery on the wall of the stomach is ruptured and bleeding, close the wound with "people tape." This, as you suspect, is similar to the tape of an elastic bandage, but is made of human tissue which grows immediately onto whatever human organ or internal area you apply it. Of course these devices exist only in your mind, but when you transmit an image of them via Medipic to the person you are helping, the inner mind picks them up and adapts itself to the instruction transmitted. As you work with such ailments as skin blemishes, rashes and irritations, you will see how quickly they will respond to the projected image of a simple washing in an antiseptic solution followed by an application of healing oil. So keep your Televisual messages simple.

6. The secret psychic technique for diagnosing and healing ear, nose and throat problems

When you tune in on the subjective mind of the person you wish to help, you will get an "impression" as to the nature of the problem. This impression will express itself to you in different ways at different times. Most often it will be visual. In other words, you will appear to be looking at the troubled area in the subject's body and will see there some malfunction that is clearly the cause of the difficulty. Sometimes this impression will translate itself to your active consciousness in terms of the physical sense that is troubled.

An example of this is the case referred to in Chapter 1 where Nell Crossen, the healer, experienced a sharp pain in the left side of her neck as she successfully attuned herself with a woman patient she had never seen. She diagnosed this as a "wry neck," which was later confirmed.

A similar report of an "impression" other than a visual one is found in the healing of Ann Stone by May McLaughlin of West Palm Beach, Florida. Lou Stone was worried about his wife, Ann. She didn't seem well, but to his inquiries she said, "Oh, I'm all right," Nevertheless, it seemed clear to him that something was troubling her so he asked May McLaughlin, a Seventh Sense healer, to try to find out what was bothering his wife and to cure it if she could. Here are May McLaughlin's exact words:

> I had difficulty making contact with Ann but when I finally got through to her, I got a terrible whistling and pain in my right ear along with a splitting headache, mostly at the base of the brain. I waited for other conditions to reveal themselves but received nothing. For a moment I thought this experience might be subjective—that it was something I

alone was experiencing. Then I realized it was but my recognition of the distress Ann was suffering, and I was able to identify the source as her ear.

I hastened to clear out the infection, for such it was, and was pleased to note that the ringing stopped immediately. I sent a beam of gold light energy into her ear to correct and heal it and followed this by enveloping Ann in a blue aura to soothe the pain and calm her nerves. As an extra precaution I then mentally wrapped a towel saturated in blue energy around her head. I asked the Universal Mind for a complete healing for Ann, and I was sure that this was so.

All this was reported to Lou Stone. When he later asked Ann about her headache and the ringing in her ear she looked very surprised and said, "They're both gone—but how did you know?"

Most often you will receive a visual impression of what is wrong. When you are asked to help someone who complains of an ear affliction, a sore throat, nasal trouble, a bad sinus condition or any other problem, first relax in a quiet place and then reach out mentally to contact the subjective mind of the sufferer. With your eyes closed, you will get the impression that you are looking at the person who needs help and you will see directly into his or her head, almost as if it were transparent. Your attention will be drawn to the area that needs correction and there you will see exactly what is causing the discomfort or pain. It may be that you will see the sinus cavities blocked with mucus, dark red colors moving up and down the throat which would indicate a sore throat, or the inner part of one or both ears may appear to be throbbing, indicating pressure on the nerves in the eustachian tubes and ears. In a word, you will get a visual impression of what is wrong and where the malfunction is located. Your next step, of course, is to correct it.

As an example of what might be done to cure an earache, let us take a specific case, that of six-year-old Timothy Miller of Plainfield, Connecticut. His mother, Frances Miller, is a graduate of one of Ben Bibb's classes. Here is her report of the case:

CURING AN EARACHE

In the wee hours of a cold winter morning, my six-year-old son, Timothy, woke up crying with an earache. My first thought was to ease his pain, so I placed my right hand over his ear and sent turquoise pain-killing energy right into the affected area. With my left hand I directed soothing blue energy into his solar plexus. In a few minutes he experienced relief and was calm enough to go back to sleep.

It was then that I sought out the cause of his pain in order to correct it. I relaxed, contacted his inner mind, and observed a great deal of liquid in his ear. I mentally drained this fluid out with a tube and swabbed up the remaining droplets of moisture with cotton.

At 9:30 a.m. when our pediatrician's office opened I called and was told that the symptoms I described were typical of an ailment many children were suffering from at that particular time. The doctor did not think it would be necessary for me to bring Tim in unless he got worse, but said he would telephone prescriptions to the local druggist for medication to ease the pain, and penicillin to clear up the infection. I could pick these up later. He said that should take care of the infection in two or three days and asked me to bring Tim in for a check in about ten days if all went well. If not, I was to call him again after forty-eight hours.

When he awoke, Tim's ear was much better but still bothering him a little. About 10:30 a.m., Mrs. Grace Grissom of Plainfield, Connecticut, another Seventh Sense graduate, telephoned me and when I told her about Tim she said, "I'll try to help him, too." Ten minutes after I hung up the phone, Tim yelled, "Mommy, my ear doesn't hurt any more." I phoned Mrs. Grissom with the good news and she said she had contacted Tim moments after our first telephone conversation and had seen more fluid in his ear. This she set in motion, directing it to flow out through the eustachian tube and down the throat. This appeared to work because Tim had no more pain or discomfort from that moment on.

Meanwhile I had the two prescriptions to pick up, or so I thought. I telephoned finally about four o'clock to the drugstore to find out about them and learned they had not received any instruction from the doctor. So I called the doctor's office and was told the prescriptions would go to the druggist in a few minutes and I could pick them up after 4:30. When I walked into the druggist's with Tim, it seemed a little comical. A little boy presumed to have been in severe pain for twelve hours, and who should have his eyes all swollen from crying, came walking in with me all smiles and looking as happy and healthy as a boy could be. I'm still wondering what the clerk thought as she saw him.

As has been explained, the inner mind of the sufferer does the healing in most cases. All that you need do is to indicate through mental pictures what needs to be done. Quite often, though, you will find that extra energy must be provided by you if the healing is to be accomplished as quickly as desired. This case is a good example of a mistake many healers make. They assume that once they have successfully reached the inner mind of the sufferer and instructed it in what to do, they can retire and assume their work is done. Not so! Sometimes the victim does not possess sufficient energy to get the healing completed properly and quickly, so you should always apply healing energy. This woman, Frances Miller, did supply healing energy to her son but not enough. When at 10:30 in the morning his ear still hurt a little, she should have made contact again, repeated the treatment and sent him more energy. Fortunately for her and for small Timothy, Mrs. Grissom called at just that time. It was her additional effort that finally resulted in a complete cure—a cure within a few hours and not three days as the anticipated result of the medication prescribed by the pediatrician.

I was curious about the medicine, as you too probably are, so I checked. Mrs. Miller said that she had bought it because the drugstore had made it up and she felt obligated to pay for it. But as for giving it to Timmy she said, "No way. Why should I? He didn't need it." He certainly didn't.

CURING A SORE THROAT

A sore throat is usually symptomatic of something more serious, frequently a viral infection which may attack the entire respiratory system. Thus it is advisable, as always, to check beyond the sore throat when someone so afflicted comes to you for help. Heal the aching throat, yes, but look around for other symptoms. Are the nasal passages filled up? Do the lungs show signs of malfunction? Does the subject have a fever?

When you are asked to help someone with a sore throat, first find a place where you can relax without being disturbed. Take three deep breaths, letting each one out slowly; then establish mental contact with the inner mind of the sufferer. See there not only the condition of the throat itself, but take note also of all contributing factors.

Proceed then to first heal the throat by painting it mentally with a strong germicide followed by white healing oil; next flood the area with blue energy to take out the pain and soothe the inflamed parts. When this has been done, the patient should begin to experience some relief and you can go on to the next step, which is to clear out the cause of the sore throat. In almost all cases this will be a virus of some sort, often a "flu" virus. Seek out the focus of this infection, which may be in the throat itself but could be elsewhere, and proceed to destroy it. The best way to convey this need for action on its part to the inner mind of the patient is to mentally bathe the infected area with a powerful germicide like Listerine or Lysol.

Follow this immediately with a bath in white healing oil plus a shot of healing energy. You can then withdraw, but check back in six hours or so. If necessary, repeat the treatment then and follow it with a bath in blue energy to take away all pain and soothe the nerves.

The case history of a healing of this type may help to clarify the foregoing instruction. The healer is Wilda Beidler of Danielson, Connecticut, who at the time was still a student of Ben Bibb. The subject was H.E., age 50, of South Killingly, Connecticut. Here is her report:

> A call came for Ben Bibb, who was at that time in my home. It was from Mrs. E., who said that her husband was very sick with a tight chest, a sore throat and fever of 103 degrees. She asked Ben Bibb for help. Ben looked at me and said "You can do it" and told me what he had been asked to do. Ben had to leave then for a meeting and since the E.'s are old friends, I decided to do what I could for H. But I was a little nervous because this was the first case I had tried out of class.
>
> I sat down and drew energy to myself, took a few deep breaths, closed my eyes and mentally called H's name. I received him loud and clear and got a good mental picture of him in person. His lungs had a lot of fluid in them, so I made a broom of white energy and swept them clear. This took a little time but when I saw that all the mucus was gone I flooded the area with a golden sunshine aura to kill all the germs. I then wrapped him in a blue pain-killing aura and sent it through his entire body, including his throat, which was sore, and the nasal passages, which had been clogged up. Following this I poured life energy into the brain stem and into the solar plexus. I stimulated his heart action with pink energy and swept blue energy up and down his body once more, telling it to cool off. Finally I put him in a blue paper room with blue bedding and felt he was fine.
>
> At seven that night his wife called and said that his temperature was back to normal, right on the button, and he was feeling fine. He came to the house the following night wanting to know what I did and if I could give him some more energy because he felt just fine.

As you proceed with your healing work you will find that in a great many cases the inner mind of the subject just doesn't know what to do. It is then up to you to show it via Medipic (a mental scenario) what needs be done. In other cases you will find that the inner mind knows how to correct the problem, but either it cannot because of insufficient energy, or it is forced to proceed very slowly. In these cases it is important that you send it energy, particularly of the quality most needed. Sometimes, too, you can show the inner mind a quicker way to correct the problem so that it can accomplish in a day or two what might normally take weeks or even months. In every case it is best to not only send mental pictures to the inner mind of the subject but also to send additional energy. This can always be done with no loss to yourself, for life energy is all around us in boundless quantities. As a matter of fact, when you send energy to a patient, when you tap this infinite reservoir to help someone else, you will invariably find that you end up with more energy yourself.

HOW TO CURE HEAD COLDS
AND SINUS PROBLEMS

Let us now look at some practical approaches to healing head colds and correcting sinus problems. Most of these difficulties arise from infections of various sorts, but some occur because of allergies. The infectious types are much more common, so we will discuss their treatment first and get to those caused by allergies later in this chapter.

When the body recognizes any type of infectious germs building up in the system, it hastens in its own way to correct this. As you know, it starts releasing extra white corpuscles in order to surround these germs, render them inactive and carry them out of the system—whether the germs be streptococcus, staphylococcus, influenza, pneumococcus or any similar type. This method of correction and elimination is lengthy and puts a heavy drain on the human energies, but it is the only method the inner mind was originally programmed to employ and turns to in all cases. Usually the conscious mind of the victim does not become aware of the infection until the white corpuscles have built up to a point where his nose is stopped up or his sinus cavities are in pain. From this point onward, the course of the infection is not always predictable. If left to itself, the white corpuscle army can usually throw off the infection in fourteen to sixteen days, provided the victim gets plenty of bed rest during that period. Without sufficient rest, energies may become deficient to the task at hand and as a result, the infection may degenerate into a serious or even fatal ailment. If, however, a physician is consulted in time, he can prescribe antibiotics and other medication that will usually bring the infection under control in three or four days.

Since everyone is different from everyone else, some people have a higher natural resistance to these infections than others. Their

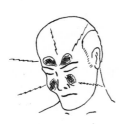

1. This is possibly the way the sufferer's head will appear to you on making mental contact with the inner mind.

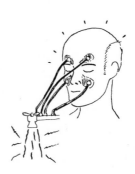

2. Your first task then is to clear out the clogged sinuses and give the patient relief from pain. Mentally blow out, drain out or swab out these cavities in whatever way suggests itself to you as best at the time.

3. Next kill off the germs. This can be suggested by mentally washing out the sinus cavities with a powerful germicide. Remember that you are not actually using this germicide but merely suggesting to the patient's inner mind the need for vigorous and thorough action on its part. Follow this procedure with a flow of white healing energy.

4. See the sinuses completely cleared out, free of mucus and infection. Instruct the subject's inner mind to repeat this process every twelve hours until there is no longer any need to do so. Finally, send a powerful surge of energy to the entire body, washing it in sun-gold energy from the head to the feet and then back from feet to head; then withdraw.

systems throw off the germs quicker and they suffer less inconvenience. It is your task as a healer to so stimulate the inner mind of the victim that it will expel these germs as rapidly and efficiently as might a person with the very highest natural resistance—or maybe even quicker and more thoroughly. As an example of what to do and how to do it, the standard Medipic healing procedure for sinus infection is pictured.

The treatment for a head cold due to infection is similar. First, clean out the clogged nasal passages; then perform a prophylaxis (kill the germs), and finally mentally flood the passages with healing oil plus either white or sun-gold healing energy. As always, finish by giving the subject a shot of powerful energy to help him or her carry out the treatment you have suggested to the inner mind.

Here as a practical example is the case history of a healing performed to cure a sinus infection. The healer is a woman named Vi Holtberg, who operates a real estate agency in Boynton Beach, Florida. The man with the sinus problem is Kenneth Kruchek of Lake Worth, Florida.

Vi Holtberg reports as follows:

> Kenneth Kruchek told me that he had been afflicted with sinus troubles as far back as he could remember. In Ohio, where he grew up, it was worse than here in Florida, particularly in damp and cold weather. Here it was still an annoyance and often painful, but he was resigned to the belief that nothing could be done about it. I decided to see if I could help him.
>
> Without telling him, I tuned in one night on his subjective mind. Since I had success curing a head cold using a sea water treatment, I decided to use it again on Kenneth. I began by rinsing all of his sinus cavities with ocean water, asking that whatever of the trace minerals were useful should be absorbed in or by the interiors of the sinuses—and that the unused or unwanted particles be flushed away, carrying with them all injurious cells and particles.
>
> Then I beamed rays of sun-gold healing energy into the cavities, followed by an injection of sinus healing oils which were to penetrate the linings of the sinus cavities. This treatment was repeated every three or four days, but it was almost three months before Kenneth got any real relief. Once started, however, the complete healing came rapidly. Recently I asked him about his sinuses. He said, "It doesn't seem possible after all these years to finally get relief, but it's marvelous." When I told him what I had done, he found it difficult to believe. But when I asked if I could use his name in a report, he grinned and said, "Sure. Go ahead."

Sometimes you will find that the subject's nasal passages or sinus cavities have filled up because of an allergy. In these cases, clean out the congestion in the affected areas in whatever way seems best to you at the time. This could be by draining them, by blowing out the mucus, by swabbing it out or some other way suggested to you by your intuition. Let me remind you that you will on occasion be led to suggest unusual and original picture sequences to the inner mind of the patient. This is your intuition working, so follow its guidance.

After the congestion has been mentally removed by your suggestion, ask the subject's inner mind about the cause. Usually it will reveal in picture form the substance causing the allergic reaction, but sometimes you will receive the message via smell or taste. You will recognize it if you will give it a moment's thought. For example, dog hair might be revealed visually, but garlic would usually strike your sense of smell. Once this is identified you must explain to the inner mind that this is a basically harmless substance which should be ignored. Tell the inner mind there is no need to become upset or frightened when in its presence. While tremendously powerful, the inner mind can be likened to a child. Once it becomes convinced you desire only to help and gives you its confidence, it will accept and act on the suggestions you give it.

AN UNEXPECTED DIVIDEND

Occasionally a healing effort will not only achieve its objective but also pay unexpected dividends. This occurred in the case of Natalie Ambrose of Monterey, Massachusetts. Natalie had a sore throat and asked Ben Bibb to help her if he could. On contacting her inner mind, Ben discovered that the sore throat came from her thyroid gland, which had been underactive and out of balance for some time. When he established the proper normal balance, her sore throat went away and did not return. For Natalie there was an unanticipated and very welcome dividend. At the time Ben balanced her thyroid gland she weighed one hundred and seventy-five pounds. Six months later she weighed one hundred and thirty pounds and never felt better in her life.

In a letter to Ben Bibb she says:

> At the time you treated and healed my thyroid gland, six months ago, I weighed one hundred and seventy-five pounds. I now weigh one hundred and thirty pounds. During this time I have eaten everything and all that I wanted to. It was the easiest weight loss I ever heard of. You know I'll be forever grateful to you.
>
> Sincerely, Natalie Ambrose.

HOW TO LOSE WEIGHT

On the subject of weight loss, you should know, as a healer, that when it is necessary to the good health of the subject, you can suggest that he or she lose weight. This alone will usually result in a weight reduction of the required amount, but sometimes it is necessary to add other suggestions to achieve the proper objective. For example, you might suggest mentally to the inner mind of the subject that certain high-calorie foods are distasteful, as Annie Zvengilas of Plainfield, Connecticut did for her friend May Richards, who needed to lose weight.

One day May Richards confided to Annie Zvengalis that she was supposed to lose at least five pounds and asked if she could help. Annie agreed to try and said she would aim at getting her weight down that amount in a week. Here is her report.

> May Richards asked me to work on her to get her weight down, so that evening I tuned in on her and commanded her inner mind to reject as distasteful all high-calorie foods. I also suggested that she automatically confine herself to 1000 calories a day until further advice. I then visualized May on a mental scale losing a pound a day after I had instructed her to do so. The next day she was actually a pound lighter and said she had no desire for her usual snacks the evening before. Before the week was up she had lost five pounds and has asked me to help her lose five more.

The foregoing case is not unusual. When it is convinced you mean it only good and no harm, the inner mind of a subject will accept your suggestions and act upon them. This is a precious gift to be used wisely—so cherish it.

7. Seventh sense psychic healing methods for correcting eye troubles

This chapter presents tested mind power methods for treating various eye afflictions such as glaucoma, cataract, etc., and psychic treatments prescribed for their relief and cure.

The eye is one of the most intricate and delicately adjusted organs in the human system. As a natural consequence, it is subject to a great variety of malfunctions. These range from common nearsightedness and farsightedness to cataract, glaucoma, corneal ulcer and other afflictions including accidental eye damage. It is our purpose, therefore, to consider here as many of these problems as space will permit and, in addition, provide a technique which will enable you to resolve competently any other situations you may encounter.

NEARSIGHTEDNESS AND FARSIGHTEDNESS

These are the commonest of all eye afflictions. Most people over forty are troubled to some degree by either one or the other. Both are caused by a weakening of the ciliary muscles which focus the lens of the eye. This is usually a deterioration due to the normal aging process of the individual, but in some cases it is an inherited characteristic or may be caused by injury or excessive eye strain.

Whatever the cause may have been, you can in almost every case either remedy or cure both these afflictions and astigmatism (eye imbalance) as follows:

1. Tune in on the inner mind of the subject and examine the eye structure. If the muscles surrounding the lens appear slack or loose, you then know you are on the right track; go on to the next step.

2. Treat each muscle individually by supporting it with tiny elastic threads.

3. Then strengthen the muscles by giving them a jolt of bright red energy.

4. Conclude by bathing both eyes in cooling, soothing, healing blue energy as you withdraw. Check again in twenty-four hours and repeat the process if necessary.

This Medipic technique should work successfully in all situations except where there may have been damage to the eye or eyes. In these cases, examine further until the traumatic condition discloses itself and then set about correcting it according to the method described later in this chapter.

Floaters. Another fairly common eye affliction is a phenomenon described as floaters or spots before the eyes. This starts as small black specks that appear to float around between the eye and the object it is focused upon. Since there is no pain involved and only a slight inconvenience at first, most eye specialists ignore these and encourage their patients to do the same. This affliction has a tendency to get progressively worse, however, particularly in people past middle age, so that eventually it will seriously impair sight itself.

As a Medipic healer you can correct this regardless of what stage it may be in when the victim approaches you for help. As an example of a satisfactory technique to follow, here is the case history of a cure. The healer is Isabel Cusack, a Seventh Sense graduate who lives in Lantana, Florida. Her subject asked that her name not be used because she is a trained nurse and presently employed, so we will refer to her as Mrs. B. Here is Mrs. Cusack's report:

> A friend of mine, Mrs. B., complained one day about "floaters" in her eyes and said that the condition had worsened in the past year to a point where she had to look very closely at certain types of printing to avoid making a mistake. She knew I had been doing some psychic healing work but regarded it with the skepticism normally held by members of the medical profession, but when I offered to try and help her she shrugged her shoulders and said, "What can I lose? No one else has been able to do anything about it."
>
> At the time she was seated right before me, so I mentally placed one hand on each side of her head at the temples to act as magnets. I then silently instructed the floaters to move to the outer corner of each eye, where my fingers attracted them and magnetically plucked them out. When I saw mentally that all had been removed, I covered her eyes with white healing energy and terminated the treatment.

At the time Mrs. B. made no comment, but she telephoned me the next day to say that the floaters had disappeared. That was several months ago and they have not returned.

These three eye problems for which healings have been described, nearsightedness, farsightedness and astigmatism, are normally regarded by ophthalmologists as either incurable or not serious enough to be concerned about. Glasses are usually prescribed for these conditions. As the affliction progresses, the glasses have to be changed to gradually increasing strength in order to maintain an acceptable visual standard, but once a satisfactory correction is achieved by the Seventh Sense Medipic technique, the patient's sight is usually normal for many years thereafter.

Floaters, or spots before the eyes, are also usually regarded by eye specialists as having little or no significance, but if they should appear as brown or red they may indicate a vitreous hemorrhage or an impending retinal detachment. You, as a healer, should always examine the eye carefully before leaping to any conclusions. Any disturbance of vision demands an explanation.

QUICKLY HEALING EYE INJURIES

The eye is a very sensitive organism and may be injured in many ways. It may suffer a blow on the eye or near it; foreign matter, like a cinder, may imbed itself in the eye, causing irritation, pain and sometimes infection; or, worst of all, a sharp instrument may penetrate the eye causing lacerations, contusions and sometimes hemorrhage. In almost all such traumatic conditions, you can suggest healing to the subject's inner mind by sending it visual instructions (mental pictures) describing how the healing is to be accomplished.

Lacerations and hemorrhages of the eyeball or eyelids should be treated by drawing together the lips of the wound or severed blood vessels and mentally sealing them with transparent healing tape after first having removed all foreign bodies. The entire area should then be thoroughly washed out with white healing energy to prevent infection and stimulate a rapid return to normal.

Contusions. The damaged blood in the bruised area should first be mentally drained off and replaced with fresh clean blood and, where necessary, with fresh new tissue. Green healing energy should then be flooded into the affected area and followed by a flow of blue energy to ease the pain and soothe the nerves.

To help clarify these processes for you, here is the report of a cure of serious eye damage to a boy named Scott who lives in New York City, as reported by his mother, Gloria. At her request their last names are not used, but they are on file. The healer was Ben Bibb. Here is Gloria's case history report:

> Scott, age ten, accidentally jabbed the tip of a pen into his right eye and required immediate surgical attention. This was on October 10.
>
> At this first operation there were five doctors present: the junior resident on duty in the emergency room, the senior resident who performed the trauma surgery, an attending physician as required when a resident operates, our private ophthalmologist and his associate.
>
> The diagnosis was a torn cornea (a three-centimeter wound requiring four stitches), protruding pigment jelly and a detached and tilted lens. The X-rays fortunately revealed no foreign bodies. All five doctors reached the same general conclusions. The junior resident for one was excited that he had independently reached the same conclusion offered by the senior resident. All told us there was no way in the world a detached lens could be medically or surgically corrected and all concluded that Scott would never again be able to see well with that eye. In fact, the attending physician strongly urged that "removal of the lens" be added to the surgical permission for the immediate repair work. This we refused.
>
> The doctors told us that a cataract in that eye could almost certainly be expected to form within six or seven months due to the lens damage, and that to remove a cataract from a detached lens would be like bobbing for apples. This could mean a complete removal of the lens at that time. A further possible complication, they pointed out, was the danger of post-operative infection which would then require the removal of the eye itself.
>
> The day after the surgery, October 11, I was telling a dear friend, Lydia, about poor little Scott and she offered to contact Ben Bibb and ask him for help. I knew nothing of this man but when Lydia told me of his many remarkable healing achievements, I pleaded with her to ask his help, which she did that very day. Lydia called back two days later, on October 15, and said she had seen Mr. Bibb the night before and he had said, "Don't worry about little Scott. I've got his retina all glued tight. It's okay."
>
> I didn't know what she meant, so she explained about Mr. Bibb's mental healing technique, and how he had suggested to Scott's inner mind to reaffix the retina by sending it a picture of gluing it back in place.
>
> The next day, October 16, the attending physician and our private ophthalmologist, his assistant and the senior resident all examined Scott's

eye and were candidly amazed. "It looks great!" said one. When I asked about the lens, the senior resident said, "It looks solid, but we will have to wait and see." I had to bite my tongue to keep from telling him why.

On October 20, the day before Scott was released from the hospital, our private doctor examined him and found his vision to be 20/30 in the injured eye. He was amazed and said to Scott several times, "God has been good to you. He has performed a miracle for you," whereas on the day of the operation he had said to me, "It looks bad, very bad. He could lose that eye."

On October 25 I took Scott to our doctor to be checked, as he had requested, and he found then that Scott had 20/20 vision as it is today, four months later. On February 28 the doctor told Scott it would no longer be necessary for him to come in for checkups since he was completely cured and there was no danger of a cataract forming or, as far as he could determine, of any other complications arising.

For this I sincerely thank Ben Bibb.

HOW TO REMOVE AND HEAL
A CATARACT

One of the commonest eye afflictions, particularly in people over forty years of age, is the development of a cataract. The so-called degenerative cataract, which occurs most often, is characterized by a gradual loss of transparency in a normally developed eye lens. When the lens reaches a point where the eye can no longer delineate the outlines of objects, the clouded lens may be surgically removed and replaced by glasses or a contact lens.

As a Medipic healer you can frequently correct a cataract without recourse to surgery. As in most cases where Medipic is employed, you merely suggest to the inner mind of the subject a method which, if followed, will reverse the degenerative process and restore the eye to normal sight. The basic technique is here illustrated with a series of pictures suggesting the mental images you might employ to show the inner mind of the subject what should be done.

The illustration is a basic technique for removing all cataracts. Cataracts have many different causes, however, and it is wise to look for the cause of the cataract when you have the subject under mental observation. If you discover its cause was simple senile degenerative change (just growing old), or a trauma (injury) caused by a blow, by previous X-ray treatment or by an infected tooth, you need do nothing further. The removal of the cataract itself is all that is necessary. However if the cataract should be the result of some

EYE HEALING MEDIPIC

1. Here you can see the affected eye as it will appear to your inner sight at first contact. Note the clouded lens before the eye.

2. First remove the lens from the eye. Remember that this is a mental operation only.

3. After removing the lens thoroughly, wash out the eye with an antiseptic solution to clear it of all germs and prevent infection.

4. Install a new, perfect, clear lens in place of the old one and glue it firmly in place.

5. Flood the eye completely with white healing energy to speed up the acceptance of the new lens and restore normal sight as soon as possible.

systemic disease (like diabetes), chronic inflammation of the iris or the presence of some toxic substance or drug, you should take steps to correct the cause itself or the cataract may form again. Since each of these possible causes is a problem in itself, it is recommended that you consult the chapter where its correction is described.

TREATING GLAUCOMA VIA MEDIPIC

There are many causes of glaucoma, a gradual deterioration in vision in both eyes which, if not corrected, may lead to total blindness. In order to permanently correct or cure glaucoma these causes must be sought out and, if possible, eliminated. Regardless of cause, you can relieve glaucoma quickly and easily by using the Medipic technique here described. This relief will only be temporary, however, unless the aggravating cause is sought out and either modified or entirely removed.

Whereas the tendency to glaucoma may be hereditary, it is usually aggravated by worry, fear and similar destructive emotions which produce tension. This increased intraocular tension is related to, and may be said to cause, an imbalance in the production and outflow of the aqueous or eye fluid. The tension acts to block off the outflow of the fluid, resulting in pressure which causes the pain and distress of glaucoma. Your first consideration as a healer should thus be to eliminate this pain by reducing the pressure on the cornea and pupil. Here, then, is the Televisual method to employ.

RELIEVING THE PAIN OF GLAUCOMA

1. Make contact with the inner mind of the sufferer.

2. Locate the tiny canal (called the canal of Schlemm) which drains the eye fluid from the cornea. You will find it in the lower part of the cornea in each eye.

3. The next step is to mentally clear out this canal so that the fluid, when released, will flow out easily and quickly. This can be done by blowing out the tube (or canal), by running a tiny wire through it to clear out any blockage and to slightly enlarge the aperture, or by any other similar set of pictures which will show the inner mind what has to be done.

4. When you are satisfied that the canal is clear, send a flow of blue soothing and relaxing energy through it and then bathe the entire eye in the same blue light. In almost every case this will restore the canal of

Schlemm to its normal function and relieve the intraocular tension and pain of glaucoma.

Sometimes the foregoing Televisual treatment will give a sufferer from glaucoma permanent relief, but more often the nervous tensions of everday life will bring about its return unless they are eased. A friend of mine suffered a very painful and distressing attack of glaucoma while he was negotiating a new union contract. When I treated him as described the pain went away, but the negotiations continued and after a week the glaucoma attacked again. By then the contract was almost settled, so when I repeated the treatment it gave him relief which has continued to this day, some three months later. I do not deceive myself, however. My friend is relaxing now, but as soon as some serious problem presents itself, he will start to worry, become tense and have another attack of glaucoma. In a case like this there is not much you can do. You can relax him, yes—but this is a temporary expedient. It is not possible or practical to stay at a person's side twenty-four hours a day, so it is the responsibility of the individual to control himself and his emotions and thus free himself from these tensions.

While nervous tension and its accompanying high blood pressure are the most frequent causes of glaucoma, there is no doubt that the presence of an intraocular tumor or an infection of the iris must also be considered. Here again, the best methods of handling these problems will be found respectively under the chapters dealing with tumors and with infections.

There are many other eye afflictions, far too many to be detailed here, but most of them can be relieved once the eye has been examined mentally and the real cause of the problem ascertained. A good example of what can be done, and how to do it, is this case history described by D.A. of Riviera Beach, Florida. The healers in this case were Ben Bibb and his wife Margaret. Their account of the healing will follow D.A.'s report, dated June 30.

My eye trouble began last July, nearly a year ago. At that time I noticed a cloudy growth on my right eye which was beginning to impair its vision. I consulted a doctor and he took blood samples, injected dyes, prescribed creams and drops and treated it periodically until October.

Since it was no better, he then sent me to a special eye clinic in Miami. From July until October I had many days of constant eye irritation. Sometimes my eye would become so swollen it would be entirely shut. Even on the good days the eye would be red and irritated. Light sensitivity increased constantly and finally reached a point where I was wearing dark prescription glasses indoors as well as out.

At the eye institute a laser beam was focused directly onto the eye. This gave me some relief. I finally reached a stage where I could go about three days between serious attacks. However, I used medication four times daily. This condition continued until almost four weeks ago when I met Ben and Margaret Bibb and told them of my trouble. They offered to try to help me. The very next day there was an improvement. This change continued rapidly; in a week my eye was back to normal size and it hasn't swollen shut or become irritated since then.

Now even indoor fluorescent lighting doesn't affect it. I don't use medication any more and I can now use any makeup I choose without irritation! This tremendous improvement took place in the first week after meeting with the Bibbs. I am eternally grateful to them for their wonderful help.

Here is Ben Bibb's description of his action and that of his wife, Margaret, in connection with this case. Ben writes as follows:

Margaret and I knew nothing of D.A.'s problem until we met her in Florida when we were there in May. Noticing her swollen eye we inquired and she told us the story. When we offered to try to help her she accepted gratefully. Margaret and I worked on the problem separately.

Observing her eye mentally, we both got the same impression, a symbolic image of a blob of something dark clutching at the optic nerve just behind the eyeball. Each of us in our own way set about removing the "blob." Margaret erased it steadily and slowly by rubbing it mentally and I by sending a ray of pure energy into it until it disappeared. After everything looked normal behind the eyeball, each of us sent healing and soothing energy into the eyeball itself until the eye appeared normal to our mental vision.

This is a most interesting case because it points up your value as a mental healer. Here is a situation where the medical profession with all of its experience, skill and amazing instruments had no way of pinpointing the cause of D.A.'s eye trouble, much less curing it. By contacting her inner mind, both Ben and Margaret Bibb were able to see the cause of the problem independently of one another and then take steps to correct it. You also can accomplish these seeming miracles when you have learned to contact the inner mind of the person seeking help.

8. Instant relief from headaches—how televisual healing can cure their causes

This chapter pinpoints various reasons for headaches and examines them in detail. Psychic healing techniques are then given with explanatory case histories.

Most transient or infrequent headaches are related to fatigue, excessive use of alcohol, or some form of digestive disorder such as might result from overeating. In these cases the headache is just the human system's way of saying, "Stop it. I can't take any more." If the sufferer is sensible, he or she obeys the warning, cuts out the overindulgence or gets the necessary rest, and the headache departs, not to return again until the offense is repeated. These cases do not require psychic healing. Usually a few hours' time is all that is needed. In an emergency, however, or if the headache persists, it can usually be healed in a few moments by the Medipic treatment for the elimination of head pain which is described in this chapter.

More serious problems are involved in cases of chronic or recurring headaches. The cause here may be a systemic infection, a head tumor or a head injury, or it may be related to an infection of the ears, nose or throat—but these conditions are relatively rare and by far the greatest number of chronic headache sufferers are the victims of migraine or emotional disorders. All of these conditions can be corrected by the Televisual healing methods you have been taught. Let us examine each type of headache ailment and the recommended method for handling it.

Simple nonrecurring head pain. This type of headache can usually be eased in a few moments when due merely to fatigue or an upset stomach. Here is the simplest and best method.

1. Make contact with the subject's inner mind and discern there the cause of the headache. If it is due merely to fatigue or an upset stomach, proceed as follows.

2. If the sufferer is in your presence seat him or her in a straight-backed chair and stand behind it. If the subject is at a distance, create this position mentally.

3. Place your right hand alongside the subject's head at the level of and about an inch from the right ear and position your left hand similarly on the left side of the head. Both your palms should be turned inward, or toward the subject's head. Mentally run white healing energy swiftly down your right arm, out the palm of your right hand, into the head of the subject at about the ear level, through the head and directly out the left side, into the left hand up the left arm and out. Keep this rapid flow of white energy going for two or three minutes without a stop.

4. Pause for a minute or two and then repeat the white energy flow for another three minutes. Pause again and then send a light blue soothing, pain-eliminating flow of energy through the subject's head in the same manner for thirty seconds and then withdraw.

You will find this procedure most effective in relieving all headache pain regardless of its cause. If the pain is nothing but the result of overindulgence or fatigue, it will not return, but if there is some chronic disturbance causing it, this should be sought out and eliminated. Louis Stone of Riviera Beach, Florida, a graduate of Ben Bibb's classes, has had great success in touching the sufferer's ears lightly while following the foregoing Televisual healing technique. His method works very well but it is not necessary for you to copy it. The basic technique will work for you, although you also may hit upon some variation which appeals to you and works well for you. If so, by all means use it.

Here is a case history reported by Mrs. Donnabell Carter of Glastonbury, Connecticut. The subject was a personal friend whom she identifies only as Joann. As you can see, she in turn has her own way of treating a headache. It is a little unorthodox—but it works! Here is her report.

One day Joann and I were sitting at a tiny table having ice cream sundaes, when Joann said, "I can't eat any more. I have a splitting headache." Without saying anything I bowed my head in concentration. I saw the pain as a cloud of gray around Joann's head, so I directed this cloud to lift up through her head and go up and away while I brought down a cloud of blue light into her head to take its place.

She squealed, "What are you doing?" and described how the pain felt as if it were being sucked up out of her head and a soothing feeling coming down from above and replacing it. Right then the pain came crashing back. I told her to shut up and let me concentrate. Then I went through the treatment again and upon completion I put a protective light of gold about her head and shoulders. This did it. She had immediate relief and no return of pain.

As you can see, Mrs. Carter has her own method of handling headaches, a method which works for her and may work for you—or you may devise some different technique adapted to your thinking and experience. In the beginning it is usually best, however, to start with the standard formula described earlier in this chapter.

Curing headaches which come from accidental damage. Sometimes headaches come about as the result of an accident and resulting head damage. Here is such a case, described by the healer, Mrs. Frances Miller of Plainfield, Connecticut. The victim was Donald, her younger son, age three. Here is her report.

Recently I was working in my home and my two sons, ages three and five, were playing in the back yard. Suddenly I heard screams and cries. Running outdoors, I saw Donald, my younger boy, with blood all over the back of his head and a large red stain spreading down his shirt. Tim, the older boy, said later that Don looked like a rooster with his hair all red. Out of the terror-stricken atmosphere, I managed to grasp the fact that Donald had fallen off the swing and landed on a sharp rock. Blood was everywhere. At first I had some difficulty in finding the wound; then I discovered a gash about an inch and a half long from which a red stream poured steadily.

I pressed my fingers on the wound to stop the flow. Result? The blood ran down my hand, arm and onto my skirt but the bleeding didn't stop. I thought of my Seventh Sense training and closed my eyes while I mentally visualized my thumb and forefinger closing the wound, and white healing energy pouring into it. In a few seconds I opened my eyes and saw a red, jelly-like substance form right over the wound, sealing it off. That was it: no more bleeding! And Don, whose back was toward me said right then, "Mommy, it doesn't hurt any more."

How practical can you get? I had no car and the nearest hospital emergency room was over twenty miles away. I hate to think what might have resulted if I had not had my Seventh Sense training. Later, to be sure all was well internally, I made another mental contact and found no brain damage, just a depressed blood vessel which I inflated to its normal diameter. The next day, a scab about three quarters of an inch long was the only evidence of injury and even that had disappeared entirely within forty-eight hours.

Almost any accident involving head injury will result in headache pain, so be prepared to first ease that pain before proceeding with the necessary Medipic treatment. This will give the sufferer quick relief and will in no way impede the final complete healing.

Here is another accident case involving severe head pain which was relieved rapidly by means of a Medipic treatment. The healer was Julia Whitten and the victim of the accident was Molly A. Rickenbrode of Ripley, New York. At the time of this healing Mrs. Rickenbrode was in New York while Mrs. Whitten was in Florida. So you can see that the headache relief technique can be applied even when the sufferer is not in your presence. All that is required of you is to make mental contact and visualize the victim sitting before you. Proceed then with the mental treatment, exactly as if he or she were actually there. Here is Molly Rickenbrode's account of what happened.

I wish to testify to an almost unbelievable "cure" by Julia Whitten. I was visiting in a hospital when I slipped and fell on a newly waxed floor. I landed on the right side of my face, cutting a big gash on my forehead, badly twisting my neck and hurting my shoulder. The X-rays taken by the Emergency Department of the hospital showed no broken bones, so they sent me to be treated by my own doctor. For a whole month he had me coming in for head traction. While in traction I had some relief from the excruciating head pain, otherwise it was almost unbearable. The neck brace did not help. Unable to endure laying my head down, I sat in a chair night and day, sleeping fitfully only a few moments from sheer exhaustion.

A friend of mine wrote to Julia Whitten of Seventh Sense asking help for me. I was in New York State and Mrs. Whitten was then in Florida. I figured she had just about time to receive the letter when I went into a deep sleep, the first in over a month. When I awoke there was no more pain. A miracle!

Now there was no more headache and I could move my neck without it hurting. Only then did I realize that my shoulder had been injured and hurt when I moved my arm. Again I got no response from the doctor's treatments and he was frankly puzzled. I had corresponded with Julia in order to express my thanks for her help, so when she came north she stopped by to see me. I had said nothing to her about my shoulder, but when she met me at the door she told me that the fascia of my shoulder socket had been injured. When the doctor, at my urging, took an X-ray of the area, the verdict was an injured fascia; the treatments and exercises he had given me were the wrong therapy for such a condition.

When she told me, the nurse laughed a little and said, "It took the doctor two months to find out what your friend saw in a minute." We decided not to tell him for fear of hurting his feelings.

Mrs. Whitten's treatment was the standard Seventh Sense relief for head and neck pain. She discovered the sprained neck muscles and corrected them, but since no mention had been made of shoulder pain, she did not give it any thought. As her husband drove her towards Mrs. Rickenbrode's home, however, she reviewed what she had previously done. Sitting in the car, she mentally explored Mrs. Rickenbrode to see if she could help in any other way. It was then she observed the damaged shoulder which she described to Mrs. Rickenbrode when she opened the door to receive them.

RECURRING HEADACHES

Chronic or recurring headaches may be caused by a blood infection, a head tumor or some other traumatic condition, but these cases are relatively rare when compared to the far greater numbers who suffer from migraine or emotional disorders. Migraine headache attacks are devastating, as anyone who has ever suffered one can testify—so it is important that you learn how to relieve such pain and prevent its recurrence. The immediate cause of pain in both migraine headaches and nervous headaches is pressure upon the nerves in the head. You as a healer should make mental contact with the inner mind of the sufferer and observe there the reason for this pressure and the nerves that it is affecting. For your information, these pain-sensitive head areas may lie in the tissues covering the cranium, in the large cranial or upper cervical nerves, in the intercranial venous sinuses, in the large arteries at the base of the brain, or in the dura matter at the base of the brain; or it may occur during the dilation and contraction of the walls of sensitive vascular channels. You can observe this by making the usual mental contact which will enable you to single out the exact point or points to be treated.

How to relieve the pressure of migraine. In migraine headaches, the primary cause of pain-creating pressure is glandular imbalance. This could involve but two or three glands but more often you will find five or six to be involved. Thus the Medipic healing technique is to balance the entire upper glandular system. The treatment is as follows.

1. Make televisual contact with the inner mind of the sufferer and then proceed at once to relieve pain by streaming white healing energy in one ear and out the other to be followed by then streaming light blue calming and pain-relieving energy in the same manner. This is the pain-killing method described earlier in this chapter.

2. When you are confident the sufferer is experiencing relief from pain, proceed to the next step. This is to balance and bring into harmony the following glands: the pituitary, the thalamus, the hypothalamus, the thyroid and thymus glands. You do this by sending blue peace-producing energy to each in turn and then tie in the pineal gland to the group thus connected.

3. You then instruct the pineal gland to take charge and continue with all necessary energy corrections until the entire group is completely and properly balanced and functioning normally.

4. Finally, bathe the entire head with blue energy to calm all nerves and relieve tension. Continue this blue energy flow until the patient relaxes and all pain is gone.

Here is a case history report on a migraine healing by Mrs. Cleo Mitchell of Oneco, Connecticut. The subject was her daughter, Mrs. Carol Ann Wiltrout of Scotia, New York. Mrs. Mitchell writes as follows:

On May 25 I received a phone call from my oldest daughter, Carol Ann Wiltrout, who said she was in the fourth day of very severe pain from a migraine headache. She had been experiencing these attacks for over a year and had gone through all sorts of tests by a neurosurgeon who had put her on three very potent drugs. Since the onset of these attacks her general condition had deteriorated. She had lost weight and was becoming increasingly nervous. She was working as a broker for a realty company, so it was necessary for her to be active evenings, as well as days, showing houses to prospective purchasers. I finished the conversation with my daughter at 5:20 p.m. and immediately went to work for her using the knowledge I had gained in the Seventh Sense classes of Ben Bibb. Here is what I did:

After several deep breaths I felt relaxed and reached out with my mind to my daughter. After making mental contact, I used the fingers of my left hand to touch the pituitary, thalamus and hypothalamus glands, charging them with blue energy. I then directed the pituitary to act as governor to make all glands function properly, and directed a powerful stream of blue energy into the center of her forehead to glow in her mind and brain and relieve all tension there.

Following this, I blended blue and green energy (I call it aqua) for the relief of pain and sent it as before into the center of her forehead, but then expanded it to glow very brightly through her entire body. I asked it to relieve all pain immediately and then I bathed her once more, this time in a pure white aura to kill all foreign bodies that might be causing her distress. After sending a golden aura to surround her with spiritual protection, I wrapped her in a pink blanket of universal love.

It was about 5:30 p.m. when I finished. It seemed to me I had been busy for an hour, but it was only ten minutes. I called Carol the following morning to find out how she was feeling and she said that her headache started to let up about 5:30 the evening before, so she went to bed. She woke up at 3 a.m. and found her headache entirely gone. She did not even have any soreness which she usually had after a migraine attack. I then told her I had worked on her from 5:20 to 5:30 p.m. the day before. She said, "I have to know what did it, Mom, you or the medication, so I'll cut out the medication and see what happens." She gave the three potent medicines to her husband and told him to keep them until she asked for them. He did this, but she never asked because she hasn't had a migraine headache from that day until now, nearly three years later.

The medical books list thirty-eight possible causes of various types of recurring headaches, but of migraine they say simply, "The cause is unknown." This accounts for the average doctor's well-meaning but stumbling efforts to relieve it. How much better it would be for doctors and their patients if they would learn how to look into the patient's inner mind, as we do in our Seventh Sense Healing Techniques, and observe there directly the cause of the malfunction.

How to cure nervous headaches. Another type of recurring headache which appears quite often is called a "nervous headache." The pain causing pressure on the cranial nerves is here brought on by attacks of extreme nervousness and corresponding increases in blood pressure. Once you observe and understand this type of headache you can heal it permanently with a little cooperation from the sufferer—or sometimes with complete ignorance on the part of the patient and no cooperation at all, as in an actual case which will be described later.

As in all cases of head pain, regardless of cause, you should first relieve the pain; then, if you should observe that the headache had been the result of an acute nervous attack, proceed as follows:

1. Relieve the pain as earlier indicated.

2. Send a vigorous charge of red vital energy into the subject's nervous system via the spinal column. This is a primary essential since most nervousness is closely allied to lack of energy. Repeat this charge if it seems necessary.

3. Then flood the patient's entire body and nervous system with a wave of soothing, healing peace-producing blue energy. Do this again until the subject is relaxed and at ease.

4. Finally put an aura of sun-gold energy around the subject. This should extend from twelve inches above the head to six inches below the feet and four or five inches out from the body. This is to maintain a protective shield about the subject until the energy charge you have given takes effect.

The foregoing Medipic treatment will in most cases bring immediate relief from head pain. However, in order to build up the subject's confidence to a point where he or she will suffer no more acute nervous attacks, it will probably be necessary to repeat the treatment three or four times, depending upon how run down and lacking in confidence the subject may be. Also, after each treatment put the patient on automatic, which means to instruct him or her to automatically repeat the Medipic series every six hours until it is no longer necessary.

Here is a case history which may make this clearer. It is reported by Jean Danahy, who was for years a very nervous woman and, in the last year before her cure, suffered greatly from nervous headaches which would strike without warning and flood the right side of her face and head with pain. The interesting part of this report is not so much the curing of the pain, but the change in her whole personality which came about as a result of her treatment by Ben Bibb. Here is her report.

> I had been suffering a great deal of pain which was spasmodic. The attacks had become more and more frequent, settling in the right side of my head and face, when I made my first visit to a Seventh Sense meeting. On my first meeting with Ben Bibb, he touched his fingers to my right shoulder and neck two or three times during the session. This surprised me because I had told no one of the pain in that area. The pain left me then and I have had none since, although that incident was over a year ago.
>
> This was a new beginning for me in another way too, although I did not realize it at the time. Today I am not the same person mentally or physically as I was then. It's been a year now and the change has become

noticeable to all around me. From childhood, I had always considered myself dumb and stupid. Any small situation would really upset me and send me running to someone for help to solve it. Recently I came to realize that I have been solving far more serious problems without even thinking about asking for help. Now, for the first time in my life, I am using my own mind. Also, my physical appearance has improved to a point where people are saying to me, "I don't know what you're doing to yourself, but you sure look great!" A year ago if someone tried to pay me a compliment of any sort I would think they were making fun of me. Now I can smile and say, "Thank you." My experience in being healed and the other changes in me and my reactions may not be what one would call miracles, but to me they are.

It is clear what took place. In addition to having the pain relieved that first night, Jean Danahy has since then been stimulated with new energy to a point where she now has self-confidence. She is no longer nervous and, as a result, has improved greatly in her personal appearance. Some people, including Jean herself, would call this a miracle, but it is just one more evidence of the remarkable results that may be achieved by you working with the techniques of Medipic.

9. Secret medipic methods for handling tumors and parasitic internal growths, leading to their elimination

In this chapter we will set forth tested Medipic techniques for dealing with tumors and other internal growths. There are several ways in which these problems can be efficiently handled. We will here describe those that have proved to be most successful. As you may realize, there is a widespread fear that any internal growth may be malignant. The averages, though, indicate the opposite. Only a small percentage are malignant, and even some that may originally appear so eventually turn out to be benign, so when a person comes to you for help you should first dispel his or her fears, for they may be groundless. For this reason, here, at the very beginning of this chapter and before any healing techniques are described, is a case history which supports this. It is but one of many such which prove the wisdom of an optimistic approach.

The case is reported by Nell (Mrs. Lloyd) Crossan of West Palm Beach, Florida, who is a Seventh Sense healer. The subject is Alice (Mrs. William) Curtis, age 44, of Lake Worth, Florida. Mrs. Crossan relates that Alice came to her home on January 20 and told her she had just come from her doctor, who had given her bad news. She had been having difficulty in moving her bowels, sometimes passing blood, and she had gone to her family physician for a checkup. The complete physical he gave her included a Pap test, which was positive. So when Alice Curtis came to see Mrs. Crossan she was very frightened.

Her doctor had suggested that she see a specialist, but she delayed and it was not until February 19 that she visited a Palm Beach gynecologist. After a rigorous examination including X-rays, he told her she had a tumor about the size of an egg in her rectum which was pressing into the wall of her uterus. He wanted to put her in a hospital immediately to have it removed, but again she delayed, saying to Mrs. Crossan that she wanted to go to the Mayo Clinic. When she asked Mrs. Crossan to help her, Nell said she would do what she could.

Nell Crossan reports she had actually started to help Alice back on January 20 when she first learned of her trouble, but because of Alice's fears and low energy level, she did not feel she was making much progress. When Alice again postponed a decision on surgery, Nell doubled her efforts and asked Ben Bibb to help her. She was using one of the recommended Medipic treatments for the removal of a tumor which involves shrinking it down until it disappears, but results were slow in appearing.

Mrs. Curtis finally made an appointment to visit Mayo Clinic on April 2. The X-rays there showed the tumor to be very small, about the size of a lima bean, and the examining doctor said he only recommended surgical removal because of the previous diagnosis of malignancy by the two Florida doctors. When the operation was performed, the tumor was found to be quite small and not malignant. At this writing, nearly two years later, Mrs. Curtis is entirely well and there has been no recurrence of her trouble.

The point made here is that if you are optimistic and do your best to help anyone who comes to you in distress, you will frequently find that the situation turns out to be not nearly so serious as it may at first have seemed. A second point is—always do what you can to help even though others may believe the situation to be hopeless.

The treatment that most student healers find easiest in relieving a subject of an internal growth, like a tumor, is to mentally pluck it out. As you gain experience you may find other techniques more to your liking, but since this method seems to work well for most students, it will be pictured here.

Earlier we referred to Mrs. Crossan's attempt to remove the internal tumor of her friend, Mrs. Curtis, by shrinking it down, because that was her usual method. This technique is usually employed in eliminating external growths and is not so often applied to those inside the human system. The standard method for remov-

MEDIPIC FOR REMOVING AN
INTERNAL GROWTH

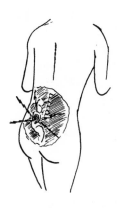

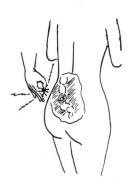

1. Upon making mental contact, observe that a tumor is located in the lower bowel, partially blocking passage.

2. With your fingers, reach in mentally and pluck out the growth, making sure that all connecting blood vessels and tissues are removed with it.

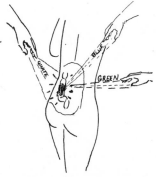

3. Roll the tissues, blood vessels and tumor into a ball and destroy the entire mass in whatever way seems best to you. You could plunge it into a bucket of alum, or burn it in a stove, or throw it up to the heavens with instructions to return to the Greater Life, as one healer did.

4. Into the hole left after the removal of the tumor, pour enough green healing energy to fill it completely. Then seal it in place with "human tape." When this has been done, flood the entire area with white healing energy and follow it with a similar flood of soothing, pain-removing blue energy before ending the contact.

ing internal obstructions was followed by two women working together on the following case. Note that while both healers visualized an immediate removal of the obstruction and the inner mind of the subject obediently followed the visualized instructions, it took nearly two weeks before it could accomplish what had been visualized for it in minutes. This is because the inner mind works in ways known only to itself. Once convinced of the urgent need to act in a specific direction, it proceeds to do so. Sometimes the objective can be reached by it in a few hours; in other situations weeks may be required. The complexity of the task and the amount of energy available are the deciding factors.

Here is the healing as reported by Virginia Sullivan of Jupiter, Florida. She worked with Carroll Owen on the subject, George X.

A very dear friend, George X, phoned me from Washington in January to tell me he was feeling miserable and to ask my help. He had been to the hospital for tests and the X-rays disclosed a large mass which was creating an obstruction in the appendix area. The doctors surmised that a ruptured appendix several months earlier had become encapsulated and was now beginning to cause trouble. His blood count was bad; he had lost weight and was running a temperature, so they recommended surgery if a new series of X-rays to be taken a week later showed the same condition.

Carroll and I went to work on him that same night. I got a good mental contact and saw a large dark mass low down on the right side of his stomach. I lifted this out with my mental fingers, separating it carefully from the surrounding tissue and wrapping it in the many threadlike ends that adhered to it. I put the entire mass in a bucket of lye where it was quickly destroyed. There was quite a large cavity in his stomach which I filled with bright green body-healing energy and covered it with "people tape" to hold it in place. When finished, I cleaned out the entire stomach and intestine area with dazzling white healing energy. At that point I felt certain that the task was accomplished, so I broke the contact.

Carroll later told me she had followed the same general procedure but had finished by bathing him in a blue aura to soothe all the pain and bring his temperature down to normal.

George telephoned after the second set of X-rays had been taken and gave me the report. Apparently on the new pictures the mass appeared to be only about one-half its original size but the doctors still worried. They postponed the operation and sent him for another series of X-rays and tests six days later. This third set of X-rays showed no trace of the mass that had been present in the two previous series of X-rays. Moreover, his temperature and blood count were normal and he had gained some weight. When he asked the doctors what they thought, they told him they could not understand what had taken place, much less explain it. It was something beyond their knowledge and experience.

HOW TO ELIMINATE
SURFACE GROWTHS

By far the greatest number who come to you for treatment of tumors, lesions and other growths will have them on their skin or close to the surface of their bodies. For these, the simplest and best method to employ is to shrink or in some way diminish the growths until they disappear. Once you get the general idea, almost any such visual suggestion you give the subject will achieve the result desired. The following Medipic technique is a good example of the method used by many Seventh Sense healers.

1. Make mental contact with the inner mind of the subject who has come to you for help. Note there the location and nature of the growth to be eliminated.

2. With a small brush, somewhat like a paint brush, paint the tumor or growth with shrinking paste. Paint it two or three times to make sure the idea of "shrinking" penetrates the subconscious mind of the subject. Shrinking paste is suggested but almost any other visualization that will convey the idea of diminishing to the point of disappearance will be satisfactory. One healer even uses a soft rubber eraser and rubs them out.

3. If there appears to be a hole or small cavity where the growth has been, fill it with green living tissue paste and seal it over with people tape.

4. Pour white healing energy into the affected area until all possibility of infection has been eliminated and the tissues appear to be healing in a normal way; then flood the area with soothing, pain-relieving blue energy and terminate the contact.

TERMINAL CASES

Occasionally you will be approached by someone who asks your help for a relative or a close friend who is considered to be a so-called "terminal case." This means that the medical prognosis is negative and only death can be foreseen. This ultimate may appear to be a week off, or a month, or some uncertain interval—but the end is regarded as inevitable. In a situation like this offer to do what you can, but inform the petitioner that at this late stage there is very little that can be done. This petitioner will understand because he is probably fully aware that every technique known to science has been already employed without success. He or she has come to you as a last resort, feeling that there is nothing to lose, so do what you can.

Frequently at this stage there is not very much that can be done. We are not miracle workers, but depend upon the willingness of the patient to help. If they will do this, the amount of energy its inner mind can summon and control may aid us. You will, in some cases, when you make visual contact, see that the entire physical body has so degenerated that the best that can be done is to reduce or eliminate pain. Here is a case of this type in which the healer was able, not to cure, but to buy an extra year of time for the sufferer in addition to relieving her of most of the pain. The healer is Joyce Dix of West Palm Beach, Florida and the subject was Mrs. G. of Lansing, Michigan. Here is Mrs. Dix's report.

> When I first heard of Mrs. G.'s plight she was thought to be dying. Her entire abdominal area was infected and the doctors had given her radiation treatments. She was in bed, not eating and unable to get up. Her daughter told me about her and her condition, and said she was planning to go to Lansing to be with her mother on her last days. I said I would like to see if I could help her any and her daughter said, "Please do anything you can. I'll be so grateful."
>
> My first step was to contact her subconscious mind and implant in it the idea that it was to return all body functions to normal, or as close to normal as possible. It was also to reject everything that might be harmful to the body in any way. I could see plainly there were many areas in her body in pretty bad shape. Her intestines were all but blocked with what seemed to be a network of a vine-like material that was wound about everything. She had sores over large parts of her body and she had no hair left as a result of the radiation. All in all, her condition was very poor.
>
> After suggesting to her subconscious that it return the body to normal functioning I next took out the magnetic field and aligned it as well as I could with the etheric body. Both were in bad shape, particularly the magnetic field, which was anything but magnetic. The etheric body appeared to have lots of holes in it; I patched these up. This I did every day, as well as clearing the entire system as best I could. I used a golden aura and also did the body washout several times. I disengaged the vine-like mass in the intestines, wadded it together and sent it up into the sun. Every time I worked on her, and that was just about every day for about a month, I suggested that the food she ate would prove useful to the body and provide necessary energy. I repaired body tissue whenever I observed this was needed and on each contact I sent auras of energy into her magnetic field.

The result was encouraging. She gained strength gradually and started eating more. Eventually she got to a stage where she could get out of bed and eat at a table. Soon she was able to go out and do some shopping, but what was most rewarding to me was that now she was almost entirely free from pain. This condition continued for several months, to the delight of the doctors, who were convinced it came about because of the radiation treatments (which had been discontinued when they deemed her case hopeless almost a year before). Her blood tested so good they decided to resume these treatments, but after two weeks she died. I am convinced I bought her an extra year of life and I am happy about it.

As you can see, not every case you may work on will end as a complete success. Sometimes, as in the case just described, only a partial success can be attained, but even that in itself is a reward for your efforts. You should always try.

Here is another case, not too different, which has a happier ending. The healer is Mrs. Donnabell Carter of Glastonbury, Connecticut and the subject is a 74-year-old woman, described as Mrs. B.E., who lives in New Jersey. When first contacted by Mrs. Carter, the patient was weak, confined to a wheel chair and in great pain most of the time. Due to the nature of her ailment and her extreme weakness, the doctors regarded her condition as terminal.

Here is Mrs. Carter's report.

After reaching a meditative state, I thought of Mrs. E. and in my mind saw her lying on a bed. As she lay there sleeping I talked to her body cells and I felt them listening. I called to the cells that were doing all the damage and told them they were no longer a part of the entire body, but were forming their own structure. I told them they could do better and grow more rapidly if freed from the body's limitations and called them to me. They appeared to rise up as bubbles from various parts of the body. They came up towards my hands, which I was now using as magnets to attract them. As they came into my hands, I shaped them into a large ball and, after covering them with a pale purple cloud, I sent them up and away in the care of the Almighty.

Now I addressed my attention to the body and went over the major bones, dusting them with salt and scrubbing them clean. I scrubbed and rinsed the internal organs out as you would a dirty sponge. After I saw bones and organs clean, I gave them a bath in nourishing sugar water. The body was still weak, but I instructed the healthy cells to keep up this good work. This entire healing sequence was repeated six times over a month before I felt that it was taking effect, but take effect it did, and I can tell you it is pretty exciting to see a woman once considered to be dying to be doing her own gardening and social entertaining just as she did before she fell ill.

This chapter would not be complete if conditions considered inoperable were not discussed. Sometimes you, as a healer, can provide the cure because you can see without a doubt just where the offending cause lies. At other times you can achieve a healing because through Telepic you can persuade the inner mind to make a physical correction impossible by external mechanical (surgical) means. Here is a case which illustrates this.

HANDLING A PROBLEM
CONSIDERED INOPERABLE

Some neighbors told Mrs. Nell Crossan of West Palm Beach about Mrs. T.E. and asked her help. Mrs. E., who also lives in West Palm Beach, is in her late twenties and has two children. For some time she had been suffering from severe head pains which apparently were the result of pressure within the skull caused by an accumulation of fluid which was not draining normally because of the presence of a tumor. The doctors had performed a spinal tap to drain off the fluid, but it continued to accumulate and the pressure built up again. Mrs. E. was told that the tumor was inoperable because of its location. She was facing the possibility of another spinal drainage when Mrs. Crossan was asked to help. Here is Mrs. Crossan's report on the method she used to relieve Mrs. E. of pain and eventually eliminate the cranial pressure.

> The treatment started with my calming the nerves throughout her body. I started with the head and worked down to her feet by psychically placing my hands on her body and telling the nerves to calm down. I did this in back and front. After completing this calming procedure, I told the pituitary gland to keep the nerves calm; then I gave the body a complete washout front and back. I next turned my attention to the tumor in her head. I pulled out the roots gently and rolled them up into a bundle towards the tumor. After pulling out all the roots with my fingers, I packed them around the tumor and saturated the entire mass with alum to kill it. To keep the alum powder soundly packed around the tumor and to prevent it from spreading to the brain I encased it completely by wrapping it in human tape.
>
> After I opened a gland to drain off the lymph fluid, I went back to the tumor which was now destroyed and filled the cavity with green aura

paste. I asked the liver to produce new cells to prevent the tumor from reforming and finally left her body wrapped in a spinning green aura to continue the healing process.

The first week I repeated this treatment once a day. Her pain gradually went away, and by the seventh day I felt that the tumor had vanished. She had no more pain, but as a precaution I repeated the Medipic treatment twice a month for the next two months. I am happy now to report there has been no recurrence of her trouble since the last treatment over a year ago.

It is now eighteen months since that report was written and Mrs. E. has had no recurrence of her trouble. This is a good example of how an apparently inoperable problem can be solved by contacting the inner mind of the sufferer and persuading it to heal the body it occupies.

These reports by Seventh Sense healers are but a few of a great many similar successes in curing or inhibiting internal growths. You can perform similar seeming miracles through the secret techniques of Seventh Sense as taught by Ben Bibb and described in this book. They are not miracles but the employment of human body resources. You, or any one else willing to try, can bring about healings similar to the ones described. All that is required is an open mind and sincere effort. The incredulous, though, will always bring about their own failures.

10. Medipic methods
for strengthening and healing
the heart

This chapter presents mind power methods for giving the heart new energy by raising the vibratory rate of the energy body and repairing heart damage and related problems by mental instructions given to the inner mind.

All heart problems are serious—and there are many kinds. Some are birth defects, either actually present in the infant or there in potential to develop into a serious problem years later. By far the greatest number of heart difficulties other than external injuries are those caused by the subject himself. Commonest is an ailment called atherosclerosis, which is usually the result of overindulgence in eating, drinking or smoking plus hypertension and/or lack of exercise. As it develops, atherosclerosis tends to prevent adequate blood supply from reaching critical areas like the brain, the muscles—particularly the heart muscles—and the arteries leading to the important body organs. Our concern is with the blockage or reduction in blood supply to the heart muscles, which may result in coronary thrombosis, angina pectoris, myocardial infarction and similar serious and potentially fatal ailments. Important: in almost all of these serious situations the basic cause is lack of adequate blood supply, a situation which you can correct. Illustrated is the method to employ.

HOW TO "STOP TIME"

For all mental heart operations and for certain brain Medipic operations, it is necessary to "stop time" in order to accomplish the healing without interfering with the regular functioning of the organ involved. The heart, for instance, must not be allowed to stop its

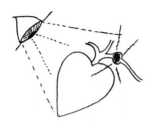

1. After making mental contact, first examine the subject carefully in order to identify the exact location of the blockage. There may be more than one point involved, so be sure to make a most thorough examination.

2. Having located the artery affected and made certain that it is the only one being blocked, then proceed. (If you have discovered more than one blood restraint, take care of both in the same manner.) Let us assume that in this case you have discovered only one obstruction, in the coronary artery, which you are now to clean out. Your first step is to "stop time" in order not to interfere with the normal functioning of the heart. This method will be explained at the completion of these instructions.

3. During the "stop time" period, open the coronary artery and clean it out thoroughly with a long, flexible, very narrow brush. The obstruction must not only be removed from the path of the blood but completely destroyed and eliminated.

4. When you see that all the blood clots and any other obstructions have been removed and the artery is clean, wash it thoroughly with white healing energy to stimulate it and prevent infection. Then end "stop time" and start the blood flowing freely once again.

5. Before breaking contact, flood the entire heart cavity with bright blue energy to eliminate all pain and soothe the nerves.

regular beating. Therefore, as soon as the mental connection has been made and you have concluded your survey of the affected area, command time to stop. This is the technique. Just *command* time to stop.

What actually takes place without you realizing it, is that your own activity is so speeded up that the entire operation is performed within the time of one heartbeat. You have no physical realization of this. You proceed to the cleaning out of the artery and its subsequent repair just as you would normally work on a broken leg. Don't hurry: be completely relaxed and confident because you will have all the time you require—but until you end "stop time" everything you do will be so speeded up as to be almost simultaneous. Your conscious awareness will be at normal but your subjective (inner mind) activity will be rapid.

The Medipic technique described can be applied in every situation in which you find an artery partially or completely blocked, regardless of cause. If, however, there is damage to the artery or to the heart itself, repair work must also be done.

LONG DISTANCE REPAIR

Here is a case of some "long distance" heart repair which illustrates an interesting approach to healing heart damage. A young woman living in Lantana, Florida, whom we will call Fay, because she does not want her name used, had a history of painful heart attacks dating back over a period of years. The doctor treating Fay never told her exactly what was the cause of these painful seizures but it was probably angina pectoris.

One morning when Ben Bibb was teaching a class of student healers in Connecticut, he received a telephone call from Fay in Florida. She said she was experiencing a most painful heart attack and pleaded with him to help her. Ben concentrated mentally on her and observed that she was indeed having an attack. Her heartbeat was fast, erratic and labored, and she was in considerable pain. He said to her, "You are lying down, aren't you?" and when she answered "Yes," he said, "Place the telephone receiver over your heart, let go of it and relax. Then after five minutes, pick it up and speak to me."

She did so; then Ben Bibb, still holding the telephone receiver to his ear, put the mouthpiece to his forehead between his eyes and poured mental energy through the telephone into her heart. Since quick relief was the primary objective, he poured a powerful beam of white healing energy to her steadily for about three minutes, then switched to blue energy for soothing and relaxing, then to green energy for cellular rejuvenation, then to red energy for vitality, and finally back again to white energy.

After about five minutes Fay spoke very sleepily saying, "I'm back." When Ben asked, "How do you feel?" she answered: "I'm sleepy. But the pain is gone and my heart seems to be beating slower, more steadily." Ben then told her to hang up the telephone, go back to sleep for two hours and then call him again. Two hours and five minutes later she called, entirely calm and relaxed. All pain was gone and had not recurred. Ben told her then to see her doctor as soon as she could. She argued a bit about this, but finally agreed. In a letter about two months later she reported that she had seen the doctor who had treated her from childhood. After a thorough examination he told her she was in good physical condition and her heart was sounder and stronger than at any time since her first attack many years before.

The average new student cannot be expected to have the confidence to command as much energy as an experienced healer like Ben Bibb, but you, even as a beginner, can heal an angina case by clearing out the obstructions in the artery in the manner earlier explained. Don't hesitate to heal this and similar heart problems. You can do no harm, and if you use the Medipic technique properly, you can do a great deal of good.

There is a chapter devoted to self-healing later in the book, but since it is a subject in which every student naturally has great interest, we include here a report on self-healing of a heart condition. The student-healer is Patricia Glennon of Plainfield, Connecticut. Here is her report.

> For several years I have been sorely troubled by bad attacks of palpitation of the heart. They usually last about two hours, but sometimes longer. I have been going to the Ben Bibb Seventh Sense classes and decided that I would try the Medipic treatment the next time I had an attack. One hit me last night, so I went to work.
>
> I lay down and did my best to relax. This was not easy with my heart fluttering in my breast, but I finally succeeded in calming myself down. Then I visualized pink energy all around my body, and while I was doing this I suddenly saw what appeared to be a beautiful waterfall of white energy. It responded to my will and I directed it to flow right into my heart with instructions to return my heartbeat to normal. In less than ten minutes my heartbeat was back to normal and I felt just great. Many thanks to Seventh Sense and Ben Bibb.

HEART BIRTH DEFECTS

It is unfortunate that the amazing healing powers of the human body have not yet been explored to any degree by the medical profession. They still put too much dependence upon surgery and medicines. Most often these will effect satisfactory cures. There is no doubt about that. There are some situations, however, where even if the problem is intensified, the surgery required for correction is as risky as the ailment itself.

A good example of this is the case of little R.V.E. who was only four months old at the time. He was born with a heart defect. When his grandmother, Mrs. F.V.E., heard he was scheduled for open heart surgery, she called Ben Bibb for help. The doctors at the University Hospital in Gainesville, Florida, believed that he had a malformed valve and probably a ventricle wall hole in his heart. They set an operation for eight days later.

Here is Ben Bibb's report:

> When little Bobby's grandmother called me I told her that children of his age usually responded very well to open heart surgery and asked her not to worry. She said she was afraid he would not survive the operation and implored me to work on it. Eight days seemed a short time for such a serious correction; I was afraid the surgeons would go ahead with the operation before I could could effect a recognizable improvement. I told her this and said I would speed the healing as much as possible.
>
> I made mental contact with little Bobby and caused time to stop so that I could open his heart and look at the problem. I found there that two valves on the right side of the heart simply had not formed, or grown, completely. Since they did not close, the contraction of the heart forced blood partially backward into the incoming vein as well as outward into the outgoing artery. My inner mind saw this symbolically in the form of small "flapper" valves which were simply too small to completely close the "pipes" of the veins and arteries. Mentally, I felt the material of the valves and produced a similar material in plastic form with which I enlarged the "flapper" valves. This putty-like material was easy to shape, and it adhered to and blended with the tissue of the valves. Using the energy from my mental fingertips I made this material merge with and become part of the valves, enlarging them to the proper size. I started time again and observed that the valves would then close completely.
>
> However, I mentally still heard a foreign noise from the heart. Upon examining it again I found that the wall between the ventricles had a small hole in it. Using the same putty-like material with which I had enlarged the

valves, I formed a fleshlike "plug" and pushed it into the small hole. I then flattened it on both sides so that it was secure and smooth on both sides of the wall. This stopped the small hole securely and the noise could no longer be heard. I then started time once again and withdrew.

His grandmother called me on the eighth day. Bobby had been taken to the hospital on the seventh day for examination and preoperative planning. The surgeon inserted a catheter into a vein with an optical device in it, so that after getting the observing end into the heart itself, he could look at the malformed valve and make his operation plan. After nearly two hours, the doctor came out of the treatment room and told the parents: "I have made a mistake. This boy does not need open heart surgery at this time and probably never will—certainly not until he is past five years old!" A slight heart murmur remained with Bobby for about six months. It was smaller each time it was checked and finally disappeared entirely and has not returned since.

In reading this remarkable healing you must understand that at no time did Ben Bibb touch Bobby's heart or in any way actually shape its interior. The pictures he describes were mental pictures sent into the infant's subjective mind so that it would understand what needed to be done. Ben Bibb's concern about the time element was because he knew that this repair work by the infant himself would take time and he did not know if it could be accomplished before the dangerous open heart operation would be performed. Fortunately for all concerned, the infant's repair powers worked rapidly enough and fortunately also, the doctor who attended him was a careful, completely honest man. These careful, honest, self-sacrificing doctors are the unsung heroes of our time.

Here now is the story of another heart healing by Ben Bibb, also of a birth defect. This was the problem of a young woman, a widow about thirty-three years old, with a small son. Mrs. J.L., as we will call her, had been troubled for many years by a heart murmur.

For about twelve years, I had been told at my yearly physical that I had a heart murmur. At first, I was told not to worry, that many people had them. Later, though, when I saw a heart specialist in the process of getting insurance, I was told just what kind of murmur it was, and that it was more serious than I had been led to believe. I didn't get the insurance, naturally, and I later began to have some vague pains upon occasion.

About four years after this I met Ben Bibb and asked him if he could heal my heart. He did, and on the next physical I had there was no indication of a heart murmur. I have had three annual physicals since then

over a period of three years and there is still no murmur. Moreover, I now
have the life insurance I need to protect my young son.

Ben Bibb's report on this healing is very similar to his healing of
little Bobby described earlier. Here is what Ben writes about it:

> Upon mentally looking into J.L.'s heart and listening to it, I found
> there was a small hole in the wall between the ventricles. It was apparently
> from lack of completion before birth, rather than from deterioration or
> damage, for it appeared to be small but perfectly round. The edges
> seeming to be "finished off" as would the edges of any completely formed
> tissue.
>
> Mentally, I produced a flesh-consistency piece of matter that I have
> named "people putty," to describe the fact that it can be molded into any
> shape by the mental fingers. I made a short plug of it, firmly called for a
> "stop time," and inserted the plug in the hole. Then with my mental
> fingers on each side of the hole and on the ends of the inserted plug, I
> mashed the plug of "people putty" flat on each end. This now had become
> a leakproof plug, solidly closing the hole. Then I used my finger tips to fire
> energy into both ends of the flattened plug until it appeared to have
> merged into, and become the same as, the surrounding flesh.
>
> I told Mrs. J.L. that the murmur should be completely undetectable in
> a month or two. In about two months she reported that she had once
> again applied for insurance, had taken a physical including an EKG and
> had passed.

While Ben Bibb does not specifically state so in his report, he fired
a lot of energy into Mrs. J.L. in order to stimulate her physical body
to more rapid and efficient healing efforts in response to the Medipic
instructions which he gave to her subconscious mind. This is
particularly important in all heart cases. Actually, you should start
every Medipic healing by giving the subject energy, but in cases of a
weakened, damaged or malfunctioning heart, the subject's life energy
is usually at such a low ebb that this stimulation is a basic necessity.
There are a number of ways to do this. The simplest, and often the
most effective, is to collect the energy yourself from the great
limitless energy supply all around us, and then send it as a white
invigorating charge into the subject's etheric body or as a red
stimulating charge into the subject's physical body. To do this you
must have plenty of energy of your own right and must also know
how to visualize control and manipulation of the etheric and life
energies.

For the beginner and for the average healer, one with normal energy supply and control, the following method is recommended. Immediately after making mental contact, visualize a great ball of white light, like sunshine, forming above the subject's head. When this appears to be about three feet in diameter, lower it into the subject's body so that it envelopes the head and upper torso. Maintain it in that position until it dissolves into and merges with the etheric body of the sufferer. Usually this will provide the subject with enough additional energy to enable his or her subconscious mind to carry out the instructions you give it via Medipic, but if in your judgment (your intuition will tell you) it is insufficient, repeat the process. This should do it.

There is still another technique for increasing the patient's energy. This is to be employed only after you have given complete instructions to the subject's inner mind and feel they are understood and will be carried out. This method is to raise the rate of vibration in the subject's etheric body. All energy manifests as vibration and in a human body, the average rate of vibration sets the tone or life quality of the entire body. You can raise the vibratory rate of a subject by ordering—yes ordering—his or her inner mind to do just this. Say before breaking mental contact: "I order you to raise your vibratory rate twenty-five percent." In most cases, a twenty-five percent lift will be more than adequate, but sometimes a raise of one half again, or fifty percent, may be necessary. Don't decide this on a whim, but look to your intuition for guidance. If you are attuned, as you should be, you will know with certainty just what rate of increase will be most beneficial.

As you realize, I am sure, nearly everyone who comes to you for help is already depleted in one way or another before you see or hear of them. You should therefore first endeavor to help every sufferer to bring his or her energy supply back to normal. While heart patients usually are in need of immediate help, this may also be true in many other afflictions. Be prepared to supply support to the energy bodies of all your petitioners. It is always better to be sure.

11. Secret psychic healing treatments for banishing gall bladder and liver ailments

Effective methods to successfully cope with these often related gall bladder and liver problems is what this chapter is all about. We will support these with actual cases of miraculous cures via the Medipic System.

When your mental examination of a sufferer indicates that the gall bladder or the liver or both are causing the pain and difficulties, the simplest and best treatment is to first wash out or clear out both organs. Very often, this will be the only remedy required, but sometimes it is necessary to look further after the "washout" has been performed. Very often you will find the emotions involved, but injudicious eating or drinking could be large contributing factors in upsetting the liver. Gallstones are the usual cause of pain in that organ; these will require special attention after the initial washout. The liver itself may be afflicted by jaundice, hepatitis, cirrhosis and other serious ailments, all of which should receive special attention as soon as you have identified them. Your careful mental examination is vitally important here, as it is in almost all cases involving internal malfunction. Once you have completed this examination and have identified the problem with certainty it is well to first give the sufferer what relief you can. This is best performed with a "washout" as described.

In some cases, this cleansing of the liver and gall bladder will relieve the sufferer completely. Where there is no organic damage or infection involved, the washout just described will restore the organs to normal functioning and the patient to good health, but when cirrhosis, jaundice, hepatitis of the liver or stones in the gall bladder

LIVER AND GALL BLADDER
WASHOUT

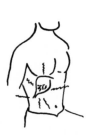

1. When after making contact with the inner mind of the sufferer, you trace the problem to the liver and observe it to be cloudy and cluttered, proceed then to "wash it out."

2. This, as always, is a mental action. You create a spray-gun, fill it with white healing energy in liquid form and spray the interiors of the liver and gall bladder thoroughly until they look fresh and clean to your mental eye.

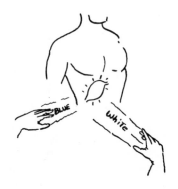

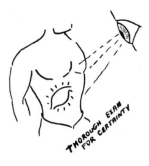

3. Flood both organs with light blue soothing, pain-killing energy. Repeat this process twice more.

4. The pain should now be gone, but before withdrawing, give the patient another thorough mental examination to ascertain with certainty whether or not additional specialized treatment may be necessary.

are observed, further work on your part is required. Before we get into these problems, here is a case where a liver "washout" healed the liver and eliminated the pain. The healer is Ben Bibb and the subject Pauline Shaffer of Palm Beach Gardens, Florida.

Here first is Mrs. Shaffer's account of what took place. Ben Bibb's report will follow.

> I was having a great deal of internal trouble: there was a lot of pain in the rib cage, occasionally accompanied by nausea, and it was getting worse. I was hospitalized for tests which were indefinite and only added to my discomfort. Finally I called Ben Bibb, whom I had met, and asked him for help.
>
> I explained my symptoms to him over the telephone and he immediately told me what the problem was, just as I was talking to him. He said it was a malfunction of the liver and he would handle it as soon as he could. I knew he was very busy and I was embarrassed that I had asked him to help me. The very next day I became sick to my stomach and threw up a great deal of rather horrible fluid. But after this the pain left and I steadily improved. Now I am in perfect health and have had no further trouble.

Reporting on this case Ben Bibb writes that when Mrs. Pauline Shaffer telephoned him he became aware at once that the chest pain she described was caused by a liver malfunction. Being then in the midst of some other work, he told her he would get to her with help as soon as he could. Here is his report.

> When Pauline Shaffer telephoned me and described her "chest wall" pains, I intuited immediately that this was a case of referred pain from both liver and gall bladder—but I was tied up in other work at that moment and told her I would get to her as soon as I could.
>
> When I was finally able to work on her, I surrounded her with a heavy aura of white healing energy and then, in my creative imagination, I used a reflector to project the energy in a moving stream through the liver and gall bladder—sweeping back and forth with the beam to cause a washing effect to clear the liver and gall bladder of all sedimentary matter. On completion of this, I mentally saw the liver and gall bladder fresh and healthy looking. I then gave her inner mind a reminder to continue the healing work as demonstrated, every evening on retiring and every morning upon awakening, as long as necessary.

In this case, as in most that will come to your attention, a simple cleansing of the liver and gall bladder sufficed to heal the patient and prevent a recurrence of the painful experience, but if your examination discloses imbalance or infection or damage, further work on your part will be necessary. Here are some of the problems which will require special additional treatment.

TREATING JAUNDICE

You can usually detect jaundice in a subject by looking at physical manifestations. The skin will usually have a yellowish or greenish-yellow tone, but sometimes a jaundiced person will not exhibit this symptom to any noticeable degree. It is better to depend more upon your psychic sight than the physical. While jaundice is, in itself, seldom considered fatal, it can, if neglected, cause permanent liver damage, which is serious. When your examination reveals jaundice, therefore, proceed at once as follows:

1. Give the liver a complete washout with white healing energy as described.

2. Since jaundice is directly due to an oversupply of bilirubin, proceed next to correct this. Since this oversupply can be caused either by overproduction, or by defective excretion, two different treatments should be considered.

3. If your examination discloses overproduction, balance out the controlling glands immediately after the washout.

4. If defective excretion is indicated, find the block and remove it mentally with your fingers.

5. Repeat the washout with white healing energy and conclude by giving the liver a cool bath of soothing blue energy.

The balancing referred to in Step 3 may be accomplished by several different visual instructions to the patient's inner mind. Just remember that a glandular imbalance existing in that area should be pointed out to the inner mind with a suggested method of correction. You could visualize a set of balance scales in which you set up pairs of glands and correct them two by two until they all balance out. You could visualize a pool of water on which all the glands involved are made to float evenly, or you could just order them all to come to a point of equilibrium. Use your imagination and your intuition will not fail to suggest a workable method.

The blockage referred to in Step 4 may be caused by debris of some sort. In that case plucking it out will usually suffice. If it is the result of damage, you must ascertain the extent and again use your intuitively inspired imagination to suggest a satisfactory correction.

Jaundice symptoms may be the result of other liver problems such as hepatitis, cirrhosis, etc., which are treated here separately.

HEALING HEPATITIS

Hepatitis is inflammation of the liver caused by infection or toxins of some sort. The infections may come from viruses, bacteria or other predatory germs. The toxins could be household items like carbon tetrachloride, phosphorus, anesthetics or antibiotics. Regardless of cause, the important first step is to get the liver thoroughly cleaned out.

To your inner eye, the liver may appear to be flaming or to have waves of heat emanating from it. This will clue you as to the best treatment, namely, to first flood it with soothing, cooling, pain-reducing blue energy. This will ease the inflammation and give the sufferer some measure of relief. It should then be followed by a thorough washout with white energy as described at the beginning of this chapter. When your inner eye can see the liver clean and free from foreign matter, examine it once again to determine whether the hepatitis was induced by a poison of some sort or by an infection.

If you find that the inflammation resulted from some form of toxic intruder, no further work will be required because you will have already cleaned out all such sedimentary poisons. If you discover infection, seek out the virus or germs causing it and destroy them with white energy, or just command them to leave the system of the sufferer. Always conclude by giving the patient an extra shot of white healing energy and instructions to repeat the treatment at intervals until it is no longer necessary.

An exact medical appraisal of the ailment, while helpful, is not always necessary. We have on record a great number of successful healings by Seventh Sense workers with no medical knowledge and no sure way, other than what they see, of determining an underlying cause. These workers send healing energy and instruct the inner mind of the patient to employ this energy in the best possible manner to correct the malfunction. This usually works, occasionally with very rapid efficiency. Here is reported a case of this type. The healer is Mrs. Yolande Scott of Lake Worth, Florida and the subject a woman in her forties identified as E.G.

HEALING A LIVER AILMENT

A friend of mine telephoned me and asked me to help her neighbor, Mrs. E.G. She was very sick, could not hold any food in her stomach, and had very bad cramps. This had been going on for about a week. She had gone to a doctor who gave her medicine which did not help. My friend said Mrs. E.G. looked worn out and she was worried about her. I told her I would work on it right after dinner, which I did.

First I put blue energy around her to calm her nerves. Then I looked into the stomach area and I could see that a lot of bile was pouring into the stomach, causing nausea. I ordered the liver to stop producing so much bile and I mentally poured antacid into her stomach to stop the nausea. I then poured lots of white healing energy into her stomach, liver, gall bladder and intestines. I finished by covering her in sun-gold energy and telling her inner mind to repeat this every day for a week.

The next day Mrs. E.G. called me and said: "Thank you so much for what you have done for me. I was so sick. You don't have any idea how bad I felt. But this morning I got up feeling so good I had bacon and eggs, toast and coffee for breakfast and kept the whole thing in my stomach. This is fantastic. May I keep your number and call you again if I need you?" I told her, yes, of course, but apparently she is all right because I haven't heard from her in over two months.

In this case the inner mind of the subject responded to the instruction given it by stopping the excessive flow of bile, and then accepted the healing energy as an aid to a permanent correction of the liver disorder. Neither the healer nor the patient ever knew exactly what caused the trouble or how it was corrected. You will find in your Medipic healing work that this will frequently occur. You should not depend upon it, of course; whenever possible, seek out the cause of the malfunction and give the inner mind of the patient instructions which will stimulate it to correct the condition in its own way.

CORRECTING LIVER
CIRRHOSIS

According to the most recent government statistics, cirrhosis of the liver is the fourth most dangerous and fatal affliction in all people over 45 years of age. As a cause of death it is exceeded only by heart disease, cancer and arterial brain damage. When you encounter it in a sufferer, therefore, you will find it necessary to instruct the inner mind to rebuild the damaged areas in addition to the usual cleansing process. Overindulgence in alcohol is probably the major cause of cirrhosis of the liver. In addition to the actual healing, you should, in all such cases, do what you can to help the subject free himself from this craving for alcoholic stimulants. Later in this chapter you will find some suggestions as to how this may be accomplished. After alcoholism, the most frequent causes of liver damage are obstructions caused by hepatitis, malnutrition or insufficient blood supply. Sometimes you will find that the entire architecture of the liver had been changed and will require instructions from you to set it back in order.

Here, then, is a suggested Televisual technique for correcting cirrhosis of the liver.

1. First give the liver a thorough washout as described earlier in this chapter.

2. Then examine it carefully with your inner eye in order to determine the cause of the liver malfunction.

3. When the extent and nature of the liver damage is observed, give the patient's inner mind visual instructions on the best methods to repair it.

4. Flood the liver and adjacent stomach area with white healing energy and follow this by pouring into the patient an aura of light blue soothing, pain-killing energy.

5. Before breaking contact, instruct the patient's inner mind to repeat this entire healing procedure every twelve hours for three days, and then every twenty-four hours for a week thereafter.

Very often you will find evidences of fibrosis in the liver, as well as the presence of scar tissue and sometimes nodules. All of this obstructing material must be cleaned out, swept out by the employment of white healing energy. The open holes and wounds that are left must then be immediately filled with green building energy until they return to normal. If you find the cause or causes of this damage to have been a previous attack of hepatitis, or chronic hepatitis, no further treatment will be necessary once the injured areas are healed. If the cause is malnutrition, however, steps should be taken to reinforce the blood. If the blood supply is actually insufficient, a heart stimulation may be required.

If the cirrhosis is the result of prolonged overindulgence in alcohol, you should seek out some way to help the patient overcome this craving. One way is to suggest to his or her inner mind that the taste of alcohol is displeasing. In most cases, if the individual is sincere in a desire to stop drinking, this will suffice. When an individual has been an alcoholic for a long time (a period of years), sterner measures are necessary to help him or her break the habit. In such a case the implanted suggestion that alcohol in any form is nauseating usually works.

Here is a case history which shows how this may be done. The healer is Pauline Shaffer of Palm Beach Gardens, Florida. When she was cured of a liver ailment by Ben Bibb, as described at the beginning of this chapter, she became so interested in the Medipic methods that she took a course under the instruction of Mr. Bibb and developed into a most successful healer. Here is the way she handled the problem of an alcoholic, a man in his fifties described only as A.M.

> Help was requested by a family member without the knowledge of the man himself. The problem was alcoholism, and was a long-standing one. It was only when it became clear to him that he was breaking down physically that he tried to stop drinking, but he could not. His daughter came to me and asked if I could help.
>
> This man was quite difficult for me to reach. It was only after several tries that I was able to get the attention of his inner mind. When I did, I instilled the thought he would become nauseated when he imbibed. For a while he continued to drink but each time he became more ill than the previous time. Finally he cut it out entirely for over three months before temptation overcame him. On that occasion he was very nauseated, so he hasn't had a drink since. He is perplexed and bewildered because he has no knowledge of what happened, but at the same time he is getting better physically, which delights him. He takes full credit for his strength of will in breaking the habit; no one in his family has let out the secret. They are too happy with the improvement.

Along with this case history and several other healings reported by Mrs. Shaffer, she sent the following list of her observations since she became a Seventh Sense graduate healer.

GENERAL FINDINGS BY
PAULINE SHAFFER

1. Mental fingers can be used as a surgeon uses his instruments.

2. A soft mauve light appears at times when a stabilizing influence is needed.

3. The Seventh Sense training opens the inner mind to other sensitivities in addition to healing.

4. People who do not believe in the Seventh Sense healing techniques can often be helped—but I find I cannot help those who ridicule it.

5. Emotional lesions can be healed as well as physical ones.

6. Protective shields can be applied and are very effective. I encase a person in a very bright white light.

7. I wash my hands mentally before working on different cases. I feel that in this way contamination is avoided by me— and also that between the auras of the people served.

You can see from the foregoing that Mrs. Shaffer is a thoughtful and observing person. The Seventh Sense training has helped her to a much broader understanding of life and of herself. You can be benefited in the same way and to the same degree if you apply yourself conscientiously to your healing work.

It may be helpful if we include one more case history. This was a very bad cirrhosis condition experienced by a woman about 57 years of age whom we will call E.A. The healer is Vi Holtberg of Boynton Beach, Florida. Miss E.A. has supplied us with the copy of a medical report on her condition when she applied for Social Security disability benefits. It was written by Dr. Richard Frey who had been treating her for many years. The report is very complete and therefore rather lengthy, so we will only reproduce significant parts of it. In addressing the Medical Head of the Social Security board in St. Paul, Minnesota, in behalf of Miss E.A., Dr. Frey says,

I have followed Miss A.'s illness since November of 1968 at which time I made a diagnosis of a cholangiolitic cirrhosis. The patient has had the usual course since that time with a gradual progression of her disease with increased hepatomegaly, increasing jaundice and melanosis, with decreased functional capacity as measured by her ability to perform any type of sustained physical activity during the course of a day, and more recently during the course of even 30 to 60 minutes. The diagnosis was originally confirmed in March of 1972 at the Metropolital Medical Center.

Miss A. was admitted to the hospital seven months later because of increasing fatigue due to the cirrhosis. There she was found to have an active duodenal ulcer.

It is obvious that this has been a progressive course and I cannot anticipate functional improvement in the future.

When Miss E.A.'s condition had shown no improvement in five years, she telephoned Vi Holtberg and asked for help. Mrs. Holtberg did a liver washout and mentally removed the ulcer. Although she continued to send white healing energy daily, there was no noticeable improvement for nearly a month, but by the middle of March, E.A. began to feel stronger and started to regain some weight. In April she wrote Mrs. Holtberg as follows:

> Your energy seems to be doing great things—I have really improved so much (the doctor says unbelievably). Feel great most of the time, though I still tire after a few hours. I can now do so many things I thought I would never be able to do again. My most heartfelt thanks.

This case points up the fact that some ailments and some people take longer to heal than others. In such cases it is the subject who actually performs the healing under Medipic suggestions, and if his or her energy is low and the ailment is of long standing it may be more than a month before any beneficial results are noticed. With older people, therefore, several treatments may frequently be required.

In addition to the liver ailments of jaundice, hepatitis and cirrhosis just discussed, there are many others too numerous to classify here. Nearly all of them can be handled temporarily and some permanently by employing the liver washout described. There is one other ailment in this area which deserves attention—this is gallstones.

CORRECTING GALLSTONES

Most doctors will agree that there is no known medical treatment for gallstones. Most medical books make this statement and indicate that removal by surgery is the only solution when the gallstones cause pain and create a problem. We have demonstrated complete and often what appears to be permanent relief of this condition through Medipic.

It is estimated that over fifteen million people in the United States have gallstones; possibly more, because gallstones have been found in twenty percent of all routine autopsies. In most cases the presence of stones in the gall bladder causes no discomfort and therefore goes unnoticed. Gallstones may be formed in three different ways, but no one knows why they form. Certainly we need not concern ourselves with the reason for or the character of their formation, since our sole interest is to rid the patient of the discomfort they bring about. This is usually an effect of what is called cholecystitis, which means in ninety-five per cent of the cases that a gallstone has become caught in the neck of the gall bladder or in the cystic duct. The simple cure is to remove it. Since we are not surgeons and do not cut open the gall bladder or remove it entirely, we must use another method. Here is one.

1. Having achieved mental contact and ascertained that the pain is the result of inflammation caused by a stone being impacted in the neck of the gall bladder or in the cystic duct, our first step is to remove the stone with our mental fingers.

2. The next step is to prevent the stone, or another stone, from slipping again into the aperture. This is best done by mentally gathering all the stones in the gall bladder into a sack made of people skin. They will thus be prevented from wandering off to create another blockage.

3. Now the inflammation and the pain must be eliminated. Pour blue soothing, pain-removing energy into the gall bladder and all the adjacent areas.

4. Finish by flooding the area with bright white healing energy and by instructing the inner mind to repeat the entire healing every twenty-four hours for five days.

Of course you realize that in Step 2 you could mentally remove all the stones from the gall bladder and destroy them, but this would present two problems. First, it would create a void that would have to be filled in order to prevent a sudden imbalance. Second, and this is more serious, it might take the inner mind of the patient several months to dispose of these rock-like intruders with the normal dissolving equipment at its disposal. The wrapup is thus better and just as effective.

There are many other afflictions of the gall bladder but only one, other than gallstones, is important enough to be discussed here. That is chronic cholecystitis and is the result of repeated inflammatory gall bladder attacks that have gone untreated. The gall bladder becomes shrunken and scarred and sometimes adheres to nearby viscera. When you find this to be the case, mentally remove the gall bladder, scrub it clean, inside and out, massage it with green healing oil until it feels supple under your hands and then return it and connect it properly as before. Finally, wash it inside and out with white healing energy and finish with a blue soothing energy treatment and the instruction to repeat the entire healing every twelve hours for three days. This should do it.

12. Amazingly successful psychic healing treatments for kidney, bladder and prostate malfunctions

The kidneys, bowels and the organs associated with them have the responsibility for carrying off the body's waste products. Since hardly anyone eats and drinks properly, this in itself puts a heavy work load on them. When you couple this normal wear and tear with the damage created by emotional stress, it is not surprising that they appear to break down frequently, particularly in people past middle age. In fact the genito-urinary system is so complicated and delicately balanced that it may be said to constitute the major area of disease in all age groups, particularly in the very young and the aged. Statistics show that urinary tract infections, congenital anomalies, adrenal diseases and other afflictions of the GU system account for almost ten percent of all general hospital admissions. When you are approached by a person with a problem in this area, be careful to make a most careful and searching mental examination before starting the actual healing instructions.

Most often you will find the trouble to be a kidney or bladder infection caused, as a rule, by improper elimination and the decomposition of the residue. The physician must make many tests in order to determine the actual location and type of the disturbance, but you only need to look. If upon mental inspection you discover an infection to be the cause of the disturbance, you can handle this most effectively in the following manner.

MEDIPIC FOR CURING
KIDNEY OR BLADDER
INFECTIONS

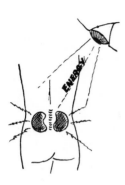

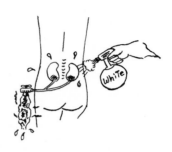

1. Make a thorough mental examination. If this discloses an infected kidney or bladder or both, send a powerful charge of energy to the sufferer to help build up his or her natural resistance.

2. Proceed then to visualize a complete cleaning out of the affected organs. This can best be done by mentally spraying white healing energy into them until you see that all of the debris, pus and infecting particles are being carried out.

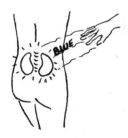

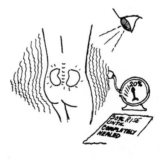

4. Re-inspect the affected areas to make sure all traces of infection have been eliminated. If you find this to be the case, raise the vibratory rate of the subject's energy body twenty-five percent, and instruct it to maintain this vitalizing activity until a complete physical healing has been accomplished.

3. Bathe the kidney and/or bladder in blue soothing, pain-killing energy until all inflammation subsides and the organs once again assume their normal condition.

This is a most effective cleansing technique which can be employed often in connection with the treatment of other kidney and bladder malfunctions. In all problems involving the kidneys and bladder, there is almost always the need to flush them out clean before moving on to the more complicated repair work. When you encounter infection in the genito-urinary system it may be the result of bacteria, in which case the foregoing washout procedure should suffice. If it is a secondary effect of a venereal disease, tuberculosis or some other more widespread infection, the cause must be identified and balancing instructions given mentally to the patient. Cases of this type may require several treatments before the subject is able to overcome and correct the initial cause.

In cases of venereal or tubercular infection, and in cases of fungus or parasitic diseases, you can help the patient greatly if you supply extra energy to aid him or her to work out the healing in accordance with the visual instructions you have given. This is best done by surrounding the subject with a cloud of white healing energy so that he or she appears to be enveloped in a scintillating white aura projecting out about two feet in all directions from the body. Gradually compress this white energy cloud into the body itself in order to raise its energy level to a point where a complete and rapid healing is possible. In cases involving virus infections it will often help the subject to heal himself if you mentally suggest that he coat the kidney and bladder walls with a paste of bicarbonate of soda before washing them out with the white healing energy. A virus is acid in character and the bicarbonate will help to neutralize its virulence.

The following report of an actual healing of a kidney infection will make this clearer. The subject was Claudette R. Marquis, age 27, of Jewett City, Connecticut. Since she was at that time a Seventh Sense student, she first asked the class for help, but later Ben Bibb himself looked into her case and completed the cure. Here first is her report. It will be followed by the file report on her healing.

> About the middle of October I began to experience a lack of bladder control, but I delayed doing anything about it, thinking it was probably only a temporary condition. On October 26, while engaged in household chores, I began to feel faint but again I shrugged it off and went back to work. On October 28, about 4:00 a.m., I was awakened by a burning sensation in my urinary tract. I went to the bathroom and then back to bed but was aroused again five minutes later. This happened twice again

before I thought to light the bathroom light and examine my urine. When I saw it was full of blood, I panicked and awoke my roommate, Nancy, to drive me to the hospital. The emergency room physician was quite nonchalant and said that urinary infections were quite common. He told me not to worry and prescribed an antibiotic.

After two days I felt better and went back to work, but after four more days I began experiencing some pain in my left side around the ovaries. I called my doctor for a follow-up exam on November 8. After the internal exam, his face was quite somber. He said it indicated infection of the left fallopian tube, probably caused by the virus which was the original cause of the urinary infection. He said he would try another antibiotic, but if that didn't work, surgery would be required. At my age I didn't want to be barren and I felt desolate.

On November 14 I went to a Seventh Sense meeting and told them for the first time about the trouble I was having. They all went to work to help me. I had walked in feeling chilled and had kept my jacket and coat on, but after a few moments I got so warm I had to remove them. I left the meeting burning with heat and the conviction I was going to be entirely well.

On November 22 when I went back to the doctor for a check-up, he seemed amazed. "Your unpleasant condition is almost entirely cleared up," he said. When I told Ben, he said he would give me one more treatment, just to make sure. It is now March and I have been just fine ever since then.

Here now is the Seventh Sense file report on the case of Claudette Marquis.

At November 14 meeting, Seventh Sense student Claudette Marquis of Jewett City, Connecticut, asked for help saying that her doctor had diagnosed an infection of the left fallopian tube which had been precipitated by a virus infection of the kidneys. The group poured a lot of sun-gold healing energy into Claudette for the kidney, bladder and ovary infection with each member using his or her own visualization for cleaning out the infection. Some used mental syringes and others swabs to clean the infected areas, while still others mentally rubbed in salves made of solidified healing energy. When she left the meeting she said she felt hot, undoubtedly an effect of the energy she had received. Later that evening, after she had gone home and the meeting was over, Ben Bibb gave her the following treatment. Here is his account:

"I checked her mentally and found she had completely recovered, so I gave her instructions to relax and accept the instructions I would mentally give her. I visualized her lying down and generated a huge white healing aura all around her. Using a mentally produced reflector, I caused the white healing aura to become a flowing beam of energy directed by the reflector. I swept out the ovaries, bladder and the entire urinary and reproductive systems with this strong beam of healing energy, making sure that all residual infection was being cleaned out. Then I changed the aura to green, the clear green of cellular regeneration, and went over the entire system again making sure that everything looked completely fresh and normal when completed."

Before moving on to other genito-urinary problems, here is the case history of the cure of a kidney infection which you will find interesting and instructive. The subject is Dan Meyers of West Cornwall, Connecticut, who raises and trains horses. The healer was Ben Bibb. Since Ben Bibb's account shows a most thorough analysis of the problem and a most detailed account of the methods he used to effect this cure, it is given here in the belief that all students will profit by his instructive lecture. An acknowledgment of the cure by the wife of the subject will follow his report.

Ethel Meyers (Ethel Johnson Meyers, the psychic) called me on a Sunday evening, saying she was calling in spite of her husband's objection. She stated that Dan Meyers, her husband, was in serious pain and had considerable swelling. He had been diagnosed as having a bladder infection, his right testicle was swollen and pains were radiating down both legs from both sides of the groin. She said he had had two vertebrae fused several years before and wondered if that could be a contributary cause.

After a quick mental survey, I told her on the telephone that the basic problem seemed to be the kidneys, a rather serious viral infection which referred the pain and tension into the back muscles. The swelling in the right testicle was not related to that, I said, but the pains in the groin were, in that the muscle tension and strain affected the area of the fused vertebrae and put pressure on the pain nerves in the vicinity of the twelfth thoracic vertebra, and lower, with resulting referred groin and sciatic pain. I advised her that I did not anticipate any difficulty in clearing all of the problems.

A BEN BIBB LECTURE

A short time later, I relaxed into my working state and mentally contacted Dan Meyers. Inspecting the kidneys, I found symbolically swollen and darkened organs, and inside them I could see spots of pus. The muscles alongside the spinal column were rigid with stress, and the pain-reporting nerves at the small of the back and just lower were pulled against the vertebral bones and were inflamed with irritation. In the right testicle there appeared to be a viral infection in the membrane covering the testicle itself, with resultant fluid buildup around the testicle. (This is somewhat similar to a condition of the heart called pericarditis.)

First, I mentally surrounded the body with a large and very thick white aura of pure life energy, visualizing it as a thick brilliantly white cloud. This "white energy" has the pure quality of healing. I made a pronouncement to the kidneys to "stop time" and used my mental hands to open them up. I sprinkled baking soda inside of them, because since a virus is an acid life form, the alkaline property of the baking soda would serve to counteract the virus. By mental will power, then, I caused the white energy to congeal to liquid thickness and mixed it with the soda; then I closed the kidneys and pronounced "start time." With a mentally created small reflector in my hand, I began focusing the ray of moving white energy through the kidneys, flowing it through and back and forth. After three minutes of concentrated effort, I again checked the kidneys and found that the pus was gone, the swelling had gone down and the kidneys were of normal color.

I then went to the right testicle, using baking soda and white energy in much the same manner and completing by mentally creating a small tube to drain off the fluid and thereby reduce the swelling. On completion, the testicle looked normal.

Next, I turned my attention to the back and the pain referred from it. I mentally surrounded the white aura previously created by a new cloud of blue auric energy, a life energy which has the qualities of soothing and harmonizing as its major healing factors. I caused the blue to shrink, pushing the white energy into the body. I then took "human tape," mentally created and reinforced the sheath which surrounds the vertebrae and discs, particularly in the area where the fusion had taken place some years before. Then I caused some of the blue energy to congeal to a paste-like consistency and, making sheets of this, I wrapped up the reddened pain nerves coming from the spinal column and radiating around the groin and down the legs. With the reflector once again in my hand, I focused a flowing ray of blue energy into the back muscles and along the pain nerves, moving it slowly back and forth until all tension was gone from the muscles and the pain nerves had resumed their normal color. Then I once again inspected the kidneys and testicle and found them to be normal looking.

Finally, with my hands acting like magnets over the physical body, I willed the etheric body (the life force field) to rise out of the body. Placing my hands far apart, one above the head and the other below the feet, I began transmitting energy from my right hand to my left through the etheric body, and simultaneously began sounding a mental note. As I gradually caused the pitch of this note to rise, I pronounced, "I am now raising the vibration rate of this etheric body to fifty percent above normal to speed the healing. Upon completion of the healing, return to your normal vibratory rate." That concluded the treatment.

In this account of the healing of Dan Meyers, you will find a number of suggestions which will assist you in achieving cures in similar circumstances. Remember, never jump to conclusions; always look. It would have been easy for Ben Bibb, having found the major problem to be a viral infection of the kidneys, to clear it up and let it go at that, but he did not. You can see that his most thorough inspection disclosed other problems which required attention. This he gave—and so Dan Meyers was rapidly healed, as you will read in this report from his wife, Ethel Johnson Meyers.

> My husband, Dan Meyers, had been suffering for a week before I called you, with horrible pains in the bladder or its environs. He had gone to see a doctor who told him it was a bladder infection and gave him some antibiotics. These made him feel somewhat better and reduced his fever for a couple of days, but by the weekend, when I returned from New York, he was much worse. By Sunday night when I called you he was terrible. The pains now extended to all the surrounding parts. When I told him I was going to call you, he tried to talk me out of it, but I just walked into the next room, picked up the telephone and called you in spite of him.
>
> When the alarm woke us the next morning, I turned to ask him if it would be all right for me to go to New York or if he would prefer me to stay with him. To my surprise he said: "Do you know this is the first night I've slept through in a long, long time? I feel great!"
>
> He really was feeling fine and began tearing around getting his horses, ready to go to the track, doing hard work trimming and doctoring their feet. He has been going strong ever since. Now he is very grateful and is looking forward to the time when he can meet you in person.
>
> Ethel Meyers

It was indicated at the beginning of this chapter the whole genito-urinary system is so delicately balanced and so complicated that a great number of different afflictions can strike it. One may trigger off another or several other ailments, as is evident in the case described by Ben Bibb.

Kidney infections use many disguises which often make it extremely difficult for the medical profession to diagnose them accurately, but you can usually get a clear picture with your first mental look. This will enable you to set about correcting the problem with no waste of time. The following report will help make this clear. The subject was William A. Copeland, Jr., 57, residing in Nashville, Tennessee. The healer is his daughter, Judi Jones of West Palm Beach, Florida, who was assisted by her husband, Charles Jones. Here is her report of the case.

A few days after New Year's Day, my father entered the hospital in Nashville suffering from very high blood pressure, blood in the urine, an enlarged left kidney and apparently complete failure of the right kidney. He was in a lot of pain. After X-rays and other tests, a mass was found in his left kidney which the doctors believed to be a tumor. My husband, Charlie, and I began to work on him, each using our own methods, and in two days we observed that the right kidney was functioning normally. Also his blood pressure had come down some and the bleeding was diminishing. After another set of X-rays the doctors decided that the mass in the left kidney was not a tumor but a kidney stone. As far as we could see there was no sign of cancer—only a kidney infection. Even though his blood pressure had dropped substantially the doctors continued the same prescription. Fearing overmedication, I telephoned my mother (I was in Florida and my father in a Nashville hospital) and asked her to get the doctors to cut back on the blood pressure medicine, but they refused.

A day later my father had a heart attack and thereafter was placed under the care of a heart specialist. This doctor cut out all medication and told my mother that excessive medication to relieve blood pressure can cause heart attacks in some people. We then began working to correct the heart damage; soon some progress was noted. The blood in the urine cleared up and the blood pressure continued to drop. Before the heart attack the doctors treating him had decided to operate on the kidney; when he was released from the hospital after it appeared he had recovered from the heart attack, they still wanted to operate to find out what the problem was. We told my father his kidneys were now clear and normal, so he delayed. Later, under pressure, he went back for another set of X-rays, which confirmed that his kidneys were indeed back to normal—no internal mass, no bleeding, no pain. His heart is also stronger and seems to be recovering nicely.

My husband and I worked on him at different times and used different energies directed at the diseased and injured areas. In addition to the energies, I also worked on the etheric body, clearing up dull areas and raising its vibratory rate as seemed indicated.

In this case there undoubtedly was a mass present in the left kidney as disclosed by the X-rays; this was removed by Medipic suggestion. The primary cause of all the problems was the kidney infection. When that was cleared up, the rest of the symptoms also disappeared. The bleeding, the high blood pressure and the pain all were gone when the kidney infection was cured. Charlie and Judi Jones used very different methods to effect this remarkable cure, and cure it was, for that was well over two years ago and the problem has not recurred. Charlie just pours pure energy into the subject and leaves it to the inner mind to make use of this energy in the best way. He can do this because he is physically a very powerful man and can command vast stores of energy. His wife, Judi, depends more on visualizing (sending pictures of the healing method to the inner mind of the sufferer) and then instructing the subject's vital body to pick up its own energy by raising its vibratory rate.

Use Your Intuition. Even though a standard visualization technique is suggested in many chapters, you are free to use any visualization or any method that may seem appropriate at the time. On this same subject of kidney problems, another healer, Julia Whitten, uses a very different approach. This is not the only method she uses, for Julia is a most successful and sensitive healer who unerringly employs the technique that appears to be best adapted to each situation. Here is her report of the elimination of a kidney stone. The subject's name is not on the report but it can be obtained (if necessary) by contacting Mrs. Whitten in Statesville, North Carolina.

> Several weeks ago, a fellow student handed a card to me with the name of her brother. He had a large stone in his kidney which was causing him pain and the doctors said it would have to be surgically removed. I said I would try to help. As I reached my "working state," a pair of golden hands appeared, pulsating with energy. They seemed to enter the young man's kidney and caress it. Each time they withdrew the stone was smaller. After three sessions it was about the size of a radish seed. The day after my last (third) session for him, he was driving along and had an unusually great desire to urinate. He stopped his truck and in the process of urination he expelled a small stone. Later X-rays confirmed that the kidney was clear and the stone no longer existed. Results like these are most gratifying, and the technique is something anyone can learn. You do not force these things to happen. It is a quiet <u>knowing</u> that it <u>can</u> be done.

Like any other human organs the genito-urinary system is subject to birth defects and also to injury. Almost all of these problems can be far more easily corrected by Medipic methods than by medication or surgery. However, damage to the external genitalia can often be more easily and more quickly repaired by surgery and medication.

PROSTATE TROUBLE

Prostate difficulties of one sort or another trouble many men as they advance in years. The cause or causes are unknown. Usually the first symptom is a retention of urine or its painful passage. This is caused by enlargement or hardening of the prostate gland to a point where it cuts off the passage of urine or makes it difficult. Since most men so afflicted are past sixty years of age, its relief or correction presents two problems to the healer.

1. Since this enlargement and hardening of the prostate has been many years in process, it cannot be corrected quickly.

2. In people over sixty, lack of physical energy and elasticity make healings more difficult and they therefore take longer.

Be prepared to face these problems squarely when your help is sought by a prostate sufferer, and take the best measures to overcome them. Your first step should be to endow the subject with as much additional energy as you can provide and as he can retain. Once this has been done, proceed to send to his inner mind visualizations designed to show it how to soften the gland, reduce its size and facilitate the flow of urine past it. Here is a simple method.

1. Mentally massage the prostate with green healing oil designed to soften it and reduce its size.

2. At the same time, enlarge the tube which passes the urine and strengthen it so that it will remain clear under pressure.

3. Flood the prostate, the testicles, the penis and the entire area with brilliant white healing energy. See that this is accepted and absorbed by the organs involved and then finish by bathing them with soothing, pain-removing blue energy.

It may be and often is necessary to repeat this treatment several times before any improvement becomes evident. Remember the two basic problems that are to be met and overcome here: age and lack of energy. Keep working and success will crown your efforts, as it has the efforts of many other healers faced with the same difficulties. It has been done before many times and it will be done again by you. On the other hand, we have on record several almost instantaneous corrections (within twenty-four hours) of prostate pain and blockage of urine. Everyone is different, so never assume that one person will react in the same way as another. For example, in some persons a thorough bowel movement will release urine seemingly dammed up by the prostate and result in an easy flow.

MENOPAUSE

This is a problem that causes considerable difficulty for some women while others seem to sail right through it with very little discomfort. It occurs at the time when the woman's ovaries decide to stop producing live ova. It may occur as early in her life as the mid-thirties, or as late as the sixties. Until her system once again balances out after this "change of life," the average woman has a pretty miserable time. This pain, upset condition and general discomfort can last from a month or two in some cases to a matter of two or three years in others. There apparently is no certain medical way to alleviate this condition, but since the basic problem is one of hormonal imbalance, you as a Seventh Sense healer can usually restore this balance and effect a "cure" in a matter of hours.

In order to know what visual suggestions to offer the inner mind of the subject, you should first comprehend what is taking place within the woman's body to cause her all this discomfort. So here is a rough general description of it. When a woman is functioning normally, every twenty-eight days (approximately) her pituitary gland will trigger the production of new live ova. At the same time, it directs the "throwing off" of the ova from the previous month and also the uterine lining in order to have the reproductive system ready for a new ovum. But when the ovaries do not then produce new live ova, both the pituitary gland and the uterus overreact. As the result of years of habitual action, both resist the change. The pituitary gland keeps on signalling, by means of hormone release, for the ovaries to discharge the ova and the blood supply, and for the uterus walls to "slough off," so that a fresh potential placenta wall can grow in the old one's place. What usually results is excess bleeding coupled with cramps, uterine pain and concomitant tension.

Your job as a healer is to correct this artificial imbalance as rapidly as possible. The quickest and simplest technique is to contact the subject's inner mind and instruct her pituitary gland to stop sending hormone signals to the pelvic area. This should be followed by flooding her nervous system with blue energy to kill the pain and calm her, so that her blood pressure will return to normal. With the cessation of the hormone stimulus, the bleeding and convulsive action of the uterus will stop. What follows will depend upon the woman's physical condition. If she is no longer capable of producing live ova, her periods will stop. But if her system is still capable of creating live ova, her periods will usually resume after a twenty-eight day delay. To make this clearer, here are the reports of two "healings" by Ben Bibb.

CORRECTING MENOPAUSE PROBLEMS

The first report concerns Mrs. Rose Chamberlain, 51, who at the time was a resident of Ann Arbor, Michigan. She came unannounced to Ben Bibb's home and asked him for help saying she had to drive back to Ann Arbor from Florida (where Ben Bibb then lived) the next morning and didn't think she could make it in her weakened condition. She said she had lost a great deal of blood and was even then bleeding profusely. Although he was busy on another project, Ben stopped it and proceeded to help her. Here first is Mrs. Chamberlain's account; following it is Ben Bibb's report.

> I want to thank you for the help you gave me the Tuesday after Easter. I had been to the emergency ward in the hospital on Sunday night for the heavy bleeding but they did not help me much. My neck and back were knotted with pain and tension and I had to drive to Ann Arbor the following morning. I didn't know what to do.
>
> I had been treated by a doctor at home (in Ann Arbor) who explained to me that my problem was a thickening of the uterus walls which frequently happens to women at "change of life." This gets "sloughed off" at each period. I had started out with three days of confinement and bleeding but later it often went on for three weeks. I was anemic and getting weaker each month. The doctor at home said the only cure was the removal of the uterus, but when I consulted a doctor in West Palm Beach the week before I saw you, he said I ought to go into the hospital immediately to have the uterus removed because it was so terribly enlarged. He was afraid my heavy bleeding would give me chronic anemia from which I might not recover.
>
> All that is fine now since you treated me. It was amazing the way I felt when I left your home that Tuesday: strong and relaxed and confident. By nightfall the bleeding had stopped and I drove home the next day without any trouble. I have felt fine ever since; my last period was as close to normal as I've had in years. I want you and Margaret to know how much I appreciate your help in my great need.

Here is Ben Bibb's report on this case.

> Mrs. Rose Chamberlain of Ann Arbor, Michigan came to my home one afternoon when we were living in Florida. She said she had read an article on me in one of the local West Palm Beach papers and had come because she desperately needed help. She was scheduled to drive to Ann Arbor the following morning, but was so weak she was afraid to attempt it. She had been a victim of heavy menstrual flow and accompanying pain and weakness for some time, and now it seemed to be worse than ever. It was, of course, part of the malfunctioning that can occur at and during menopause.
>
> Because of her obvious pain, weakness and distress, I went to work to help her immediately. I used direct energy from my hands, first into the pelvic area with a gentle flow of blue energy to soothe the pain and relax the ovarian-uterine system. Then I sent white energy into the same area to give the total healing effect. Alternately, with my fingers bunched, I sent a beam of the same energies into the pituitary gland between her eyes. She appeared stronger, thanked me and left. After she had gone, I sent her a mental flow of the same energies with mental instructions to her to relax and to stop producing the menstrual-signalling hormone. She reported by letter that within a short time after leaving the house, the blood flow stopped. She was able to leave the following morning, driving to Michigan, and grew stronger during her trip as the blood loss was replenished.

In almost every case of distress during menopause, the triggering cause can be traced to the automatic repetitive action of the pituitary gland. Always be sure to bring it into balance and, if necessary, order it to stop releasing hormones into the uterus. There may be other problems which you can and will discover when you make a mental examination, but in most cases you will find that a complete hormonal balance is all that is required.

In order that you may know more about these critical hormones and how they work, here is another menopause healing which Ben Bibb described in his class instruction. It is included because a lecture by Ben Bibb on hormonal balance is part of the report. The subject of the healing is Mrs. Iola Maher, 49, of Kinnelon, New Jersey. The healer is Ben Bibb. Here first is Mrs. Maher's report. It will be followed by Ben Bibb's and include the descriptive lecture he gave to his class. Mrs. Maher's report is in two letters, the first describing her problem and asking for help, the second reporting her experience of the "healing" and its outcome.

Here is her first letter.

I need your help—badly! The past three months or more (it seems forever at this point), I have felt just rotten. My doctor says it is because I am going into menopause and my estrogen output is on the decline. I'm 49. My main complaint is tiredness. I have to force myself to do housework and I end up exhausted when I'm finished. I have been up two hours now and I could go right back to sleep.

I have hot flashes, especially at night, plus aches and pains. My eyes pain me and I have a pain in the back of my head sometimes. I had a blood test taken after I almost passed out in the doctor's office, but he said the results were fine. I had a pap test last month—no problem there. My blood pressure then was 140 over 80.

I'm a physical wreck. All I can say is this is not me. I always had energy to spare, but not now. Can you help me?

That letter was written on May 13. Ben Bibb received it four days later and started his work for her that evening. He heard nothing from her until July 23, when he received this letter dated July 19.

It's me again, feeling better and younger each day. I'm sorry I didn't write you sooner, but knowing how busy you are, I didn't want to bother you. As you know, my doctor's attitude was that this was just something I would have to put up with until it passed, if ever. I not only looked but felt like death warmed over. I was never so tired in all my life. I believe I could have slept every day around the clock.

Three or four days after I wrote to you, I started feeling better. At times I would feel this terrific heat all over my body, like I was sunburned all over. This would last for maybe a half hour and would occur two or three times a day. I felt better afterward. I feel like my old self now, only younger. I wonder if you have discovered the fountain of youth. I have no problems with menstruation any more, only sometimes a slight ache in the back of my head when I start my period.

Monday we are off for more vacation—this time to Maine and Canada. Earlier this month we went to Disneyland and Myrtle Beach and Virginia Beach before coming home. If it wasn't for you I could never have made it.

Love, Iola.

Since Mrs. Maher's case was typical of many other women's menopausal problems which are uncomfortable, annoying and debilitating but otherwise not so serious, Ben Bibb chose it to discuss in his class instruction. Here is a transcript of his remarks.

A BEN BIBB CLASSROOM LECTURE

The first letter from Iola was dated May 13 and pointed up the problem fairly well. Menopause in the woman creates a usually permanent hormonal imbalance, since the estrogens and androgens from the ovaries are no longer being supplied. The result is the classic "hot flashes" as the body tries with various reactions to adjust to this missing hormone flow.

However, the adrenal cortex, which is located atop the kidneys and is the center section of the adrenal glands, has the ability to produce sex hormones. Usually this production is diverted to aid in the production of cortisones, but it is my concept that, upon cessation of the production of the sex hormone by the ovaries, the adrenal cortex is supposed to pick up this production and thereby maintain the hormonal balance. This would explain why some women pass through menopause, or through ovary removal, with little of the usual side effects. Their adrenal cortices responded properly. In only one case of menopause have I used the technique of reversing the onset of the menopause and bringing the patient back to normal menstrual flow. It was successful, but was done only at the patient's specific request.

With Iola Maher I first made mind-to-mind contact and checked her physical body. I found the ovaries had become rather dormant and I got the impression from them that the inner portion was beginning to atrophy. There was overactivity of the adrenal medulla, the outer covering of the adrenal glands which is separate from the cortex, which was causing the excess adrenalin to be produced. The pituitary gland was behaving erratically. This is the master gland which directs the entire hormonal system. It signals the ovaries for the start of the menstrual period and the adrenal medulla for the production of adrenalin. We must remember that the hormonal system is a system of harmony and balance and every hormone must either be used for its specific purpose or inhibited by an equal-but-opposite hormone. It must be remembered that these hormones are all-powerful chemicals which cause action in the body.

I then did a hormonal balancing of Iola Maher's body. I mentally placed the forefinger of my left hand on her pituitary gland, my middle finger on her hypothalamus gland above and to the rear of the pituitary, my little finger on the pineal gland and my thumb on the brain stem below the glands. I then demonstrated to the Inner Mind of the subject that there was a hormonal imbalance by checking the blood stream with my right hand fingertips to show that the blood felt hot and "spicy" instead of warm and neutral. I then used the same right hand to point out to the Inner Mind the dormant ovaries, and led a symbolic wire energy-link from them to the interior of the adrenal glands, their cortices.

At this point I began a pulsing rhythmic energy flow from the fingers of my left hand into the glands in the head and sent them the thought of harmonizing and balancing. These head glands are the governing glands, so I instructed them to produce everything needed in the proper amounts and at the proper times with nothing extra and nothing left out. Then, with my right hand fingertips, I began energizing the thyroid gland which is wrapped around the windpipe, plus the four small parathyroids embedded in it, pulsing the energy in unison with my left hand, harmonizing and balancing.

As soon as I was satisfied that it was in harmony, I went to the thymus gland, located in the forewall of the chest. This governs the autoimmunity system, so I balanced it and brought it into harmony with the other glands. Then with my right hand I mentally went to the Islets of Langerhans on the surface of the pancreas. These produce insulin and regulate the glucose content of the blood. I harmonized and balanced them in the same manner. Then I went to the adrenals themselves and balanced them as they would be with fully functioning ovaries, bringing them into harmony with the rest of the glandular system. I went then to the ovaries, touching them mentally with my right fingertips, and traced the "wires" upward to the adrenal cortices, all the while pumping energy into them with the idea they should start producing sex hormones. This I repeated several times until I felt that the message was getting through. Finally I went over both the liver and kidneys with my right hand and instructed them to filter and adjust the bloodstream to relieve it of toxins and poisonous elements. At that point I again tested the bloodstream with my fingertips and found it to be normally warm and neutral.

Before terminating the treatment I instructed her Inner Mind to call for, receive and execute the foregoing entire sequence of harmonizing and balancing three times daily until her system became fully adjusted and the hormonal flow proper. I then bathed her in a heavy flow of blue-colored life energy for soothing and calming, and then released her.

This lecture presents in capsule form almost a full course in hormone direction and glandular balancing. It will pay you to study it carefully. You will learn a lot.

13. Psychic healing remedies for stomach and bowel disorders

Most of the people who come to you with pains and other distress in the stomach will be found to be experiencing some form of indigestion. They can all be helped easily! Your examination may show the problem to be more serious. It could be caused by appendicitis, gastroenteritis, diverticulitis, some form of intestinal obstruction, ulcers, dysentery, dyspepsia or food poisoning. Some of these malfunctions may be cleared up with the standard healing procedures with which you should now be familiar, but others may require special attention. In most such cases, you will find that any cure will take time. You must be patient and be prepared to perform the Medipic treatment more than once. The following ulcer healing is a typical example.

HEALING A STOMACH ULCER

The healer in this case is Frans M. Eyberse of Lisbon, Connecticut, and the subject a woman named Paula, age 27. Her last name is not given, but she works for the same organization as Frans Eyberse. Here is Frans' report.

> Paula is 27 years old and a co-worker of mine. She had been afflicted with an ulcer for about six months when I first heard about it. Her doctor had put her on a diet and the normal medication for ulcer cases, but Paula, being young and liking to "live it up," resented the restrictions and occasionally strayed from the diet. This made her miserable. So one day she asked if I could help her with her ulcer. I said I thought I could and would try.
>
> I worked on Paula on three separate occasions. Each time I got the same picture. There was a sore in the wall of her stomach and it had worn the wall very thin until it was almost perforated. On each occasion, I mentally took white "people tape" and placed it over the sore area on each side of the stomach wall. Then mentally placing my hands on each

side of the wall over the tape, I pressed them together to "fuse" the tape and make it a part of the wall itself. I then packed the whole stomach area with white healing energy and commanded her Inner Mind to use this energy to heal the ulcer. At the end of each "operation" I asked her Inner Mind how long the healing would take. The first two times I received no discernable reply—just a sense of confusion as to the length of time and even as to the success of the operation itself. After the third session, however, I asked the same question of her Inner Mind and immediately got the reply "no pain—three days." I also got a good sense of accomplishment this time, as if something had finally "broken loose," and there was no longer need to be concerned.

This third operation was done late Wednesday evening; counting three days from then would bring us to the weekend. I didn't say anything to Paula about the three days, merely that I had worked on her. Friday, when she left for the weekend, she still had some discomfort, but when I saw her Monday morning she told me that the pain had stopped over the weekend. She had even gone off her diet somewhat without any ill effects.

Since then she has returned to a normal diet, has stopped the medication and has had no recurrence of the ulcer pain. The time elapsed is now several months, and she and I both feel that the ulcer is healed.

This case report is included here in complete detail because it points up a situation which some healers do not handle properly. In this case, it was not until the third repetition of the Medipic healing that the subject's Inner Mind responded. Once its attention was attracted and it understood what had to be done, the healing was accomplished by it in a period of three days. When you are working on a sufferer, particularly one with an internal problem, always keep trying until you are sure you are reaching the Inner Mind and that It understands what It is to do. Never assume that because you have given the proper Televisual technique for a healing that the subject's Inner Mind understands and will act on it. Always ask and keep demonstrating the proper Medipic healing method until you get a satisfactory response.

Here is the report of another ulcer healing which was performed during the seventh month of the subject's pregnancy. The healer is Pauline Shaffer of West Palm Beach and the subject is her daughter Mrs. Carol Thompson, 32, of Orlando, Florida. Here is Mrs. Shaffer's report.

During my daughter Carol's last pregnancy, she telephoned me to ask my help. It seems she was suffering a great deal from a stomach ulcer and asked if I could give her some relief. She also asked me to check on the baby and I said I would try. I found the stomach area very inflamed and with blood very close to the surface in one area. This I repaired with "people tape," and then flooded the entire stomach with white healing lotion. The turquoise aura was then used to calm her and relieve tension. She had no more pain after that.

The fetus was male and rather thin but with an abundant head of hair. I had a strong feeling that something was wrong with it but could not pinpoint it. There was no sign of deformity and the problem did not appear to be mental. A definite time, August 1-3, was imbedded in my mind. My grandson was born August 2. He looked exactly as I had seen him but was slightly jaundiced at birth—a malfunction which I had not been able to ascertain.

Since by far the greatest number of stomach problems stem from overindulgence of one sort or another, from food poisoning or from a cold or virus infection, the best procedure for you to follow is to first wash out the stomach with white healing energy. This can cause no harm whatever the problem may be, and in many cases it may be the only healing treatment required.

This treatment will in many cases serve to effect a relief from pain and a correction of the problem, but do not assume this is the only attention you need give the subject. After this washout, always make sure to re-examine the patient to determine if further attention on your part may be necessary. The primary cause of the pain may be an inflamed appendix, diverticulitis, ulcers or food poisoning, or it may be elsewhere—in the kidneys and just referred to the stomach area, for example. Look and make sure; then go to work.

HEALING DIVERTICULOSIS

Diverticulosis, called diverticulitis when inflammation is present, is a fairly common stomach ailment. It is estimated that thirty percent of all people over 45 have some degree of diverticulosis. You can discern the presence of this problem when you do a mental examination of the person who has come to you with some stomach pain or discomfort. It will appear to your psychic sight as small mucus-like sacs clinging to the intestinal wall. These should be removed with your fingers via Medipic and the points of contact with the intestine or colon closed and healed. Here is a report of a standard healing of a diverticulosis case. The healer is Pauline Shaffer of Palm Beach Gardens, and the subject is a woman friend of hers, 52

MEDIPIC METHOD FOR
CURING STOMACH AND
BOWEL DISORDERS

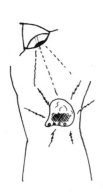

1. When your mental examination reveals a great deal of disturbance in the stomach itself, proceed first to wash it out.

2. This is best accomplished by using white healing energy. Mentally flood the area with this energy by applying it under pressure (as from a spray gun) until all particles of food, decomposed material, poisons and viruses have been loosened from the stomach walls.

3. Form this debris into a ball, mentally remove it from the stomach and then destroy it in whatever way seems best to you at the time.

4. After again coating the stomach interior with white healing energy, cover the entire area with an aura of soothing, pain-clearing blue energy; then order the Inner Mind of the subject to repeat this every twelve hours until a complete healing has been accomplished.

years of age, identified only by the initials F.B. Mrs. Shaffer's report is given first followed by a letter of thanks from Mrs. F.B.

> Mrs. B. is a friend of long standing. She had been troubled for many years by diverticulosis and this had become aggravated by an emotional upset caused by her home conditions. She appeared distraught when she came to me in June a year ago and asked for help.
>
> When I tuned in on her that night, she was so upset that I first bathed her all over in a turquoise light to calm her nerves and ease the pain. Then, when she seemed more at ease, I mentally examined her stomach and intestines. I removed the little sacs with my mental fingers and straightened out the kinks in her intestines, making certain that all blockage was eliminated and a free flow assured. I then bathed the entire stomach and the intestines and colon with white healing energy. This treatment was repeated nightly for eight days, after which time I felt the healing had been accomplished.

Mrs. B. was indeed "cured." She was also helped in other ways by the energy Mrs. Shaffer stimulated in her. A recent conversation disclosed that Mrs. B. has not been troubled by diverticulosis now in over a year. Some nine months after Mrs. Shaffer's healing efforts, Mrs. B. wrote the following letter.

> Dearest Friend Pauline,
>
> I would just like you to know how much you have helped me and in how many ways. Your power has done great things in my life. First I must tell you how much better I feel just in general, an all-over feeling of well-being, both physically and mentally. I feel free, for the first time in years. I do not have a sinus condition any more and the doctor says my sinuses are "clear as a bell." Thanks to you, Pauline, I have not had an attack of my diverticulosis since last June when I asked you to help me.
>
> Pauline, I just talked to you last week about my headache and already I am helped. I can almost tell when you are helping me because I start to feel better. I thank God that I have a friend like you and that I can feel I am your friend. I just want you to know how much I appreciate you and your help to me over the past year.
>
> My best to you always, F.B.

The method employed by Mrs. Shaffer in healing Mrs. B's diverticulosis is simple and practical. Remember always that as a healer your primary object is to get results—to help and cure the sufferer in the quickest and best way possible. You will find, as you progress in this work, that the best way is often the simplest. Go directly to your objective and leave the more complicated virtuoso performances to those less knowledgeable. In cases of diverticulitis, where there is inflammation present, look for infection. This occurs most often when the diverticular neck becomes obstructed by edema or feces. This blockage favors bacterial proliferation and resulting infection. After the diverticulae have been removed via Medipic, be sure to cleanse all of the resulting openings thoroughly with white healing energy before closing them with "people tape."

TREATING DIARRHEA

The frequent repeated passage of unformed stools is called diarrhea. It is an effect, so in all cases the cause must be sought after immediate relief has been given. Relief may be given by bathing the bowels with white healing energy while visualizing a temporary retention of the feces or mucus. The cause may be any one of many gastrointestinal disorders, parasitic infection, gastroenteritis, malabsorption, etc. Occasionally the cause may be traced to diseases of other organs (liver, adrenals, thyroid, etc.), or even simply to an excessive use of laxatives. First calm the subject and give what temporary relief you can; then seek out the cause and correct it. You now should have the knowledge and ability to initiate such a healing whatever the cause may be.

CURING APPENDICITIS

This was a dreaded affliction fifty years ago, but today it is regarded medically as of little more danger and significance than an infected tooth. It can still be extremely painful and distressing.

If your mental examination traces the cause of pain to an enlarged and inflamed appendix, the following Medipic healing treatment should correct the situation.

MEDIPIC FOR TREATING APPENDICITIS

1. Mentally clean out the appendix. Remove all foreign matter that may be lodged there. If the appendix is twisted, bent or kinked, straighten it out; then wash it clean with white purifying and healing energy.

2. Pack blue soothing, pain-relieving energy around the appendix. Mentally compress this blue energy while lowering its temperature to 40 degrees Fahrenheit.

3. Maintain this cooling, soothing blue energy pack around the appendix until it is clear to your psychic sight that all inflammation and swelling have gone and the appendix looks normal.

4. Flood the appendix and surrounding intestinal area with white healing energy and retire.

There are many other ailments that may cause stomach pain, far too many to be treated in detail here. There are, for example, intestinal obstructions of many types, including cancerous tumors. There is chronic constipation, which is usually the result of a "lazy" colon and requires only stimulation with red energy to start the bowels functioning properly. There are hemorrhoids, which should be treated like the inflamed appendix, and so on. Since it is easier to learn from the experiences of others, some case histories are included here, two involving rectal ailments and one a so-called "false pregnancy."

RELIEVING RECTAL AILMENTS

This report is by Bev Powell of El Cajon, California. He describes the successful healing of his mother, Mrs. Powell, who was suffering from a bowel impactment. Here is his report.

> In the early part of November my mother suffered her first bowel impactment. My sister was with her at the time and she, with the help of a neighbor who is a registered nurse, was able to remove it. They did it at home with the use of surgical gloves and a Fleet enema, but it was difficult and very painful.
>
> Two weeks later, my sister had gone home and I was staying with my mother in Florida, when in the evening she suffered another bowel impactment. I knew that I couldn't physically relieve her all by myself because I didn't know how, so I decided to try a psychic operation, as I had been taught by Ben Bibb. I asked my mother to try to relax and sleep and told her I would go into my room and try to help her. She had the faith of a child and she did go to sleep. Here is what I did then.
>
> Mentally, I placed her in a comfortable position on her side and then I inserted a soft small tube into her rectum through which I visualized a warm mineral oil flowing gently throughout her entire colon, bowels and intestines. I surrounded her with auras of blue to relax and soothe her, and white to heal and cure her. Then I instructed her mentally to rest and relax until the oil could break up the bowel impactment. After that I fell asleep.
>
> About 4 a.m. I awoke to find my mother standing next to me. She told me she had just had a perfectly normal bowel movement and that all the pain and discomfort were gone. She had no more problems with her bowels after that.

At the time of this report, Bev Powell was still an undergraduate student in one of Ben Bibb's classes, but he wanted so much to help his mother that he overcame the nervousness which was normal because of his lack of experience. This young man's achievement of a difficult healing should instill confidence into each student who sincerely wants to heal.

Not every gastrointestinal disturbance is necessarily fatal in character. Some are just annoying but persist in spite of the best medical efforts to correct them. In situations of this type, Medipic methods often succeed when standard medication fails. Here is a case which illustrates this. Mrs. Grace Grissom of Plainfield, Connecticut is the healer, and the subject was Frances Riley, 55, of Norwich, Connecticut.

> Frances Riley's name came to us by phone after one of Ben Bibb's radio interviews. It was given to me together with the information that this woman, now 55, had suffered for thirty years with rectal itching which had defied all medical efforts to clear it up. It was about the middle of August when I talked with her.
>
> Because this problem had not responded to local medication, it seemed to me that the cause must be elsewhere, so I decided to clean out the entire gastrointestinal and digestive systems just to make sure. As soon as I reached the meditative state and made contact with Frances' Inner Mind, I took a spray-like rotating swab filled with gentian violet energy and scoured and sprayed her entire digestive system. I started at her throat and worked downward cleaning out every crack and wrinkle, especially in the intestines, then out through the rectum, over the external area there and even into the vaginal opening to eliminate any possible pinworm infection. I followed this by mentally applying a liberal coating of baking soda to eliminate any acid condition, and then flushed out the system via the kidneys. After this I mentally took a wooden spatula and with it spread an anaesthetic paste over the entire anal area, inside and out. I then instructed her Inner Mind to raise her vital body's vibratory rate by fifty percent for one hour, to repeat the anaesthetic treatment every four hours for two days and to follow it with two liberal smearings of cold cream daily (mental) until every hint of irritation was gone.
>
> On September 9 Frances Riley telephoned to tell me that the itching had stopped. She had gone to her doctor that day and he detected no sign of irritation. Before she ended the conversation she asked me to help her sister, Barbara, who apparently has the same problem.

The medical profession identifies by name some forty-seven different possible causes of abdominal pain and disturbances of the gastrointestinal tract. Most of these can be relieved, and in a great many cases cleared up entirely, by Medipic treatments. You may occasionally find that stomach pain is referred and caused elsewhere, such as in the kidneys, liver or gall bladder. These possibilities have been discussed and methods to handle them suggested. Just remember to always look with your psychic sight and the basic cause of the disturbance will become evident. This ability you have to "look and see" will help you discover the cause of pain in situations where there is no clear medical evidence available and even, on occasion, when the evidence available denies it. The following case history illustrates this. It is reported by the Rev. Martin Grissom of Plainfield, Connecticut. The Rev. Grissom is vicar of St. Paul's Church in Plainfield and is the husband of Grace Grissom, another successful Medipic healer. Here is his report.

> I received a phone call from a woman named Elaine Rzeznikiewicz, 27, of Dayville, Connecticut, who reported she was having severe abdominal pains. I made mental contact with her and when the picture came through loud and clear that she was pregnant, I withdrew.
>
> Two days later Elaine phoned to ask what I had found as the pain was still severe. I asked her then, "Are you certain you aren't pregnant?" She said she was quite certain: her periods had been regular and as far as she was concerned it was not possible. I told her that this was all that I saw, but it bothered me. I made mental contact once again later that evening and discovered that the pregnancy was in the fallopian tube. Using my mental hands, I gently moved the fetus out of the tube into the normal position for the embryo. I then projected pure white healing energy to heal the soreness in the tube and filled her with the spiritual energy of blue to help give her a sense of calm, serenity and life-giving wholeness for the proper development of the fetus.
>
> About three months later I received another phone call from Elaine. She wanted to apologize because a doctor's checkup had verified that she was indeed pregnant. Moreover, everything was in place, she felt healthy and the fetus had begun to move. As for the pain she had previously felt, she said this had mysteriously stopped shortly after our previous phone conversation.

This one case in itself proves the wisdom of "looking," a privilege you should never ignore. Regardless of the pressure of time and other demands on your attention, carefully examine each case with your psychic sight (inner sight). The effort thus expended may result in your saving a life that might otherwise have been lost.

14. Psychic healing treatments for the relief of toothache, tooth infection and spinal afflictions

This chapter presents tested treatments for correction of bone malfunction or breakdown and the deterioration of adjacent tissue. The two areas where these problems appear most frequently are the teeth and the spine. First we will consider the teeth and after that remedial treatments for the spine.

As you know, your work is in perfect harmony with the normal healing mechanism of the body. Medipic treatments stimulate the Inner Mind of the subject to take healing action and suggest to It the quickest and best method to achieve this objective. Therefore, while you can soothe a toothache and relieve its pain, you can do nothing about a cavity or a broken tooth. In these cases, the bone structure of the tooth has already extruded beyond the gum line and can no longer be helped by the blood and other healing energies of the human system. Such problems belong to the realm of dentistry. A person with a cavity, a lost filling or a broken tooth should go to a dentist for relief.

The pain of a toothache is another matter. If the pain is caused by a cavity and an exposed nerve, you can relieve the pain—but you cannot eliminate the cause. The cavity must be closed and the nerves protected. This is a job for a dentist. If the pain is the result of an infection, such as in an ulcerated tooth, you can not only relieve the pain but also, in most cases, eliminate the cause. Here is a practical method to employ to ease pain.

MEDIPIC FOR ELIMINATING PAIN OF TOOTHACHE

1. If upon mental examination you discover that the pain is due to an exposed nerve, and nothing more, make sure the subject goes to a dentist as soon as possible to have this corrected.

2. Meanwhile, you can relieve almost all the pain the subject is suffering by packing the cavity mentally with a paste made from blue soothing, pain-relieving energy.

3. After making sure that the cavity appears to your inner eye to be filled with this blue energy paste, treat the entire tooth, root, nerve and gum area with white healing energy.

4. This should give almost immediate relief and may be repeated if and when necessary.

Here is a case history which illustrates this very problem. The healer is Mrs. Frances Miller of Plainfield, Connecticut and the subject was her husband, Frederick Miller. This is Mrs. Miller's report.

In late January, my husband, Frederick Miller, lost two large fillings, one from a molar on the upper right side and the other from a molar on the lower left side of his mouth. It was difficult for him to chew as both vacant spaces readily filled with food, causing a great deal of pain.

Much to our chagrin, we discovered that our family dentist was on vacation. One week later, when our dentist had not returned, both teeth were aching constantly. We called six other dentists, only to be offered appointments varying from April to July—and this was January. I decided then to try and help Fred as best I could via Medipic.

I succeeded in mentally contacting my husband's Inner Mind and then with my mental hands, I packed a turquoise, pain-killing filling into each of the two affected teeth and sprayed the roots and nerves involved with a turquoise solution. The pain eased almost immediately and my husband at no time suffered more than mild discomfort for the next five weeks, at which time our dentist returned and repaired the teeth with his brand of filling.

Fred Miller was naturally quite grateful to his wife for relieving the pain in his teeth over a six-week period until he could get proper treatment by a dentist. You will find, as you continue your healing work that gratitude for your help is not always expressed, however.

This is an unfortunate characteristic of human nature. Any doctor will confirm it. A person may go to a doctor complaining of great pain and suffering, but when this has been relieved and he or she feels well again, the chances are the doctor will never hear of it. The patient may even complain about the doctor's bill. Don't expect too much gratitude from those you heal. The ones who acknowledge your successful effort and express their thanks are exceptional and, unfortunately, in the minority. Here is a report on the relief of tooth pain which bears this out. The healer is again Frances Miller, who this time did not get much thanks. The sufferer is identified only as "a neighbor" in Plainfield, Connecticut.

Here is a typical example of the type of reaction you usually get. A neighbor of ours who visits us frequently enough to consider herself "a permanent fixture around the place" (her words) could not help but be aware of our Seventh Sense activities. She scoffed and laughed at first, then began asking for help but would never admit her improvement was due to any action on my part. At 9 o'clock one Sunday morning she called and said she had a terrible toothache, could not get a dentist appointment and needed help badly. "If you can do anything to help me, I'll never doubt your ability again," she said. I explained that I was busy at the moment but would get to work to help her by 11 o'clock. At that time I had a chance to be alone and performed the same mental operation on her that I had performed on my husband a month earlier (described in the previous report). Immediately after performing this psychic operation, I left my bedroom and walked down the hall toward the kitchen. As I went through the kitchen door the telephone rang. The first words I heard were "Did you just work on me?" She said that but a minute or two before, the pain had left her tooth all of a sudden after throbbing for hours—but she never even said "thank you," and from that day to this, three months later, has never thanked me or given me an ounce of credit. We have had many such cases.

People like this should not bother you. If you are successful in healing them, this in itself will provide you with a sense of accomplishment, and you will have the additional satisfaction of knowing that the world is just a little better because of your action. Every contribution to individual good is also a contribution to the general good.

If your mental examination of an aching tooth should disclose an accompanying infection, take immediate action to clear this up. Mentally wash out the infected area with a spray of white healing energy, making sure that all infected and deteriorated tissue is removed. Then pack the root of the tooth and the surrounding gum area with blue soothing, pain-removing energy. Lower the temperature of this blue energy pack until you can see that all inflammation has disappeared. Then once more, spray with white healing energy and terminate the contact. As a rule, this one treatment will do the job. Check again six hours later, or earlier if pain persists, and repeat the treatment if you observe it is necessary.

Here it might be well to include a report on self-healing of tooth pain. From our records, it appears that the need for self-healing of tooth problems has occurred fairly often, so here is a characteristic report. The healer is Althena Daly, a registered nurse living in Totowa Borough, New Jersey.

> I guess it was my own fault. I hadn't been near a dentist in nearly three years when around Christmas I noticed a little sensitivity in the right upper and lower molar areas. At first I passed this off, but when on January 4 I bit into some hard candy I knew I was in trouble. The pain nearly took my head off. I took extra aspirin and went to bed. The pain eased somewhat, but when it came back twice as strong on Monday, I called the dentist and made an appointment for the following Friday, the soonest he could take me.
>
> The aches continued and got worse, so when I couldn't sleep I decided to try to heal myself. I relaxed as well as I could and after three deep breaths I turned my mind inward and literally poured white healing energy into all the teeth on the right side of my mouth. After filling the cavities with it I then poured in green energy for rejuvenation of the affected tissues and raised my vibratory rate by fifty percent to speed up the healing.
>
> Voila! The aches stopped then and never came back. When I did get to the dentist I felt a little sheepish because I had no pain. I started to explain to him that I might have imagined the whole thing, but after examining me he said, "No, this is no imaginary problem. You have big cavities in upper and lower right side molars." He put medication in one tooth and filled the other. It is now February 3 and there are no more toothaches.

Nearly all tooth pain can be traced to either exposed tooth nerves, nerves under pressure or tooth abscesses. There are many other causes which will be reviewed briefly. One of the commonest of these is periodontitis or pyorrhea. This is inflammation and deterioration of the tissue surrounding the tooth near the surface of the gums, which can result in loosened teeth as well as eventual pain.

HEALING PYORRHEA

Pyorrhea can usually be checked and often healed by the following Medipic treatment.

1. Wash out the entire gum line area, upper and lower, with a spray of white healing energy.

2. After all germ-infected and deteriorated tissue has been removed, pack green tissue-building energy in a paste around each tooth. Be sure each tooth is treated separately and thoroughly in this way.

3. Flood the mouth with white healing energy and instruct the subject's Inner Mind to repeat this treatment every six hours until it is no longer necessary.

Less common than pyorrhea are thrush, various forms of stomatitis and neoplasms resulting from infections of one kind or another. All of these can usually be cleared up by employing the Medipic treatment for correcting pyorrhea. Special attention should always be given to the first step of this treatment, the washing away of all infectious particles by employing a mental spray of white healing energy.

CORRECTING SPINAL PROBLEMS

A common ailment, and one which you will encounter fairly often in people over 50, is back pain. The cause can vary all the way from a simple cold-induced muscular spasm to a broken or misplaced spinal disc. It is in situations involving back pain and allied discomforts that your ability to look psychically into the subject becomes invaluable. You can thus put all speculation aside, go directly to the true cause and correct it. The importance of this is vividly illustrated in the case history here reported by Ben Bibb. Ben is the healer and the subject was Mrs. Vera Gatto, 62, of Paterson, New Jersey. Here is Ben's report.

One night when I was visting Don Yott's home in New Jersey, Vera Gatto's son, Jim, brought her to me for help. She had been suffering from severe back and leg pains off and on for years. Recently they had become so bad she was unable to sleep for over two or three hours without waking from pain. Even sitting in one position in a chair for more than a few minutes brought increased pain.

As she stood there before me, I passed my left hand slowly along her back, some two or three inches out from the skin and concentrated upon the tiny sensations induced into the feeling nerves of the palm of my hand. As I did this I detected a "dull" spot just to the right of her spine, two vertebrae below the curvature of the small of her back. So I examined this area mentally and found a pinched nerve caused by a protruding spinal disc. Since she was right there before me, I decided to use manually transferred energy. I bunched the fingertips of my right hand and gathering energy from the inexhaustible supply around us, I transmitted a stream of this energy into this weakened area. At the same time I visualized that stream of intelligent energy soothing the pinched nerves and moving the disc back into place.

After six or seven minutes of this treatment, Vera said quietly that the pain was gone. I continued sending this healing energy for another minute or so and then stopped. Mrs. Gatto sat down and expressed her gratitude, but she wondered aloud if the relief was just temporary. I told her the force of the energy would continue to develop for another hour or so and that she would certainly have a pain-free night.

Three weeks later when I was again in New Jersey, Mrs. Gatto and Jim came to see me. Both were emphatic in telling me that Vera Gatto had no pain at all since my treatment of her. Her back and legs were fine. At this time, eight weeks later, there still has been no recurrence of pain.

Since Ben Bibb commands a great deal of energy, it was quicker and simpler for him to cure the woman who stood before him by direct application of the energy under his control than by instructing her Inner Mind to assume this task with the energy under her own control. As has been pointed out, when you first start your healing work the best results will be obtained by the Medipic method of showing the subject's Inner Mind what has to be done and telling It to go ahead and do it. As you proceed in your healing work and develop greater skill, you will find your control of energy improving, so there may come a time when you, too, can heal by the direct application of energy, as Ben Bibb did in the foregoing example.

Because the spinal structure is completely encased within the body and surrounded by nerves, tissue and blood vessels, it can be healed or corrected just as easily as a faulty kidney or any other inner organ. The powerful Inner Mind, which created the physical body from a single cell and keeps it alive and functioning, can also heal any imperfection that may develop. It does not always recognize these malfunctions and occasionally is at a loss as to the best method of correcting them. It is in such situations that you, as a healer, can function most effectively by pointing out to the subject's Inner Mind just what is wrong and what should be done to correct it.

Nearly everyone has suffered a pain in the back at one time or another. Usually this is musculature resulting from an injury or caused by undue strain in twisting or lifting. These situations can be corrected fairly quickly and easily by applying the Medipic techniques described in Chapter 2. If the cause of the pain is in the bones themselves, a special treatment is recommended for each different problem.

In all cases of spinal damage or breakdown, the pain is induced by pressure upon nerves in, or adjacent to, the spinal column. This may occur at any point, or points, in the spine between the neck at its top and the sacral center at its base. Most often you will find the cause to be damage suffered in an accident, either recent or remote, or inflicted by overexertion such as lifting too great a weight. The cause could also be what is called medically fibromyositis, a tenderness, pain and stiffness of joints, muscles and adjacent structures which is in turn induced by either infection, poison, damage or by exposure to damp or cold. If fibromyositis strikes the back it is called "lumbago;" if the shoulders, "pleurodynia," and the thighs, "charley horse." Each of these ailments may be cured by the Medipic method of packing the affected area with blue soothing pain-relieving paste and covering it mentally with white healing energy until the pain subsides. If the pain should recur, look further.

When a subject seeking help is suffering from pain in the lower lumbar or sacroiliac region of the back, look first for signs of injury or structural inadequacy. These are the most frequent causes. Upon examination, you may find some abnormality of a vertebra or of a disc between vertebrae. If the cause of pain lies in the bone structure, you will usually find a damaged disc at fault. Almost always this will be the result of some sort of accident. You can correct this by 'rebuilding' the disc as described in the following healing report. The healer is the Rev. Martin Grissom of Plainfield, Connecticut and the subject was Lee Blanshine, also of Plainfield. Here first is the Rev. Grissom's report. Following it is a letter from Mrs. Paula Blanshine, wife of Lee Blanshine, in which she expresses her thanks to Martin Grissom.

Paula Blanshine had told her husband's boss that Lee was in great pain, flat on his back with a ruptured disc in the lower back. The boss called

me and gave me the particulars; Lee Blanshine's name, age, address and the doctor's diagnosis. When I went to work on this case and mentally reached the subject, I could see the injury clearly. The disc was indeed cracked so I used a mental gold glue to mend the rupture, used my mental hands to press the parts together and to pick out some calcium deposits, and then squirted some penetrating warm oil into the area. I followed this by bathing the disc and its environs with strong white-gold healing energy for about fifteen minutes. The following day I repeated the treatment, followed by another fifteen minutes of white-gold healing energy. Over the next two days I went back twice more with the same Medipic treatment and energy shots at which time I felt the healing to be satisfactorily accomplished.

It was some time (about three weeks) before I heard from the Blanshines but then I got the following letter from Paula. Here is the letter.

"This letter is a bit overdue" writes Mrs. Blanshine, "and I am ashamed for not writing sooner.

"My husband, Lee, and I want to thank you for the time and work you put into the healing of his back. When we first learned he had suffered a ruptured disc, neither of us could accept it in spite of the fact that Lee was in such great pain. Even following the doctor's advice to stay in bed, and with all the pain killers, he was still miserable, but after I called you and you worked on him, the pain all disappeared within a few days—four or five—and has not returned. He is now back at work and although his job requires a lot of heavy lifting and crawling into small places, his back is still OK and has not acted up again.

"We think that what you do is wonderful and hope and pray that many people can learn about it and experience it just as we did."

Sincerely, Paula Blanshine"

Upon occasion your examination of a subject suffering "back pain" will disclose the cause to be a structural inadequacy or malformation which may have existed from the time of birth. This, as in a case of a ruptured disc, also calls for a Medipic repair effort on your part. Sometimes you may even find yourself able to help a person with a deformity considered incurable by medical or surgical means. The following case history is a practical example. The healer is Ben Bibb and the subject was Mrs. Bernadette Salvidio of Worcester, Massachusetts. Mrs. Salvidio's statement of her problem and its cure is given first and is followed by Ben Bibb's report of the Medipic method he used in healing her back. Here is Mrs. Salvidio's letter.

I had a rare, inoperable spinal condition which caused unbelievable pain and limited my every action. This had come on me suddenly eight years before when I tried to lift a heavy case onto the tailgate of a station wagon. For six of those eight years, the cause of the pain went undetected, but I finally had a myelogram done which showed that I had a rare inoperable condition. I was told that "nothing could be done" and that I wouldn't find a doctor in the country that would touch it.

Meanwhile I was in excruciating pain part of every day, particularly upon rising (or attempting to get up) in the morning. In addition to the ache, I felt as if I were carrying a 25-pound bowling ball at the base of my spine. Each night I dreaded going to bed because I knew if the pain woke me up I would be unable to move or lift my head from the pillow. In the morning it usually took me the better part of an hour to get out of bed and another hour or so before I could get to the kitchen for breakfast. I'd slide out of bed ending up on my knees on the floor and then crawl around to get the blood circulating so that I could finally pull myself up onto my feet.

Once I got going things weren't that bad. I wasn't able to do anything but the lightest housework and I could only go upstairs one step at a time. When I went to the store, about fifteen minutes was the longest time I could stand on my feet before I had to sit down. About a year before I contacted Ben Bibb, the doctors at Massachusetts General Hospital in Boston gave me some hope. They thought an operation might be possible, but when they took their own myelogram (four hours of agony) they said, "Impossible. You don't have a normal back." They sent me home after two weeks and told me to get rid of my children and hire a full-time housekeeper. Great, but how?

So my condition continued and got a little worse each week until last Christmas. We saw Ben Bibb on television and when I telephoned, wonder of wonders, I got him on the phone. It was a little after 9 a.m. the morning after I saw him on TV and I spoke to him personally. When I described my condition, Mr. Bibb said he would do what he could to help me, but that it would take a while since I had this condition so long (I was born with it). I was to call him in a week and let him know how I felt. When I called back I was disappointed to have to say I felt no better. On the following Tuesday, January 7, when I woke up, however, the left side of my back was entirely free from pain. I felt like I was cut in half; no pain on one side, severe pain on the other. When I woke up the next morning, January 8, I was entirely free from pain, but I still had that heavy, tired feeling. This continued for about a month but on February 17, just fifty-three days after my first conversation with Ben Bibb, I found I was entirely free of all pain and discomfort.

It is now the end of August and I haven't had a pain or an ache since that day. I can walk up or down a whole flight of stairs, work, bowl, play tennis and yesterday I even played baseball with the kids and got two hits. There's no more pain in my back. I am and always will be eternally grateful to Ben Bibb for healing my back, which all doctors had given up on, and making life worth living once again.

Bernadette's report is rather lengthy but it is included here in its entirety because it gives some idea of how frustrating such a back condition can be, and what joyful relief accompanies its cure. Here now is Ben Bibb's report on what he did to correct Mrs. Salvidio's spinal problem.

After Bernadette Salvidio's telephone call, I made mental contact with her and saw a pouch bulging out of the right side of her spinal column just above the sacrum, where the lowest lumbar vertebra joins the sacrum. There was an incompletely formed spinal process bone on that side of the vertebrae, obviously a birth defect, and this allowed the pouch to bulge out.

I first surrounded her mentally with a heavy white auric cloud of energy and used that energy to mentally project into the area to relieve pain and provide an incentive for healing. Then, in my creative imagination, I produced a putty-like substance and some tape, which I have called "people putty" and "people tape." I carefully wrapped the pouch with the tape, pulled it back into the spinal column and anchored it in place. Then with the putty "bone builder," I moulded a facsimile proper to the requirement and glued it into place, closing the opening which had allowed the bulge to appear. I then directed a heavy flow of energy into the area to solidify the structure which now appeared normal.

I then gave mental instruction to her Inner Mind, firmly telling It that It must not forget to continue this healing and rebuilding process that had been demonstrated to It. To make certain It would not forget, I told It that every time Bernadette thought about her back pains or worried about them, It would be reminded to renew Its efforts in completing the healing and rebuilding.

Ben Bibb is a great healer and commands a great deal of energy, yet it took fifty-three days to completely correct this woman's birth defect. He achieved a signal step forward when he was able to relieve most of the pain involved within thirteen days, but it was his firm instruction to Mrs. Salvidio's Inner Mind that effected the final and complete cure. In other words, she did it herself after being shown what to do and how to do it. Bear this in mind. Even the most difficult ailments will eventually give way if you show the patient's Inner Mind how to handle the situation and instruct It firmly to keep working at it until the complete healing is accomplished.

Nearly everyone over 40 experiences back pain at one time or another. Frequently this may be identified as *spinal osteoarthritis,* which means arthritis of the spine. This should be handled like any other arthritis attack, namely, by removing the calcium deposits mentally with an emery board and then lubricating the entire affected area with warm green healing energy.

There is also *osteomyelitis* to be considered. This is a fairly rare type of bone infection by microorganisms. It can be successfully treated by mentally disinfecting the bone marrow, first where the infection is localized and then later throughout the entire system. This cleansing treatment should be followed by an internal bath of white energy to replace and re-energize the bone interiors.

There are even more rare diseases like *tuberculosis* of the bones and joints, and *bone tumors.* The tumors should be mentally removed by hand as you would internal growths in any other part of the body. The tubercular action is almost entirely confined to the hip or knee joints and may be corrected by Medipic washouts and subsequent bathing in warm healing oil, green or white as your intuition suggests.

Some of the most painful spinal problems are the result of accidents. As a rule, you will not hear of these immediately because in almost every such case, the victim will be taken to a hospital for treatment. Once in a while the sufferer will ask you for help shortly after the damage occurs, in which case the following Medipic procedure should be employed.

Sometimes the Medipic procedure becomes clearer and easier to follow if an actual healing is described. The report given here is on a spinal repair case. The healer is Kathy Strong of Lake Worth, Florida and the subject was Susan Pine, 23, of San Jose, California. At the time of the healing Kathy was in Florida and Susan was in California. Here is Kathy's report which has also been signed and vouched for by Susan Pine.

Early one morning last summer, Susan woke me about 5:30 a.m. calling from California. She said she had been "fooling around" at the pool that afternoon and one of the boys had "cracked her back." It didn't bother her much until after dinner but then it got steadily worse until she could hardly stand the pain. She didn't know of any doctor to call in the middle of the night and had no way to get to the hospital, so remembering my work with Seventh Sense she called to ask my help. I told her to relax as best she could and think of pleasant things and I would try to help her.

I sat down, took a couple of deep breaths and relaxed. As soon as I reached Susan mentally, I ran a blue light and then a white light up and

MEDIPIC FOR HEALING
SPINAL DAMAGE

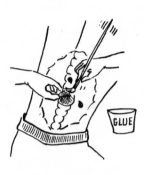

1. Examine the painful area and mentally determine the extent of the damage and just where it has occurred.

2. If you observe it to be a damaged vertebra or a cracked disc, fit the broken parts together and glue them in place. Mentally employ a good strong glue. Your purpose is to convey an idea.

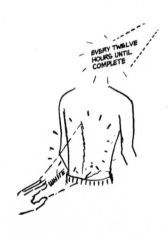

3. Hold the broken parts together with your mental fingers until the glue has set, usually three or four minutes, then bathe the injured part and the surrounding area with blue soothing, pain-relieving energy.

4. Finally, bathe the bones and adjacent muscles, nerves and tissues with white healing energy and tell the subject's Inner Mind to repeat the process every twelve hours until the healing is complete.

down her spine for about an hour. To me the white light is symbolic of healing energy and the blue the easing of tension and pain. I hoped that this would ease the pain so she could sleep. Then I took a mental look at her back to try to find the real problem. I found a bone connected to the spine that was cracked. So I took glue, applied it to the crack and pushed the bone together with my mental fingers. Then I wiped off the excess glue and put a small vise on the bone to hold it together until the glue dried.

It was then that I saw the cracked bone was slightly out of place, so I mentally popped it back into place with my fingers. It looked then like it was going to stay in place, so I didn't do anything more about it. I continued to visualize the white and blue energies up and down the spine until the glue dried. Then I took off the mental vise and instructed the white and blue energies to continue to heal and soothe the spine until they were no longer needed.

On the third day Susan called me to tell me she was back at work and feeling fine. On the night she called she finally got to sleep. Her back didn't hurt as much but it still bothered her until about noon the next day. She went to a doctor that afternoon and after taking some X-rays he said there didn't seem to be anything wrong and gave her no treatment. Everything did happen as stated.

Kathy Strong, Susan Pine.

The report in our files has both signatures on it as indicated.

15. How to psychically analyze and correct vein, artery and blood problems

Veins and arteries are subject to damage through accident or internal inducement. There are also many afflictions which attack the blood stream and its vehicles, the veins and arteries. These range from anemia, blood poisoning, hemorrhaging and leukemia to Hodgkin's disease. All can be healed by Medipic treatments, as the case histories in our files demonstrate.

One of the most feared blood disorders is the formation of a blood clot. There is always the danger that it may move and find its way to the heart or some other vital organ and block off the flow of blood at that point. This can be corrected by Televisual healing, as the following case history proves.

HOW TO ELIMINATE A BLOOD CLOT

The healer in this case is Mrs. Yolande Scott of Lake Worth, Florida and the subject was Marie Palmer also of Lake Worth. Here is Mrs. Scott's report.

> Marie Palmer came to see me at my home and told me she was greatly worried. Her left leg had been paining her and had blue marks on it. Her doctor said she had a blood clot there which would have to be dissolved or surgically removed, and she was frightened. I said I would do what I could to help her.
>
> While she was there, I examined her psychically and could see the blood clot quite plainly in her left leg above the knee. I mentally dissolved the clot by rubbing it in my fingers until it disappeared. I sent white and gold energy into the leg to make sure there was no infection where the clot had

been and to free up the flow of blood throughout the entire area. Then I told Marie to go to the doctor as soon as possible and have the leg rechecked. I felt the blood clot was gone, but I wanted her to be reassured.

She was able to see the doctor the very next day and he found that everything was fine. There was no evidence of the clot. He was surprised, but said, "You are a very lucky girl. You had a blood clot in that leg, but it just popped out and dissolved by itself." Marie says she thanked him, but didn't tell him what I had done.

In this case the healer, Yolande Scott, chose to illustrate the removal of the blood clot to the Inner Mind of the subject by mentally rubbing the clot between her fingers until it liquified and disappeared. Some healers would choose to pluck it out with their fingers, and still others to dissolve it with white healing energy. The type of visualization used does not matter as long as the Inner Mind of the subject understands what has to be done and is given the necessary impetus (or energy) to do it.

Throughout this book, the method of cure is frequently illustrated by describing a healing performed by one of the Seventh Sense workers. It is believed that a method of correction or cure is more vividly portrayed by the account of an actual healing than by a general instruction in what you might do. In line with this thinking, here is the report of a case of poison ivy that was cleared up by a Seventh Sense healer. The healer is Joyce Dix of West Palm Beach; the subject, her son, Frank, 19. Here is her report.

CLEARING UP A POISON IVY RASH

While at our summer place in Black Mountain, North Carolina, my son Frank got a bad case of poison ivy on both his arms and legs. When he asked me to get rid of it for him, I told him first to relax. I sat down next to him and took several deep breaths until I, too, was fully relaxed. I then placed the bunched up thumb and first two fingers of my right hand on the irritated portion of his arm and held it there for several minutes while I had my left hand outstretched with the palm up. I visualized white light pouring into my left palm and out my right hand onto Frank's arm causing the inflammation there to disappear beneath its brilliance. Then I put my right hand palm down directly over the affected area and felt hot energy flowing from my hand into it. I held my hand there until it became cool.

Then I went to his leg and ankle and repeated the same process. When I finished I broke contact and gave it no further thought because I was confident the healing had been accomplished. The next morning Frank's skin was its normal summer tan and all trace of the ivy poisoning was gone.

Here you see a different method. Joyce Dix is a very competent healer who often uses the Televisual instruction to the Inner Mind with great success. Here her instincts guided her to apply healing energy directly to the affected areas; this did the job thoroughly and quickly. Her son, Frank, was right there with her and, of course, this made a direct transfer of energy easier and more complete. To repeat, each person is different and thus each situation you encounter will have shades of difference from every other. It is always wise to pause and think a bit after you have mentally examined the subject and discovered the cause of the problem. In most cases the best healing technique will then appear quite obvious to you.

Several successful healers always use the direct application of energy. One of these is Glenn Whitten of Statesville, North Carolina. He says that it is the only way he can work. This is not important, as it is the results that count. Here he describes the correction of varicose veins and the elimination of the long-standing discomfort which accompanied them.

CORRECTING VARICOSE VEINS

Here are two case histories, each of which recounts the correction of varicose veins by a different method. In the first, the healer is Glenn Whitten of Statesville, North Carolina. The subject was a relative of his, Olive I. Whitten, 57, of Huntingburg, Indiana. Here is Glenn's report.

> For a long time, a relative of mine, Olive Whitten, has had a bad time getting a decent night's sleep. She has had varicose veins in both legs for several years and at night they would cramp up and become very painful. When I visited her recently and saw how badly she felt, I decided I would try to help her. The night after I saw her, I made a very good contact with the Universal Mind. The first time I ever had a breakthrough into a successful healing was at a Seventh Sense meeting in West Palm Beach about a year ago. Ever since then, the method I then employed has been the natural way for me to work. It is to be very quiet and relax until there is a deep sense of knowing I am in direct contact with the Universal Mind. The next thing that happens is always the same—I see my etheric self out in space. There is always a misty white ball of energy there which I take in my left hand. I can see and sense the energy pulsating as it rests in my hand. As this happened in the case of Olive Whitten, I mentally let the energy flow from my left hand, through me, out my right hand and into her legs and up her spine. All this time I was talking to the Universal Mind, telling It what I wanted It to do.

I repeated this treatment several times and after a few days I called to see how she was feeling. I was most happy to learn she had been sleeping the night through with no more cramps or charley horses. As is my custom, I always thank the Creator for what He does through me.

In response to an inquiry, Olive Whitten wrote as follows:

My name is Olive I. Whitten. I am the relative Glenn Whitten wrote you about. I want the whole world to know the terrible misery I suffered until Glenn visited us last year.

I am 57 years old and have had terrible burning and drawing leg cramps mostly at night due to my varicose veins, I guess. Over the years I have taken quite a bit of medication to ease this and arthritic pain that occasionally strikes, but the relief was only temporary. There has been such a change in me since Glenn's visit. The night after he left the cramps and leg pains let up and I can now get a decent night's sleep. They have not returned, and I also feel better all over. If this is an example of what Seventh Sense is all about, I'm for it.

The second case history here included is from Pauline Shaffer of Palm Beach Gardens, and the subject was Mrs. L.V., of Williamsport, Pennsylvania. This healing of a bad varicose vein and attendant discomfort took almost two years. The difference in the time from Glenn Whitten's healing is due to two factors; the age of the elder Mrs. S., mother-in-law of the healer (she was 83), and the fact that Olive Whitten's healing was a direct energy transfer. Whenever the healer and subject are together in the same room, a direct energy transfer, if possible, will achieve the desired result far more quickly than the Televisual method. The Medipic or Televisual healing method depends largely upon the sufferer healing himself and, for the most part, using his or her own energy to accomplish this. Obviously, a woman of 83 has less energy to allocate to a special healing, which as a consequence will take that much longer.

Here then is Mrs. Shaffer's report of the healing of her mother-in-law, Mrs. L.V.S.

While visiting my home town of Williamsport, Pennsylvania, a couple of years ago, my mother-in-law asked me to try to ease the pain and stiffness in her legs. While I was with her I mentally applied a turquoise light to ease the pain. The next day she said she felt better, but I was not satisfied. After returning home I examined her mentally and discerned that a very prominent varicose vein which she had had for fifty years—from the time of the birth of one of her children—was causing most of the trouble. I set about to correct this as well as easing the pain.

I gently massaged and smoothed the large vein with my mental fingers until it began to soften and shrink, and repeated the process about once each month thereafter. Each time I applied turquoise light to ease the pain and relax the muscles, and closed each session by flooding and massaging her legs with white healing energy lotion.

Her letters mentioned from time to time that her legs felt better, but it was not until this summer, some two years after the first treatment, that she informed me that the bad vein and all the accompanying pain had completely disappeared. She still has some stiffness in her knees, but that is not unusual in someone of her age.

Varicose veins are fairly common. They give little trouble to most people, but when they become become unduly enlarged and pain and discomfort ensue, they must be corrected. The foregoing illustrates two ways in which this may be done.

Accidents which affect the veins and arteries are fairly common. In most cases the damage done can be corrected quickly by Medipic methods; however, it does not often happen that a Seventh Sense healer is present or readily available when such an accident occurs. Most of the case histories on file for cuts and other arterial damage are records of self-healing. Here is one such report. The healer and subject is Daniel Sweet of Plainfield, Connecticut. His report is verified by his wife, Rosalie Sweet.

One morning recently, I went to open a can of milk. When I reached for the can opener, I picked it up with my right hand and squeezed it shut with my left. This cut a nice v-shaped piece of flesh out of the palm of my right hand. It was bleeding a lot, so I immediately pressed both sides of the cut together and held them that way with the fingers of my left hand. Closing my eyes I concentrated on the wound and shut everything else out of my mind. I forced white healing energy into it from my mind and mentally saw it healing very rapidly.

The pain gradually went away, and when a few minutes later the pain was all gone, I took my fingers off the wound and opened my eyes. The cut was no longer there. It was entirely healed; only a red spot remained the next morning that too had disappeared and the palm of my hand appeared normal. My wife saw all this and can verify it.

Anemia. The commonest form of anemia, a condition in which the red blood count is deficient, is that due to excessive blood loss usually caused by a single massive hemorrhage. Infrequently you may find the hemorrhaging to be chronic in character. In both cases your first healing objective should be to stop the loss of blood. The hemorrhage may be external and therefore obvious, but it may be hidden somewhere within the organism. In this case, examine the subject psychically in order to locate the point of internal bleeding.

There are many Televisual methods that you may employ. Probably the simplest is to mentally tie off the bleeding artery. Sometimes, if there are several blood vessels involved, a mental picture of shutting off the blood flow with a towel will prove effective. In any case, be sure to stanch the flow of blood before proceeding to the next step—healing. If an artery is severed, mentally connect the open ends and either glue them together, or bind them up with "people tape." If the blood is seeping through an intestinal wall or from a stomach ulcer, seal off the leak with people tape. In both cases, follow with a flow of white healing energy.

Anemia could have other causes. You can determine the exact one by your psychic examination. You may find that the low red blood count is due to a deficiency of red cell production, or to excessive red cell destruction. Both of these can usually be traced to improper glandular balance. The method of healing these problems can be found in Chapter 16 where hormone activity and glandular balance are described.

HOW TO HEAL LEUKEMIA

It is generally believed that while leukemia may be temporarily arrested, it always returns and usually the patient develops resistance to therapy after the relapse. When the cause is corrected, and not merely ameliorated, however, a cure can be effected. In most cases the cause of leukemia lies in an overproduction of white cells in the bone marrow of the long bones (legs, arms, etc.), but sometimes it may be caused by an overzealous activity of the cannibal section of the spleen, which under normal conditions destroys only those red cells which can no longer carry oxygen. In some rare situations it may be due to both, namely, an overproduction of white cells coupled with the destruction of healthy red cells.

If your mental examination of the subject reveals an overproduction of white blood cells at the expense of red cell production, your course is clear. Here is a Medipic treatment that may be employed to effect a cure of the resulting leukemia.

MEDIPIC HEALING TREATMENT FOR LEUKEMIA

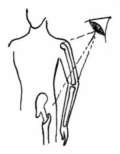

1. Mentall examine the subject. If you observe an overproduction of white cells proceed to step 2.

2. Concentrate on the long bones in the legs, arms and pelvis, sending energy from your mental hands into them with the instruction to cut the white blood cell production back to normal.

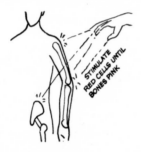

3. While still concentrating on the marrow in the long bones, send energy from your fingers into the red blood cell producing areas to stimulate them and bring them back up to the normal red cell output. Continue to pour this energy into the marrow at the ends of the bones until you observe that it is once again a healthy pink.

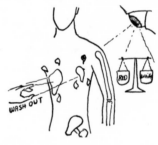

4. When you can see that the white and red blood cell productions are in normal balance, proceed to wash the bone marrow out of the liver, spleen and lymph nodes where its accumulation has created the leukemia symptoms. This is important.

5. Bathe the entire system with white healing energy and follow this with a flow of blue soothing, calming energy before ending the contact.

There are several types of leukemia, but the damage to the system is caused in all cases by the overproduction of white blood cells and the underproduction of red blood cells or their premature destruction. In all situations normal balance must first be attained and then the system cleared of the accumulated debris. The foregoing Medipic healing technique will accomplish this in almost all cases.

A case history of a leukemia healing may help to clarify this. The one that follows was performed by Ben Bibb. The subject was Roscoe Burton of Danielson, Connecticut. Here first is Ben Bibb's report. It is followed by a letter from Mrs. Burton expressing her gratitude.

> Roscoe Burton was suffering from leukemia. For many months he had been receiving a "packed" transfusion every two weeks. A "packed" transfusion is one in which a large quantity of red blood cells is strained out of other blood and placed in a pint of regular blood for the transfusion. When I was asked to help him and mentally contacted him, my examination disclosed heavy overproduction of white blood corpuscles at the expense of red corpuscle production. Using energy from my mental fingertips, I forced the white blood corpuscle producing marrow in the long bones back from the areas where it had overgrown into the red cell producing marrow. I mentally turned about one fourth of the marrow on each end of the long bones into a healthy-looking pink. Within three weeks, Roscoe's red blood count was normal and it has not varied from this now in over a year.

Here is Mrs. Burton's letter expressing her gratitude to Ben Bibb for his efforts in healing her husband.

> Ben, you have done wonders for Roscoe. His red blood is very good—normal, they say—and it has been for over a year now, ever since you worked on him. That day you worked on him was the last day he had a transfusion and his general health has improved steadily ever since. The doctors are truly amazed at how well he has gotten along—not only his own doctors but the other doctors at the hospital as well. They can't understand what they did to bring about such a change. But we know, don't we, Ben?
>
> May you and Margaret be richly blessed for the wonderful work you are doing. Thanks again.
>
> Marge Burton

Sickle Cell Anemia is one of many blood ailments. It occurs almost exclusively in black persons and is characterized by sickle-shaped red blood cells. These tend to create a semi-solid gel which makes it difficult for the red blood cells to pass through small arteries and at times will plug up vessels to create thrombosis or infarction. In such cases your first task is to free up the occluded areas and then to purify the blood through standard Televisual methods.

An increase in red blood cell concentration (but not in total mass) may result in vomiting or diarrhea. It occurs most frequently in men over middle age and is presumed to be caused by anxiety. This also occurs in long-time residents of high altitudes and may result in a heart attack. In such cases, bathe the patient in blue soothing energy and then balance the red-white blood cell production.

Polycythemia vera is the medical term used to describe a progressive increase in the red blood cell mass which may occur in men over fifty. It is usually characterized by headaches, dizziness, visual disturbances and lassitude. Here again the most effective treatment is to rebalance the long bone marrow output of the red and white blood cells and then give the subject a stimulation with white healing energy via Medipic.

Hemophilia is an abnormal tendency to bleed. It is usually an inherited characteristic but may have other causes as well. It can be corrected by Medipic methods by stimulating the blood to produce coagulants normal to the blood stream. Use red stimulating energy plus instruction, and follow with white healing energy.

Hodgkin's Disease symptoms are somewhat similar to those of leukemia, but the disease is far more serious. If not corrected, the rate of progression is rapid and usually is fatal before five years. It is characterized by an enlargement of the lymph nodes and sometimes of the spleen and liver. It occurs more often in men than in women, usually between ages twenty and forty. Medipic treatment may require a hormone balancing, but a "washout" of the lymph nodes plus a balancing of red and white blood cell production is suggested as the first step. In many cases this will achieve relief and accomplish a cure.

There are many other types of blood disorders but most of them you will seldom encounter. *Scurvy,* for example, is fairly rare today and when it does occur, you will find usually that it has been completely attended to before you hear of it. Large doses of vitamin C are normally prescribed by physicians once the ailment has been identified; this usually achieves the desired result.

Blood poisoning is usually the result of an infected open wound, but it may also result from contact with powerful chemicals such as household cleansers and disinfectants. To heal it, first mentally seek out the cause or focus of infection. If it is a wound, clean it out thoroughly and then mentally heal it. Follow the healing by cleaning out the blood with white healing energy via Medipic. If your examination should disclose an infection due to skin contact with damaging chemicals, mentally clear all traces of this poison from the blood by flooding it with white healing energy. After withdrawing from your mental contact, warn the subject verbally to avoid contact with that specific chemical in the future.

Diabetes is considered by some to be a blood disease and indeed, it is characterized by an excess of sugar in the bloodstream, but it is due primarily to glandular malfunction. Its analysis and correction are described in Chapter 16, where glandular imbalance and hormone problems are discussed.

16. New seventh sense glandular system balancing secrets for correcting diabetes and serious ailments of the thyroid and pancreas

A great many ailments result from improper glandular function. Our glands release tiny hormones into the bloodstream and these in turn stimulate our various internal organs to activity. However, these glands sometimes become overactive and at other times may become lazy or even inert. When any of these aberrations occur, the physical equipment reacts accordingly and protests in an unmistakable manner. One of the best known and most easily recognized reactions to glandular malfunction is *diabetes.* This ailment is usually regarded as a slowdown or failure to function on the part of the insulin-producing nodes on the pancreas called the Islets of Langerhans. It can sometimes be traced to the pituitary gland, in the head, which signals the Islets of Langerhans to release insulin into the bloodstream. The insulin acts as a control of the glucose (blood sugar) level in the bloodstream. As the blood sugar level becomes higher than normally required, the insulin causes a reaction in the liver which extracts the excess glucose and stores it (as glycogen) until needed.

Diabetes. A rather lengthy explanation is given here in order that you may understand and properly administer the Medipic treatment for the cure of *diabetes.* This treatment requires the balancing of the glands themselves in addition to the direct stimulation of the pancreas and its surface nodes to produce more insulin. The location of these glands is indicated in the two drawings in Chapter 1, which should be studied now, and in fact in all cases requiring hormone balancing and endocrine gland attention. Here is a very brief description of each of the important glands.

The *pituitary* gland hangs like a small berry in the center of the head approximately on a line drawn back from between the eyes. It is the master gland, signalling most of the action of the other endocrine glands by releasing hormones into the blood stream. It secretes the growth hormones, governs the action of the thyroid gland, and stimulates the production of insulin by the pancreas and the production of cortisone by the adrenals. It corrects stress changes in the body; it helps the hypothalamus and the kidneys to regulate the water content of the body, and it stimulates the production of egg and sperm cells in the reproductive glands. From this you can see that you should always stimulate and instruct the pituitary in concert with any other endocrine glands.

The *hypothalamus* is a sugar cube-sized gland from which the pituitary hangs. It is not a hormonal gland, but seems to be one of the connectors between the chemical and neural systems. It contains the so-called "pleasure center" and is involved in the control of the water metabolism in the body. It acts as the body's thermostat and internal temperature control, and produces fever when required. It contains the appestat, or appetite control, and the wake-sleep control.

The *thalamus* is slightly above and to the rear of the hypothalamus. It is not a hormonal gland but acts also as a connector between the systems. It is the reception center for touch, pain, heat and cold, and muscle sensations. Under emotion, it affects the facial muscles.

The *pineal* gland is to the rear of the thalamus in almost the exact center of the cranium, and is almost completely protected by bony structures. It emits no scientifically detectable hormones, yet it is important, being the most thoroughly protected gland in the body. It is non-automatic, but can stimulate the action of other glands (as does the pituitary) in response to the influence of spirit or soul impetus.

The *thyroid* gland is behind the Adam's apple; its butterfly shape is wrapped around the windpipe. When it becomes overactive it raises the metabolic rate (hyperthyroidism), which cause hot and sweaty feelings and a fast pulse, and may cause a bulging of the face and throat. If it is underactive it may slow body and brain growth, cause physical slowdown, swollen limbs and coldness, and create a tendency to anemia. One of its hormones may lower the calcium content of the blood.

The *parathyroid* glands are like little buttons imbedded in the thyroid, two to each side. If they are overactive they will draw calcium from the bones into the blood stream and precipitate phosphate through the kidneys and pancreas. If they are underactive, the lowered blood calcium can cause prolonged twitching of the muscles.

The *salivary* glands are not shown in the drawing. They are in the cavity above the roof of the mouth and underneath the tongue. They are not endocrine glands, but in addition to providing mucous membrane moisture, they begin digestion by enzyme action on starches.

The *thymus* gland is in the forewall of the chest, at about its center and above the heart area. In children this gland is quite large, but at adolescence it shrinks. It governs the actions of the lymph glands to fight infection.

The *adrenal* glands sit atop the kidneys. They produce adrenalin and noradrenalin, which affect the sympathetic nervous system. It releases other hormones to regulate the proportions of salt and water in the body and to control the carbohydrate, protein and fat metabolism. They produce cortisone, lack of which is found in arthritis. Underactive adrenal glands cause Addison's disease, low blood pressure and loss of body hair, and can affect skin pigmentation. Overactivity is associated with Cushing's disease, excessive hairiness and high blood pressure.

The *pancreas* is a combination endocrine and ducted gland which lies behind the stomach. The nodes on its surface, the Islets of Langerhans, produce insulin, the regulator of the sugar content of the blood. The pancreas itself produces gastric juices.

The *reproductive* glands, the ovaries or testes, are in the pelvic-pubic area. They produce estrogens and androgens (the female and male sex hormones) in both sexes. Their different balances in men and women provide the sexual characteristics. Derivatives have an effect on vitality as well as productivity.

The *lymph* glands are found throughout the body near major blood vessels. They include the tonsils. The lymph glands produce white blood cells to fight local infections. With the spleen, adrenals and pituitary, they provide hormones to reject transplants and cancer and provide valving stations to help the lymph fluid flow back upward to re-enter the bloodstream above the heart.

While they are not glands, the locations of three organs, the liver, spleen and kidneys are shown.

The *liver* is in the right front portion of the abdomen just below the ribs, and runs around the right side to the back. It produces bile for digestion and stores carbohydrates, fats, proteins and glycogen (stored glucose). It strains the blood to eliminate nitrogenous waste products, makes albumin and globulin for blood plasma, provides clotting and anti-clotting agents and stores vitamins.

The *spleen* is behind the stomach, partially under the ribs on the left side of the back. It produces part of the white blood cells, works with the lymph glands to fight infections and destroys exhausted red blood cells (those that can no longer retain oxygen).

The *kidneys* are on either side of the backbone just at and below the ribs. They strain the bloodstream to rid it of waste products and impurities, control the balance of salt and water in the body and maintain the alkalinity of body fluids.

A DIABETIC HEALING

The healer is Ben Bibb and the subject was Daniel Sweet of Plainfield, Connecticut. Danny Sweet bumped his elbow on Friday in the mill where he works. By Monday morning the elbow had a lump on it as big as an orange. When he arrived for work, he was sent immediately to the mill's doctor, who said he thought it was cellulitis. The doctor also checked for sugar in the urine; when the count showed +4, he sent Danny to the hospital. When Danny's wife was informed, she telephoned Ben Bibb to ask his help. Ben Bibb started to work on him Tuesday night and by Saturday the hospital tests showed both the urine and the blood to be completely sugar free, so he was released. The lump on the elbow remained longer, but finally disappeared the following Thursday. Here is Ben Bibb's report.

> When Mrs. Sweet called me Tuesday evening and told me the hospital tests showed Danny had diabetes, I went to work on him as soon as I could. When I made mind-to-mind contact with him in the hospital, I checked his bloodstream by feeling it between the tips of my thumb and forefinger. I found it to be sticky, which confirmed the hospital test results of glucose in the blood or diabetes. With this knowledge I then went to work.
>
> With my left hand, I mentally reached into his head from the right side and placed my forefinger tip on the pituitary gland. Tracing back and

upward with my middle fingertip, I found the hypothalamus gland, from which the pituitary hangs as if on a small stalk, and left that finger in place there. (The pituitary and hypothalamus glands are the master hormonal glands of the body.) The pituitary signals the Islets of Langerhans on the surface of the pancreas when to release insulin, and insulin controls the glucose level in the bloodstream. As the glucose level gets too high, the insulin injected into the bloodstream causes a reaction in the liver, which extracts the extra glucose, changes it to glycogen and stores it for further use if and when required. I then put the tip of my little finger on the pineal gland, which we believe is involved in non-automatic functions. My left thumb tip then found a natural resting place on the brain stem, that thick stalk of grey and white matter which connects the spinal cord with the brain. With my left hand fingers thus placed, I began a rhythmic pulsation of energy from my fingertips with the strong thought behind the pulsation to "normalize, balance and harmonize. Produce everything that you should in the proper amounts, with nothing extra and nothing left out."

My right hand then went back to the bloodstream, into an artery from the heart and, testing the blood texture again, found it still sticky. Then it went mentally to the pancreas, the elongated gland behind the stomach, and began slowly moving over it, feeling the small nodes in its surface (the Islets of Langerhans). I began pulsating energy through it, matching the pulsations being sent mentally by the left hand. After completely covering the gland twice, I again tested the bloodstream. It was not yet satisfactory. Then I sent my right hand mentally to the adrenal glands, situated above the kidneys, and pulsed energy into them with the same thought of harmony and balance. My right hand then went to the liver and moved mentally over it, slowly pulsing energy front to back and back to front. After this I again tested the bloodstream, and found it to be normal and no longer sticky.

Having established this, I withdrew my hands, examined the large lump on his elbow and decided that it was definitely an interior infection, probably viral, which had resisted cure because of the diabetic condition. I sent a heavy energy flow into the area, first blue-green to reduce the pain and then a pure golden white sunlight color to destroy the virus.

I then released him, feeling that the healing was accomplished.

You, as a healer, must bear in mind that the hormonal chemicals are very powerful. Every emission of a hormone must either be *used,* or if not used, must be *counterbalanced* by another and opposite hormone. A body unable to use the produced hormones, or unable to produce counterbalancing hormones, is in serious trouble. Therein lies the cause of many human physical ills.

This will probably become clearer if we discuss here a case of what is called "post-partum depression." As you know, when pregnancy occurs, the mother's endocrine (hormonal) system must peak up to supply the new life form within her, as well as to provide her own physical body with additional hormones to handle the new burden with which it is coping. This "peaking up" is a gradual thing which takes several months, and therefore the harmonizing and balancing system has no trouble in keeping the hormones evenly and properly supplied as required. At birth all this is changed in a matter of hours. The various endocrine glands must cease their abnormal production and retreat to the normal output for a single unencumbered body. The need for this sudden reversal comes as a shock to the entire system; the amazing thing is that most women adjust back to normal and overcome their depressed feelings in so short a time, usually not more than three or four days. Some do not, however, and therein lies a problem which frustrates the medical profession. You, as a Medipic healer, can solve this by mentally rebalancing the entire hormonal (endocrine) system and the organs it affects. Here is a case in point.

HEALING POST-PARTUM DEPRESSION

The healer is Ben Bibb and the subject is the daughter of Mrs. Mary L. Hester of Falls Church, Virginia. In December Ben Bibb received a telephone call from Mrs. Hester, who said that her daughter, 21, of Knoxville, Tennessee, had given birth to her first baby three months before and was suffering "post-partum" problems. She rejected the baby, her husband and her family. Her doctor had placed her under psychiatric care in the University of Tennessee Medical Facility, but after some treatment she left and refused to go back. Her husband and her mother were desperate and afraid they might have to have her committed. In desperation, Mrs. Hester turned to Ben Bibb for help, telling him that her daughter had secluded herself in her bedroom and was fast approaching a catatonic state.

Here is Ben Bibb's report. It will be followed by Mrs. Hester's letter of thanks.

Mrs. Mary Hester of Falls Church, Virginia telephoned me and told me that her daughter had given birth to her first child some three months before and gone into a post-partum depression which was getting steadily worse. While Mrs. Hester was still on the phone I made a quick mental contact with the daughter and discovered that her trouble was a complete hormonal imbalance which had created a chemical conflict in her system and was affecting her nerves, brain and emotional complex. I explained this to her mother and told her I would get to work on it as soon as I could, probably that night. I also told her not to worry because I was sure I could correct it.

When I made mental contact with the daughter, I found her in a confused and darkly depressed mental state, while physically she was taut but completely inactive. All of her endocrine glands were operating with a high but erratic output, while her bloodstream and cerebrospinal fluid were acidic with unused and conflicting hormones.

With this woman's mental image before me, I mentally placed my left forefinger on the right side of her head adjacent to her pituitary gland, my middle finger went up and to the rear of the pituitary and found the hypothalamus from which the pituitary stem comes. My ring finger rested on the thalamus gland, above and behind the hypothalamus, while my little finger went further back and found the pineal gland, a little-known but not-to-be-neglected gland in this situation. After my thumb was placed on the brain stem, the thick stalk above which the thalamus and hypothalamus glands are placed, I began a steady pulsation of energy through my finger tips and into the woman's brain. All this time I kept thinking "harmony, balance; produce exactly what you should—no more, no less," while my right hand mentally explored the bloodstream and the cerebral fluid and found their contents to be improper and overactive.

From there I mentally moved my right hand to the thyroid gland and the parathyroid glands embedded in it. With bunched fingertips passing along the surface of these glands, I sent a pulsing energy matching that being released by the left hand into the glands in the head, and the thought to "harmonize and balance." I went over this Medipic routine several times until a feeling of achievement came. Again I tested the blood and cerebrospinal fluid, but they were not quite right, so I sent my right hand, still pulsing with energy, to the pancreas and its surface nodes with the same general instructions to "harmonize and regulate." When a feeling of satisfaction came, I sent my right hand to stimulate and balance the ovaries in the same manner until a feeling of harmony came.

As a final precaution, I sent stimulating and balancing energy into all the other major internal organs, the liver, the kidneys, the spleen, the stomach and the heart. Upon completion I again tested the blood and the cerebrospinal fluid, and when all felt proper and normal, I withdrew.

I then wrote to her mother, Mrs. Hester, and told her that her daughter should be coming out of her post-partum depression in two or three days. On the third day her mother called me, very excited, and said that her daughter had awakened that morning and come out of her bedroom in a very puzzled state. She greeted her husband affectionately and contritely, saying that she couldn't understand what had been the matter with herself. She was very happy to see her baby and apparently was once again functioning in a normal manner.

A couple of months later, Mrs. Hester wrote the following letter of appreciation to Ben Bibb.

> **Dear Mr. Bibb,**
>
> I thought you would like to have a follow-up report on my daughter, whom you diagnosed and treated a couple of months ago. I have since then been beside myself with a sense of thanksgiving. All I can say is she is completely normal and stronger than before. She also has more energy and has become involved in outside activities in addition to caring for her home, baby and husband. She has become involved in bible study with a group of young and dynamic people and seems enthusiastic. She adores her baby and enjoys being a good mother. She apparently enjoys her marriage and is happy with her husband. I thank you very, very much.
>
> **Very sincerely, Mary L. Hester**

The technique to achieve or restore hormonal balance described in the two preceding case histories is the Medipic method taught by Ben Bibb in his classes. Every case is different, however, and some healers use different methods to achieve equally satisfactory results. One, for example, links all of the endocrine centers with a cord or ribbon and sends pulsations of energy along this ribbon until all are in harmony. Another mentally puts them into a pan of water and expands or inhibits the flow of energy to each gland until they all float evenly.

Sometimes you may encounter a case (like arthritis, for example) wherein you may effect a healing but still feel something to be wrong. Always look again and be sure to check the hormone balance because it may be the real cause of the affliction. Here is a case which illustrates this. The healer is Peg DeAmon of New Orleans, Louisiana, and the subject her mother, Cody Anderson, 57, of Houston, Texas. Mrs. Anderson had been troubled with arthritis of the spine since the age of 42, a matter of some fifteen years. This condition had grown progressively worse until the time came when she had to go into traction occasionally because the pain was so great. The doctors said the pain was caused by the deterioration of the spinal discs. In addition to the spinal pain, Mrs. Anderson had pains in both hands and a pain in the foot which she said felt like a "burning inside the bone." She had a hysterectomy in 1967, cataracts removed in 1971 and 1973, followed by high-dosage cortisone treatments which were finally withdrawn in 1974. In July 1975 her daughter, Mrs. Peg DeAmon, graduated from a Ben Bibb class in Hartford, Connecticut, and on her return to New Orleans decided to try to help her mother. Here now is Mrs. DeAmon's report of what she found, what she did, and the outcome.

My mother, Mrs. Cody Anderson, 57, had spinal arthritis for over fifteen years. In the last few years she had great pain, frequently to the point where she would have to be put in traction. When I graduated from Ben Bibb's Seventh Sense class, my first thought was to try to help her.

I played the Ben Bibb "Golden Hands" tape to start my meditation and almost immediately contacted her Inner Mind. I found much pain in many parts of the skeletal system, so I immediately put a turquoise pain-soothing aura around her entire body. Visualization was good; I could see much buildup of an off-white substance which appeared to be much like dry pie dough. We worked at cleaning each vertebra first, then we rebuilt the degenerated bone tissue by sculpting out new bones from what we call "sculpt-a-bone," which is light green in color, and replacing the worn-out bones where needed. The cleaning was done with a gold taffy-like pad and a can of golden "life dust," which was then vacuumed away.

The bones in the spine taken care of, we then proceeded to re-attach the damaged nerves. I say "we" because I follow suggestions which seem to come to me from a higher source. I always feel as if I have a "helper" right there, so I cannot take any personal credit. Next, to my surprise, the urge came to do a total hormone balancing. The duct from the pineal to the pituitary seemed closed, so it was forced open. No organ in the body was doing exactly what it was intended to do, so every organ had to be reassessed and its job redefined for it. It seemed as if the whole body had been closing down slowly. After the hormone balancing, we oiled all the joints with golden oil and received an affirmative from the Inner Mind that the healing had indeed taken place. Before leaving the body, we surrounded it with a turquoise aura to eliminate all pain, then a bright green aura for rejuvenation, and finally a gold aura for protection. Finally we gave her an order that whenever she heard a door shut, any door, the orders given to the Inner Mind would be recalled and repeated.

That treatment was given two months ago and my mother has had absolutely no pain in her back since then. She has not taken one pain pill in that time. The pain in her foot is still there, but is much relieved from what it was before I treated her. It is getting less and less painful as time goes on, as are the pains in her hands which now have almost complete flexibility of movement. The joints are shrinking week by week, and the big deposit of yellowish dry stuff that I could see in her foot with my mental vision has almost disappeared. She has no more pain in her back, for which she is joyfully grateful, and the aches in her hands and feet are gradually disappearing. Although she is in Houston and I am in New Orleans, she keeps me posted on her progress and feels certain that all her pain will be gone in a month or two.

Judging from the inspiration Peg DeAmon received to balance the hormone output in her mother's system, a project she had not even considered when starting her Medipic treatment, it seems likely that this hormone imbalance had existed for years and probably was the basic original cause of the deterioration of the spine and the arthritic pains in her mother's hands and feet. There is no way now to ascertain this for sure, but Mrs. Anderson has no more serious pain and appears to be on the way to a complete healing. It would thus seem wise for you as a healer to check on the hormone balance of a sufferer, particularly one over fifty years of age. You may find this to be the key to certain problems which are slow to respond to the more obvious healing treatments. Here is the case of a woman, fifty-seven years of age, who had been building up an arthritic spinal condition for over fifteen years, being relieved of all spinal pain within a matter of days. Unless treated by the actual physical presence of a healer who could command great energy, this condition might normally take three or four months via Medipic for a woman of 57 to correct. It seems obvious, therefore, that the hormone balance performed by the healer contributed greatly to the speed of her mother's recovery.

CORRECTING MENSTRUAL PROBLEMS

Many women have discomfort and pain at the time of their menstrual periods. Usually they accept this without question and do nothing about it except maybe take an aspirin to relieve the headache and cramps—but they need not suffer this way. These difficulties can be eliminated by bringing the endocrine system into balance via Medipic. Here is a case history which illustrates this. The healer is Robert A. Wisniewski of West Hartford, Connecticut. The subject is a friend of his identified only as Judy. This is his report.

> During the summer a year ago, I met a girl whom I will call Judy, while traveling from Hartford to New York City. We became good friends and, as she lived in New York City, I would visit her when I was in the area. As we got to know each other better, she told me that for years she had had a problem with her periods that required her to take additional hormones in pill form in order to complete her cycle.
>
> There is a standard Medipic procedure which deals with all the important endocrine glands, including the ovaries. It involves a chemical balancing achieved through control of hormone release. I decided to try to help Judy in this way, but when I contacted her for the first time she mentally pulled a black sheet over her head to break off the contact. When I tuned in again a night later, I covered her first with a pink sheet and laid her head on a pink pillow. Meeting then with no resistance, I proceeded. I

placed the fingers of my left hand on the pituitary, hypothalamus, thalamus and pineal glands, in that order, and my thumb on the brain stem. I then joined my right hand fingers to those on my left, with mental instructions to balance and harmonize, to release all the necessary hormones in the proper amounts and none that are not necessary. Leaving my left hand in place on her head, I led a white energy channel from her head with my right hand down to the ovaries and connected it there with instructions to balance and harmonize the required output of hormones. I left her in a pink aura, with the mental instruction to repeat the program at dancing class each day. I felt that her body's circulation would be really working well at those times.

About three weeks later I received a call from Judy telling me that for the first time in years she had gone through her period without taking pills. A month later, her period came and went in two days with absolutely no discomfort and it has been that way ever since.

The *salivary glands,* while not in the endocrine system, are vitally important to the digestive process. Any malfunction of these glands, or a reduction in their effectiveness, is therefore bound to result in a physical disturbance. Each time you are called upon to help a person with indigestion, particularly one who has trouble digesting milk, and wheat, oat or rye products, be sure to check the functioning of the salivary glands. This type of problem will often elude normal medical diagnosis as the following case history illustrates. You can locate the malfunction quite simply if you but examine the sufferer mentally via Medipic.

This case is reported by Fred P. Morrocco, Jr. of Bristol, Connecticut, who did the healing. It is accompanied by a letter from the subject, Ada Mason, 47, of New Britain, Connecticut, which describes her symptoms and the suffering she experienced. Here first is Ada Mason's letter.

I was admitted to New Britain General Hospital in October. "I had been suffering from diarrhea for about three weeks before going to the emergency room there. I had nothing by mouth for a few days and was put on IV solutions. In the hospital they performed a sigmoidoscopy, a proctoscopy, a biopsy of the colon, plus a BE (barium enema) upper GI and small bowel series. While there I had stomach cramps and some blood in the stools, but one day it just stopped. I felt well but weak, and was discharged with no diagnosis.

The same diarrhea, blood passage and weakness happened again in December and March and lasted about a week each time. When it came to me again in May I went back into the hospital, where they repeated all the tests of the past October except the sigmoidoscope and proctoscope. I stayed there one week, and was put on intravenous solutions for a couple of days. Again it cleared up by itself and I was discharged with no diagnosis.

My doctor then sent me to an allergist, but the best he could do was to tell me I am allergic to poppy seeds.

It started again in July, but this time not as bad after Freddie told me not to eat or drink any milk or bread products. I got through July pretty well, but it is now September. I have been feeling fine, but I am still apprehensive because it is almost two months since the last attack.

If Ada Mason's letter appears to contain certain professional-sounding references, it is because she is a medical secretary accustomed to using these terms. Here now is the report of the healer, Fred Morrocco, Jr. of Bristol, Connecticut.

On July 20 I became aware of Ada's condition from a friend of mine, who was quite concerned and asked if I would help her. I called Ada on the phone and asked if she wanted me to help her. She said she would welcome any help or relief of the condition, which had been troubling her for nearly two years. She related that for the past three weeks, everything she ate went into explosive bloody diarrhea and that she was getting weaker every day. Her doctor wanted to administer cortisone, but she refused. The last two days her tongue was swelling and she had trouble swallowing. She remarked that her diet was down to pudding and bread, that she had been in the hospital twice in the past year but there had been no diagnosis of her trouble.

I made contact with her Inner Mind and told It to accept what I proposed to do because it would be good for her. I went immediately to her digestive system to do a "washout." I made a beautiful solution of pure spring water (all mental), with aloe plant and a pure white flow of healing energy in it. I mentally had her drink it and told her to confine it in her stomach and abdomen to cure any disease or infected parts and prevent any further diarrhea. I raised her body vibration rate above normal and stimulated her adrenal glands to speed antibodies throughout her system. I then sent a flow of pure white healing energy through her whole body and then a beautiful bluish green flow to eliminate all pain and discomfort.

I then called Ben Bibb and told him about her case and what I was doing for her. He picked up on her statement that she was "living on pudding and bread." It was obvious to him she had an allergy to milk and gluten products and that in all probability her salivary glands weren't functioning since their fluids are essential to the digestion of starches, etc. I realized then that the passage of raw undigested food into the lower digestive tract would create diarrhea and an apparent allergy to milk and gluten products.

When I went back to work on Ada, I made contact again with her inner mind and instructed the pituitary and hypothalamus glands to return her digestion to normal. I told her Inner Mind to keep this locked in permanently and then instructed It that as soon as the digestive system was working normally to release the "washout" solution of aloe, spring water, etc., as waste matter through a bowel movement.

I then called Ada by telephone and told her to eliminate all milk and milk products from her diet and to stop eating bread and other wheat products and to stay off of them until further notice. I suggested she eat meats, vegetables, etc., and not starve herself. I also suggested she drink orange juice and tomato juice each day to build up potassium and create more energy. She said she would to this. I called her again on July 22, two days later, and she said she was feeling much better. The swelling in her tongue and throat had gone down and she could swallow with no discomfort. She had an exceptionally fine bowel movement that morning with no bleeding and no diarrhea and was beginning to feel stronger already.

Today, October 16, three months later, I talked to Ada again. She feels fine: no more diarrhea; no discomfort or bleeding; stronger and better in every way than at any time in the past three years. She is very grateful.

17. Healing colors and their various medipic applications for miraculous healing of people and animals

In all Medipic healings the employment of energy in various colors is suggested. The reasons for the use of specific colors is here explained. The human body is constructed of three basically different types of tissue, as follows:

1. *Endodermal* tissue. This is basically organ tissue from which the heart, stomach, liver, etc., are constructed. It is created, sustained and energized by red primary energy.

2. *Mesodermal* tissue in the primary tissue from which the muscles, bones, blood and blood vessels are created. They are sustained by green energy, which has also the capacity to rebuild any part of the body under Medipic direction.

3. *Ectodermal* tissue is basically neural and creates the sensory apparatus of the body, the brain, nerves, skin, eyes, ears, taste buds, etc. It is sustained by blue energy, which has the highest vibratory rare of the three basic energies.

These three basic energies—red, green and blue—when combined and balanced produce the complete and most powerful life energy—white energy. In brief, then, we see that the *green* energy sustains the body machine, the *red* energy provides the supply system for physical maintenance, and the *blue* energy builds and supports the communications and management systems. In Medipic healings the white energy is most often used because it is the basic life energy and is made up of all three colored energies in proper balance. However, the colored energies are often employed to serve some specific purpose for which they are best suited. For example:

Blue energy affects the nervous system and is therefore sent to a subject to alleviate pain, to calm his or her nerves and to relax body tensions.

Green energy is sent by Medipic to aid the Inner Mind to replace or rebuild damaged areas in the human system.

Red energy acts as a physical stimulus and is sent via Medipic to speed up sluggish organs and to correct those whose activity has been in some way inhibited.

These three energies, individually and in combination as white energy, are the so-called planetary energy which imbues and sustains all life forms on this planet. They are not psychic or soul energy, nor are they Cosmic Energy. They are material energies created by the radiation of the sun as it makes contact with and affects the magnetism of the earth. These are the energies employed by the Inner Mind of the subject under the Medipic instructions of the healer.

White energy is used most often in Medipic healings because it is the most powerful and also because it may be employed in so many different ways to perform a wide variety of tasks. At one time you may use it as a healing agent, and in a different set of circumstances as a cleansing agent for disinfecting and purifying a wound or an afflicted organ. It is also stimulating and energizing and can be employed to bring a debilitated or exhausted person back up to normal physical strength and action. The white energy has also many other uses which will suggest themselves to you as the need arises.

As you proceed with your work as a healer you will find yourself using still other colors. Most of these will be combinations or dilutions of the primary light colors here described. Some healers say that a turquoise-colored energy works best for them in reducing pain and calming nerves. Others find that placing the sufferer in a pink aura has a quicker and better soothing effect. The best advice that can be given you in this connection is to keep your mind open and follow the "hunches" or intuitive impressions as they strike you.

USING PINK ENERGY TO CALM AND SOOTHE

Here is a practical example of the use of *pink energy* to calm and soothe a distressed person. The healer is Mrs. Regina DeMay of Lisbon, Connecticut. The subject was her aunt, 45, name not given. Here is Mrs. DeMay's report.

We recently had a beloved uncle pass away. He was a wonderful guy, extremely well liked, and he died very suddenly of a heart attack at age 46. His wife was beside herself with grief and barely able to function.

The funeral services were delayed four days until her oldest son, who was at sea, could get there. The delay and the anxiety waiting for her son prolonged her agony. She refused to accept his death. She visited the funeral parlor several times after hours and passed out twice there from hyperventilation. The first time she was revived with smelling salts, but the second time they had to take her to a hospital.

It seemed to me she would never make it through the day of the funeral, so I set to work to calm her the night before. Since pink symbolizes Universal Love, provides contentment, and is very calming and soothing, I mentally showered her with pink rain. I put her first in a pink bathroom in a pink tub full of pink bubbles and let her soak and relax. I then proceeded mentally to put her to bed in pink pajamas, among pink sheets and blankets, in a pink room. I then put an aura of pink around her and told her Inner Mind to feel calm and soothed, and I instructed her to be strong and relaxed throughout the following day.

The day of the funeral was bitter cold and stormy. The roads iced up and driving was dangerous, but my aunt was calm and sat quietly throughout the church service. She walked out of the church on her own and from the car to the plot without assistance. When the graveside service was over she walked back to the car with little assistance and then into the house with no one to help her. At her home following the services, she ate heartily and talked pleasantly, apparently enjoying her company. She said that early that morning she wondered how she would ever get through the services, but now couldn't get over how good she had felt throughout. She said she didn't think it was right to feel so good after just burying her husband, but I felt grateful that I was able to help carry her through a difficult time.

Throughout this book there are many practical examples of the employment of various colors of life energy to achieve a healing. And of course, it is scintillating white energy that is used most often. As you know, this basic human energy penetrates and sustains all life on this planet. Since it, in turn, is the product of the interaction between the sun's rays and the earth's magnetic field, it is quite naturally affected by any changes that occur in the radiation of the sun or fluctuations on the earth's magnetic currents. As a rule, these variations are so slight as to pass unnoticed, but occasionally a magnetic storm on earth or unusual flaring in the sun can have an upsetting effect. You, as a healer, can avoid depression on one hand or overstimulation on the other by bringing yourself into balance through psychic or soul energy. Psychic energy vibrates at a much higher rate than planetary energy and can therefore dominate basic life energy when necessary. You can in the same manner stimulate or calm a patient as required.

Psychic energy, like life energy, is always available in abundance. The word that most fittingly describes psychic energy is "inexhaust-ible." Everyone has a certain amount of psychic energy as a natural endowment; this will vary from person to person. It would probably be more accurate to state that each person can "command" a certain quantity of psychic energy, for no one can possess it. It is possible to dissipate or waste psychic energy so that the amount you can control becomes less and less. On the other hand, you can build up your capacity to administer psychic energy so that more and more becomes available to your command. There are several ways in which this can be accomplished, but the simplest and most beneficial to you is to "demand" it for the purpose of helping another human being. Try it; after a little practice you will find there is more energy available for your purposes and in addition, there will be an energy surplus that will be of personal benefit.

This is one of the dividends that a Medipic healer gets when he conscientiously works to help those in distress. The more energy you demand in your effort to heal others, the larger your own energy "bank account" will become. Psychic energy has no color, as such, but it can be best visualized as scintillating bright sunlight, a sort of golden white shading back and forth into a bluish white.

Our minds are so constructed that we can concentrate better and more effectively if we accompany our effort with a visualization. It is for this reason that many healers "see" the psychic energy they employ as having some color. Actually the color used is not important; any bright color of light will do. The important element is the mental assignment that accompanies the demand for energy, namely, the task it is to perform. A healer thus may on one occasion visualize the energy as sun-gold and on another as sky blue. As long as the visualization is one of light and not pigment or shadow, it will carry through the healer's intention.

If the subject you are asked to heal is at a distance, you will most probably employ the Televisual method. This means that the subject will be using his or her own life energy in response to the Medipic suggestions you give the Inner Mind. In these cases it is life energy and not psychic energy that does the work. If the subject is in the same room with you, his or her own life energy may certainly be used, but if you have developed your ability to command psychic energy, you may find a healing quicker and easier in that way. You will become aware of the best method to employ as you develop your own skill as a healer. Psychic energy can be employed to heal at a distance also, but this requires experience and greater skill which you will undoubtedly attain as you continue with your healing work.

HEALING OTHER LIFE FORMS

All life on this planet is created from Universal Life Energy and sustained by it. This energy is given many names such as primary energy, primordial energy, basic energy and planetary energy. This energy has been described as resulting from the impact of solar radiation on the magnetic fields of the earth. It exists on this planet only—and nowhere else. The entire universe is a great sea of energies of many kinds. This planetary energy or basic life energy is but one manifestation or type of energetic activity in this vast field.

Life energy is not the only energy active on this planet. Solar energy sustains the earth itself and, of course, contributes in a large part to all life on it. Cosmic energy from other planets in our system and from stars and galaxies outside of our planetary system has some effect on all terrestrial life. There is also psychic energy, which is man's special gift and is wielded only by humankind and, of course, spiritual energy, which is characteristic of higher entities and advanced life forms. It is life energy that permeates and sustains every living entity on this earth, however, and is thus the most important energy where earth life in all its forms is concerned.

Because we human beings and all the animals and plants in the world use and are activated by this same energy, we should be able to communicate with each other on this energy level. This is just now being explored by our more advanced scientists, but it has been known and employed beneficially for some time by healers and other open-minded individuals. Many people unashamedly talk to plants and flowers and are rewarded by their healthier, hardier growth. The plants do not understand the words, but they bask in the radiance of the energy showered upon them by the human attention. Energy follows thought, and when we turn our thoughts to someone or something, even a flower, our human energy goes there. If our thought is to love or praise or admire, the recipient becomes aware of a glow of benevolence. A flower reacts to this just as a human will. It likes it and will be amenable to any suggestion that might accompany it.

The higher the life form and the more complicated its structure, the more autonomous it is. In other words, the possibility of making decisions increases. There is very little for a flower to decide, yet a chameleon, which normally will change its color to that of the surrounding area (a form of self-preservation), will retain or adopt a contrasting color if you say it looks more beautiful that way. It likes the warm glow of pleasure it receives from human attention and admiration and is even willing to temporarily surrender a self-protective device in order to have that attention continued.

Certain higher forms of animal life, like some dogs, have developed so far that they can heal themselves in response to Medipic suggestion. Of course, they can also be healed by a direct transfer of energy while in the presence of the healer, but the possibility of healing them at a distance via Medipic is worthy of your attention.

Here is the report of a Seventh Sense healer who has done a lot of work on animals, both horses and dogs. Her name is Mrs. Charles (Judi) Jones and she lives in West Palm Beach, Florida. Here is her report on several such healings.

In the spring we got a new basset hound puppy. He got all the usual shots we get for our dogs, but when he got his rabies shot he had a reaction which impressed me as allergic. A couple of hours after the shot, he broke out in a rash and by nightfall was running a fever. In the morning he was anemic, so I took him back to the vet. When I told him the dog had an allergic reaction to the rabies shot, he said it couldn't be; he had never heard of it. He maintained the anemia was caused by hookworms. I pointed out that the puppy had been checked for worms every two weeks and the last two times, the vet himself had done the checking—all with negative results. He ran three more tests anyway; all were negative. When he continued to insist that the cause of anemia was hookworms and not the rabies shot, I took the dog home and decided to work on him myself.

I used the sun-gold and purple energies overall and then I used red energy on the long bones to stimulate the bone marrow, and after that green energy to build up the red blood cells. I worked on him about ten minutes in all. About twenty minutes later, he was eating. By the time my husband came home from work, the little pup was his usual mean little self. I took him to the vet again the next day; the doctor could not believe his rapid recovery. Sometimes I feel sorry for the doctors when they are wrong and don't realize why.

Barbara Harbin asked me to work on her dog about a year ago. Her dachshund, Maggie, had a fungus infection on her feet. Barbara had taken her to several vets but none were any help. When I made contact and could mentally see the little dog, I created a soap of white healing energy and scrubbed her feet with it. I then put golden aura boots on her feet to keep her from licking them. In three days her feet were much improved and in two weeks they were entirely cured. Her feet stayed clear of the fungus for almost a year, but then one foot became reinfected. When Barbara called me about it, I did the same Medipic healing as before. The next day the fungus was gone and has not returned.

Yolande Scott asked me to work on her dog. He had dry skin and hair coming out, and scratched all the time. I made oil out of the gold energy and mentally rubbed it all over the dog. In a couple of days his skin cleared up and he has had no more trouble since.

I've also worked on the horses here for different things—cuts, springs, bruises and such—sometimes laying on hands and at other times with Medipic healing at a distance. They all healed much faster than normal. Actually I find working with animals much easier than working with humans. Animals seem to respond so much faster; also, there is no doubt or disbelief to overcome.

Most animal healings are similar to one other: they usually involve repair of damage suffered in accidents or fights. We have many such on file. Here is a fair example. The healer is Fred Miller of Plainfield, Connecticut, and the subject was his half-wild cat, Blackie.

My first experience in healing an animal was last June. That evening our half-wild two-year-old tomcat, Blackie, came home limping badly. After examining him and receiving a few claw marks in the process, I found fur missing and a long gash on the inside of his left front leg. Blackie had been in many fights before and had always chosen to care for the wounds he received rather than accept any help from me, so I just fed him and let him out for the night.

Three nights later he showed up on our front steps hardly able to move. His leg was badly infected, with a liquid dripping from the shreds of meat hanging down. That night I contacted Blackie's Inner Mind and showed him that I wanted his infection to stop and his leg to heal. I mentally sent the sun's golden rays into the leg to kill and wash out the germs; then I packed white healing salve in the cut and closed it with a green aura bandage to aid the growth of new skin and fur.

After that night, Blackie didn't show up for two days, but when he arrived for his dinner on the evening of the second day, my wife and I were happy to see there was no sign of limping. He even more or less willingly submitted to a further examination, which revealed the leg

MEDIPIC FOR HEALING
INFECTED WOUNDS
OF ANIMALS

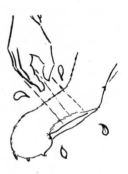

1. When he came to the door, the cat was hardly able to move. Upon visual inspection I saw his left front leg had been cut or torn and was badly infected, with a liquid dripping over the shreds hanging down from the wound.

2. When I contacted the cat mentally later, I started at that point, the left foreleg. I mentally washed out the wound with sun-gold rays designed to kill all the germs and leave the flesh clean and sweet.

3. After this I used the Medipic treatment of white healing energy which I applied to the cut in the form of a salve. I then mentally pressed the sides of the cut together and fastened them that way with green "people tape."

4. Finally I bathed the entire leg with white healing energy to speed up the growth of new skin and fur before breaking the contact.

entirely healed with only a scab an inch long remaining. Since that time Blackie has been much friendlier and more trusting and he seems to look to me for the majority of his care.

Here, in picture form, is a visualization of the Medipic healing performed by the Seventh Sense healer Frederick A. Miller of Plainfield, Connecticut, on his tomcat, Blackie.

18. Amazingly simple self-healing or self-assisted psychic methods and secrets, including the medi-automatic twenty-four hour program

The purpose of this book is to teach you how to heal—to heal yourself as well as others. *Your* physical body is just as deserving of good health as any other, so when some part of your physical equipment is damaged or fails to function properly, you should heal yourself just as readily as you would a stranger who asked your help. As you know, the Medipic or Seventh Sense healing techniques do not employ trance states, hypnotic or semi-hypnotic methods, or stylized rituals of any kind. This book shows you how to work at a *controlled level,* to be fully aware of the conscious physical happenings around you, but not permitting these conscious physical happenings or sounds to disturb or interfere. This discipline is developed through practice. In this work, therefore, you learn by doing. Your goal is to become adept at eyes-open, "two-level" work, wherein the conscious mind is disciplined to take care of the daily routine, while your Inner Mind, with full awareness, is engaging in activities in the higher sensory field.

You may say at this point, "How is this possible?" It is not only possible, but you do this all the time without realizing it. Your mind (or minds) is fully capable of doing at least three different things simultaneously, and in some cases more. You have certainly walked along a busy street, or have driven an automobile in traffic, while you were mentally solving some business problem, or even assembling a grocery list—yet your walking was controlled as was your driving. You didn't bump or run into anyone while your mind was busy at an entirely different task. Now think again. Can you remember a time when you did just that—drove a car through traffic while mentally deciding what you needed to buy at the supermarket and, at the same time, had a tune, like the theme melody of a TV commercial, running through your head? If so, when you did that, you were mentally doing three different things simultaneously. If you give it some thought, it should not prove too difficult to project your thought to a sufferer while retaining full consciousness of your physical environment. Of course, what is involved here is focus of attention. Your physical surroundings dim and blur a bit, recede into the background, so to speak, while the sufferer you are striving to relieve comes into focus, clear and sharp.

Your work as a healer, your higher sensory projection, is described as *active,* not passive meditation. We are told,

> **Therefore be on with the doing of thy works, for therein knowledge comes. A seeker will be found upon the paths and the hilltops, the rivers and the oceans, not reposing on his warm pallet.**

Therefore, the key word to success as a healer is *action.* In the early seventies, Ben Bibb was not aware of any psychic ability. At that time he had never healed anyone—nor had he even considered trying. In his reading, however, he learned that there are people called psychics who were obviously able to heal others, and he aspired to become one. He said to himself: "There *are* psychic persons and since there are, then others can become psychic, for never in history has there been an ability in humans which was limited to just one human." He then decided he would try.

Backed by the discipline of twenty-four years of naval service, he began by trying to diagnose the ills of distant persons. This required long hours of stubborn work, but he persisted. Remember, at this point he was groping: there was no one to point out the best method, as this book does for you. He selected this one path of diagnosis because his conclusions could be quickly checked. One day, he suddenly found himself observing what he knew with inner certainty was the cause of this person's suffering, and to his amazement, he also knew what he might do to correct it. Following his intuition, he suddenly found himself spontaneously doing a psychic distant healing operation on the kidneys of a woman he had never seen but had only heard about. When he learned of its success and remembered the techniques he had been inspired to employ, he used this same method on others and found that it worked for them too.

Subsequently, Ben Bibb has healed thousands of people. News of his ability soon spread; people from all over the United States, Canada and Mexico appealed to him for help. At the request of a few people, he explained his methods to them and discovered that by following his advice, they also became competent healers. Classes were started and now there are several hundred Seventh Sense graduates successfully practicing the Medipic healing methods in all parts of the United States. The full course taught them is herein described so that you, too, can become a competent psychic healer. The primary secret, of course, is learning how to contact the Inner Mind of the person to be healed. You know the method. It now is just a question of practice, of attempting to contact various different subjects until you achieve a breakthrough like Ben Bibb did—only it will not take you nearly so long because you know what you are aiming for, while at first he didn't.

SELF-HEALING

When you start to heal and as you develop your healing skill, most of your efforts will be directed to helping others. Only occasionally will you, yourself, require attention, usually for damage suffered in small accidents. In these cases of cuts or bruises, you will find that a flow of white or sun-gold healing energy applied to the affected part will heal it in an hour or two. This you can do for yourself without difficulty.

On rare occasions, you may find yourself the victim of a serious accident or a sudden attack from some form of internal disturbance. At such times the pain may be so intense that it is extremely difficult to put your conscious awareness of it into the background so that you can connect with your Inner Mind. At such times you should first envelope your entire body in a bright blue aura. See it penetrate all parts of your physical body from head to foot, and feel it soothe and calm your nerves as the pain is gradually reduced. This may take a few minutes, or it may even be several hours before your physical awareness of pain or distress is reduced to a point where you can relegate it to the background while you make conscious contact with your Inner Mind. As soon as you do, examine yourself mentally to determine accurately the cause of your pain. If you have suffered an accident, this should be fairly obvious. You can proceed at once to the work of repair as outlined earlier in this book and repeat the treatment at intervals if it seems necessary.

It is possible that in some instances your pain may have been caused by the malfunction of some internal organ such as the heart, liver, lungs or kidneys. Be sure to give yourself a good psychic examination to ascertain accurately the cause of your distress. When this has been pinpointed to your satisfaction, proceed then to correct it according to the Medipic instruction or as your intuition may suggest. Here is a report of the self-healing of a physical malfunction by a Seventh Sense healer which should clarify this instruction.

A SELF-HEALING REPORT

The healer, a man in his early sixties, describes the problem and its correction as follows:

> I had eaten heartily at both lunch and dinner and topped off both meals with a rich dessert. When it came time to retire I felt a little stuffy, but this did not stop me from falling to sleep almost immediately. About 2 a.m. I was awakened by a terrific pain all across my upper chest from armpit to armpit. My first thought was that I was suffering from a heart attack and indeed, my heart seemed to hesitate and skip or delay a beat on every intake of breath. The pain was so intense I could think of nothing else, so I sought relief by surrounding myself with a bright blue aura.
>
> An hour or so later the pain was still bad and I was beginning to feel slightly nauseous. I rose and went to the bathroom, where after a moment or two I threw up about a half pint of greenish yellow, foul-smelling, vile-tasting, mucus-like fluid. In three or four minutes this regurgitation was repeated with about the same amount of fluid, after which I felt a little better. Returning to bed, I surrounded myself once again with the blue, pain-soothing aura, and in a few minutes fell asleep. I awoke as the sun came up and was happy to find there was no pain—only a slight soreness on my right side immediately below the rib cage. Since the pain was no longer a distracting factor, I took five deep breaths and made contact with my Inner Mind.
>
> My attention was drawn immediately to where the soreness existed and there I found the offender—my gall bladder. It was full of gallstones; one was partially blocking the neck of the gall bladder, causing severe inflammation. This had been partially relieved by the blue soothing aura, but it was obvious that a correction was needed. First, with my mental

fingers, I plucked the stone from the neck of the gall bladder where it had lodged and threw it away. Then, without removing them from the gall bladder, I wrapped the other stones, of which there were many, in a porous sac made of "people skin" so that no other stone could escape and cause similar damage. I did not attempt to remove the stones from the gall bladder because I was aware they had been there for many years and the sudden change might disturb the metabolic balance that had been established.

Next I turned my attention to the duct in the neck of the gall bladder, which was distended and badly inflamed. Using white healing energy, I massaged it mentally with my fingers until it returned to normal size and the redness disappeared. With a small brush I mentally applied brilliant white energy to both the inside and outside walls of the gall bladder, the liver and the stomach to clear out all possibility of infection and speed up the healing process. Finally, I once again surrounded the area with sky blue energy to soothe the nerves and eliminate all pain. In two days, even the slight soreness was gone and I have had no trouble since, nor do I expect any.

The foregoing case is very rare; you may never find yourself in a similar predicament. Once he had overcome the pain, this man found that there was a serious and complicated situation within him for which the only medical solution is the surgical removal of the gall bladder itself, yet his intuition guided him to a Medipic method of handling the problem which has thus far proven effective and, hopefully, will so continue.

It takes a cool head and considerable experience to perform a self-healing of a serious and painful internal problem without outside assistance. It is recommended, therefore, that should you find yourself in a similar predicament, you work through the Inner Mind of another Medipic healer. Here is the way this is done.

SELF-HEALING THROUGH
ANOTHER HEALER

The person whom you decide to work through to heal yourself must be a Medipic healer and must be known to you as you are to him. A stranger will not do. As soon as you are able to dim out your conscious mind and achieve your inner state, reach out mentally for the person with whom you wish to work. Do this in any way that suggests itself to you. Use the mental telephone, if you wish, as you did in the early stages of your healing efforts. Just mentally pick up the telephone and ask by name for the person you want to reach.

Since you know this person his or her mental power will by this method be added to yours to speed up the healing you require. Remember, it is the Inner Mind of the person you have selected as a relaying contact that you will reach as a "switchboard" for the relay, and this will be below the memory level. He or she will have no conscious knowledge of it nor remember it later.

When you reach the person you have selected to assist you, merely say, "I want you to work with me on a healing. The person to be healed is myself; therefore, permit me to observe myself through your (Inner) mind. Thank you. Yes, I now see that there is an infection in the bladder which has caused inflammation and pain, so with your assistance I will proceed to spray white healing and purifying energy into the bladder to clean it out and carry off all the poisons and other foreign particles there. Now I observe the bladder is clean and is a normal pink color throughout, so as a precaution I am now spraying the kidneys above the bladder and the urethra below with the same white cleansing energy. Satisfied that all infection has been cleared away, I now bathe this whole series of eliminative organs with blue soothing, pain-relieving energy and follow it with white stimulating healing energy. A further inspection indicates that all is in order and functioning perfectly, so with thanks for your help, I will withdraw."

By looking at yourself through the Inner Mind of another healer and by performing a Medipic healing on yourself as if you were working on someone other than yourself, you achieve a confidence and a freedom of imagery difficult to attain when encumbered by the conscious knowledge of the pain and distress you are suffering. You thus evade your conscious mind's fears and doubts by conveying to it the idea you are working on another, not yourself. With a knowledge of this technique you should be able to keep yourself well at all times. It is a good idea to practice this remote control healing of yourself every now and then on trivial things, so that should a serious problem arise you will find yourself prepared.

The medical profession has a term "preventive medicine" which covers almost any sound action you might take to keep yourself well and prevent the onset of illness. In Seventh Sense, a similar "act of prevention" is recommended. It is called:

BODY WASHOUT

Body "washout" is actually one of the Medipic healing techniques which is designed to clear the system of poisons and accumulated waste products. Today's tensions of living, added to the uncertain food values in our modern diet, are inclined to create a toxic buildup which should be recognized and eliminated at reasonable intervals. Seventh Sense suggests to its healers that they give themselves a thorough *body washout* at least every six months. Here is a tested method.

Mentally prepare about a quart of pure spring water and saturate an equal quantity of white healing energy in it until the two are mixed thoroughly together, then mentally drink it all and, at the same time, instruct your Inner Mind to retain it in your system until you permit its release. After a period of complete relaxation (at least an hour) instruct the fluid to go to each of your inner organs in turn—to your liver, pancreas, kidneys, adrenals, bowels, bladder, etc., and to cleanse each completely of all toxic and foreign matter. When this has been done, instruct the fluid to carry itself and the accompanying waste out of the system by means of both bowels and kidneys. Over the next few hours you will experience very vigorous bowel and kidney activity, so don't make any special dates and stay close to home until this passes. Take a brief rest then. You will feel much better afterward.

Seventh Sense offers another suggestion for the well being of its healers. This is that each one program his or her Inner Mind to check the entire human physical apparatus at least once each day and at that time to correct any aberration or malfunction that appears. This is referred to as the:

THE MEDI-AUTOMATIC TWENTY-FOUR
HOUR PROGRAM

Actually this is a self-examination by your Inner Mind and a correction, when needed, by Medipic. Once you reach the meditative state, turn your attention to your own physical structure, observe the efficiency of its functioning (or lack of it) and give visual instructions to your subconscious mind, when necessary, on the best method to bring it back to normal. Treat yourself as you would a subject who came to you requesting help. All this is simple enough, but for the average person, the problem is to remember to do it. It is therefore recommended that you select some one point in your waking day (not in your sleep) and program yourself to check yourself each day at that time. Most Seventh Sense workers select the morning upon waking, but others like the evening at retiring time better. At these times you are more likely to have two or three minutes of privacy; as a rule, this is all the time you will need. For most people obtaining quiet and privacy at other times in the day is too unpredictable, so it has been found that the awakening or retiring time works best.

Healing others is the simplest and surest path to psychic development open to man today. It embodies in it the New Age essentials for spiritual growth. These are self-forgetfulness and compassion, and a willingness to help others in need with no thought of personal reward. This does not refer to almsgiving, although that has its place, but to personal effort put forth to attain a nonpersonal goal, usually the welfare of another. The time, energy and thought put into the healing of others brings not only the satisfaction that goes with achieving a most worthy objective, but also actually leads to spiritual advancement. Even though the realization that another human being has been relieved of pain and distress through your efforts may in itself be some sort of reward, it is a worthy one.

You will find also, as you proceed with your work as a healer, that you are beginning to unfold certain new and unsuspected abilities. You will find yourself becoming aware of what others are about to say before they say it. At times it will be quite clear to you that what a person says is not what he or she is thinking. Soon you will be able to anticipate simple events, or what someone you know will do tomorrow or a week hence. This is but the awakening of certain abilities that are inherent in all of us, usually referred to as psychic abilities. The word 'psychic' is used rather loosely, for as you will come to know, these are not soul (psychic) powers, but abilities every human being possesses which must be developed in order to be used.

The healing techniques presented in this book will, if followed, not only show you how to heal others but will also develop in you additional powers in your nature that have hitherto gone unnoticed. This is a most wonderful opportunity. Seize it—to use these proven means and methods of miraculous healing for yourself and your loved ones.